Essential Linux

Steve Heath

Digital Press

Boston • Oxford • Johannesburg • Melbourne • New Delhi • Singapore

Contents

Preface

Linux can only be described as software phenomenon. In the short space of a few years, it has gone from being a simple project to a worldwide movement, becoming one of the main academic and commercial operating system environments.

It uses the wealth of knowledge and software from the UNIX environment and combines it with the GNU copyleft software license to provide free, accessible software that can simply be downloaded or copied and then used. This has led to an explosive development of applications and drivers that have inspired others to contribute to the ever-increasing software archives.

This book provides the essential information to allow the reader to start exploring Linux using a simple IBM PC. It provides the basic software on the companion CD-ROM together with all the kernels that have been released for versions 1.3.x and 2.0.x so that the software can be installed immediately and the operating system exploration begun. The book details how to install and configure Linux, how to build new kernels to support different hardware, how to use the main commands and more.

The approach is pragmatic and down to earth, and many screen shots of the commands in action have been included to show, by example, how to use them and where the pitfalls can lie. In essence, as the book title suggests, it contains the essential Linux.

I would like to thank Mike Cash and Liz McCarthy at Butterworth-Heinemann and Digital Press for their help, encouragement and support, despite being separated by the Atlantic Ocean and a common language. Special thanks must again go to Sue Carter for yet more editing, intelligent criticism and flavored coffee when I needed it. Without her help and support, none of my books would have been possible.

Steve Heath

By the same author

VMEbus: a Practical Companion

Newnes UNIX™ Pocket Book

Microprocessor Architectures: RISC, CISC and DSP

Effective PC Networking

PowerPC: a Practical Companion

The PowerPC Programming Pocket Book

The PC and MAC Handbook

The Newnes Windows NT Pocket Book

Multimedia and Communications Technology

In preparation

Migrating to Windows NT

The Embedded Systems Design Handbook

All books published by Butterworth-Heinemann

About the author:

Through his work with Motorola Semiconductors, the author has been involved in the design and development of microprocessor-based systems since 1982. These designs have included VMEbus systems, microcontrollers, IBM PCs, Apple Macintoshes, and both CISC and RISC-based multiprocessor systems, while using operating systems as varied as MS-DOS, UNIX, Macintosh OS and real-time kernels.

An avid user of computer systems, he has had over 60 articles and papers published in the electronics press, as well as several books.

1 Inside Linux

Linux is one of the most well-known multitasking free operating system within the microprocessor and minicomputer environment because of a group of dedicated individuals, an interest in computer games, and despite an apparent lack of interest from major corporations. In these respects it has followed the early development of the UNIX operating system, which it has used for its system specification.

Origins and beginnings — UNIX

UNIX was first described in an article published by Ken Thompson and Dennis Ritchie of Bell Research Labs in 1974, but its origins owe much to work carried out by a consortium formed in the late 1960s by Bell Telephone, General Electric and the Massachusetts Institute of Technology, to develop MULTICS — a MULTIplexed Information and Computing Service.

The idea behind MULTICS was to generate software that would allow a large number of users simultaneous access to the computer. These users would also be able to work interactively online in a way similar to that experienced by personal computer users today. This was a fairly revolutionary concept. Computers were very expensive and fragile machines that required specially trained staff to keep users away from and protect *their* machine. However, the project was not as successful as had been hoped and Bell dropped out in 1969. The experience gained in the project was turned to other uses when Thompson and Ritchie designed a computer filing system on the only machine available — a Digital Equipment Corp. PDP-7 minicomputer.

The next development was that of the C programming language, which started out as attempt to develop a FORTRAN language compiler. Initially, a programming language called B was developed, which was then modified into C. The development of C was crucial to the rapid movement of UNIX from a niche within a research environment to the outside world.

UNIX was rewritten in C in 1972 — a major departure for an operating system. To maximize the performance of the computers then available, operating systems were usually written in a low-level assembly language that directly controlled the processor. This had several effects. It meant that each computer had its own unique operating system, and this made application programs hardware dependent. Although the applications may have been written in a high level language (such as FORTRAN or BASIC) that could run on many different machines, differences in the hardware and operating systems would frequently prevent these applications from being moved between systems. As a result, many man hours were spent porting software from one computer to another and working around this computer equivalent of the Tower of Babel.

By making UNIX available to the academic world in the mid-1970s at effectively no cost, AT&T had inadvertently discovered a superb way of marketing the product. However, in the commercial world it was an expensive product and frequently beyond the means of many computer users outside the academic world.

The Linux development

Linux started as a personal interest project by Linus Torvalds at the University of Helsinki in Finland to produce an operating system that looked and felt like UNIX. It was based on work that he had done in porting Minix , an operating system that had been shipped with a textbook that described its inner workings.

After much discussion via user groups on the Internet, the first version of Linux saw the light of day on the 5 October, 1991. While limited in its abilities — it could run the GNU bash shell and gcc compiler but not much else — it prompted a lot of interest. Inspired by Linus Torvalds' efforts, a band of enthusiasts started to create the range of software that Linux offers today. While this was progressing, the kernel development continued until some 18 months later, when it reached version 1.0. Since then it has been developed further to version 2.0 and has become quite a stable piece of software. In my own experience of using it for over 12 months, I can't remember a single system crash!

Inside Linux

The key to understanding Linux as an operating system is to understand how much Linux protects the user from the computer system it is running on — from having to know exactly where the memory is in the system, what a disk drive is called and other such information. Many facets of the UNIX environment are logical in nature, in that they can be seen and used by the user — but their actual location, structure and functionality is hidden. If a user wants to run a 20 Mbyte program on a system, Linux will use its virtual memory capability to make the machine behave logically like one with enough memory — even though the system may only have 4 Mbytes of RAM installed. The user can access data files without knowing if they are stored on a floppy or a hard disk — or even on another machine many miles away and connected via a network. Linux uses its facilities to present a logical picture to the user while hiding the more physical aspects from view.

While it is perfectly possible to simply accept the logical world that Linux presents, it is extremely beneficial to understand its inner workings and how Linux translates the logical world to the physical world.

The Linux file system

Linux has a hierarchical filing system that contains all the data files, programs, commands, and special files that allow access to the physical computer system. The files are usually grouped into directories and subdirectories. The file system starts with a root directory and divides it into subdirectories. At each level, there can be subdirectories that continue the file system into further levels and files that contain data. A directory can contain both directories and files. If no directories are present, the file system will stop at that level for that path.

A file name describes its location in the hierarchy by the path taken to locate it, starting at the top and working down. This type of structure is frequently referred to as a tree structure. If turned upside down, it resembles a tree by starting at a single root directory — the trunk — and branching out.

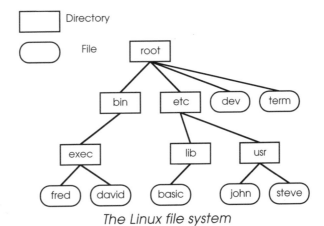

The Linux file system

The full name, or path name, for the file *steve* located at the bottom of the tree would be */etc/usr/steve*. The / character at the beginning is the symbol used for the starting point and is known as root or the root directory. Subsequent use within the path name indicates that the preceding file name is a directory and that the path as followed down that route. The / character is in the opposite direction to that used in MS-DOS systems: a tongue-in-cheek way to remember which slash to use is that MS-DOS is "backward" compared with UNIX — and thus its slash character points backward.

The Linux system revolves around its file structure and all physical resources are also accessed as files. Even commands exist as files. The organization is similar to that used within MS-DOS — but the original idea came from UNIX, and not the other way around. One important difference is that with MS-DOS, the top of the structure is always referred to by the name of the hard disk or storage medium. Accessing an MS-DOS root directory C:\ immediately tells you that drive C holds the data. Similarly, A:\ and B:\ normally refer to floppy disks. With Linux, such direct references to hardware do not exist. A directory is simply present and rarely gives any clues as to its physical location or nature. It may be a floppy disk, a hard disk or a disk on another system that is connected via a network.

The physical file system

The physical file system consists of mass storage devices, such as floppy and hard disks, which are allocated to parts of the logical file system. The logical file system (previously described) can be implemented on a system with two hard disks by allocating the *bin* directory and the filing subsystem below it to hard disk no. 2 — while the rest of the file system is allocated to hard disk no. 1. To store data on hard disk 2, files are created somewhere in the *bin* directory. This is the logical way of accessing mass storage. However, all physical input and output can be accessed by sending data to special files which are normally located in the */dev* directory. This organization of files was shown in the previous figure.

This can create a great deal of confusion: one method of sending data to a hard disk is by allocating it to part of the logical file system and simply creating data files. The second method involves sending the data directly to the special */dev* file that represents the physical disk drive — which itself exists in the logical file system!

This conflict can be explained by an analogy using bookcases. A library contains many bookcases where many books are stored. The library represents the logical file system and the bookcases the physical mass storage. Books represent the data files. Data can be stored within the file system by putting books into the bookcases. Books can be grouped by subject on shelves within the bookcases — these represent directories and subdirectories. When used normally, the bookcases are effectively transparent and the books are located or stored depending on their subject matter. However, there may be times when more storage is needed or new subjects are created and whole bookcases are moved or cleared. In these cases, the books are referred to using the bookcase as the reference, rather than subject matter.

The same can occur within Linux. Normally, access is via the file system, but there are times when it is easier to access the data as complete physical units rather than lots of files and directories. Hard disk copying and the allocation of part of the logical file system to a floppy disk are two examples of when access via the special /*dev* file is used. Needless to say, accessing hard disks directly without using the file system can be extremely dangerous: the data is simply accessed by block numbers without any reference to the type of data that it contains. It is all too easy to destroy the file system and the information it contains. Another important difference between the access methods is that direct access can be performed at any time and with the mass storage in any state. To access data via the logical file system, data structures must be present to control the file structure. If these are not present, logical access is impossible.

Building the file system

When a Linux system is powered up, its system software boots the Linux system into existence. One of the first jobs performed is the allocation of mass storage to the logical file system. This process is called mounting and its reverse, the deallocation of mass storage, is called unmounting. The *mount* command specifies the special file which represents the physical storage and allocates it to a target directory. When *mount* is complete, the file system on the physical storage media has been added to the logical file system. If the disk does not have a filing system, that is, the data control structures previously mentioned do not exist, the disk cannot be successfully mounted.

The *mount* and *umount* commands can be used to access removable media, such as floppy disks, via the logical file system. The disk is mounted, the data is accessed as needed, and the disk unmounted before physically removing it. All that is needed for this access to take place is the name of the special device file and the target directory. The target directory normally used is /*mnt*, but the special device file name varies from system to system. The *mount* facility is not normally available to end users for reasons that will become apparent later in this chapter.

The file system

Up until now, the term "file system" has been used to refer to the hierarchical structure of directories and subdirectories. For an overview, this is correct, but "file system" is also used to refer to the control structures used to locate and control the data files. File systems must be explicitly created on storage media using the *makefs* command. To format the medium so it can store blocks of data, a formatting command is used. The *superblock* and *inode* structures that allow the storage to be accessed via the file system are created by *makefs*.

Files are stored by allocating sufficient blocks of storage to contain all the data they contain. The minimum amount of storage that can be allocated is determined by the block size, which can range from 1 Kbytes to 4 Kbytes in more recent systems. The larger block size reduces the amount of control data that is needed — but can increase the storage wastage. A file with 1,025 bytes would need two 1,024-byte blocks to contain it, leaving 1,023 bytes allocated and therefore not accessible to store other files. End of file markers indicate where the file actually ends within a block. Blocks are controlled and allocated by a *superblock*, which contains an *inode* allocated to each file, directory, subdirectory or special file. The *inode* describes the file and where it is located. Using the library and book analogy, *superblock* represents the library catalogue that is used to determine the size and location of each book. Each book has an entry — an *inode* — within the catalogue.

Why go to these lengths when all that is needed is the location of the starting block and storage of the data in consecutive blocks? This method reduces the amount of data needed to locate a complete file, irrespective of the number of blocks the file uses. However, it does rely on the blocks being available in *contiguous* groups, where the blocks are consecutively ordered. This does not cause a problem when the operating system is first used, and all the files are usually stored in sequence, but as files are created and deleted, the free blocks become fragmented and intermingled with existing files. Such a fragmented disk may have 20 Mbytes of storage free, but would be unable to create files greater than the largest contiguous number of blocks — which could be 10 or 20 times smaller.

So what actually happens when a user wants a file or executes a command? In both cases, the mechanism is very similar. The operating system takes the file or command name and looks it up within the *superblock* to discover the *inode* reference number. This is used to locate the *inode* itself and check the access permissions before allowing the process to continue. If permission is granted, the *inode* block addresses are used to locate the data blocks stored on hard disk. These blocks are put into memory to reconstitute the file or command program. If the data file represents a command, control is then passed to it, and the command executed.

The time taken to perform file access is inevitably dependent on the speed of the hard disk and the time it takes to access each individual block. If the blocks are consecutive or close to each other, the total access time is much quicker than if they are dispersed throughout the disk. As is explained later, Linux also uses mass storage as a replacement for system memory and its system response is therefore highly dependent on hard disk performance. Linux uses two techniques to help improve performance: partitioning and data caching.

Disk partitioning

The concept of disk partitioning is simple: the closer the blocks of data are to each other, the quicker they can be accessed. The potential distance apart is dependent on the number of blocks the disk can store, and thus its storage capacity. Given two hard disks with the same access time, the drive with the largest storage will give the slowest performance, on average. The principle is similar to that encountered when shopping in a small or large supermarket. It takes longer to walk around the larger shop than the smaller one to fetch the same goods.

Linux has the option of partitioning large hard disks so the system sees them as a set of smaller disks. This greatly reduces the amount of searching required and considerably improves overall access times. Each partition (or slice, as it sometimes called) is created by allocating a consecutive number of blocks to it. The partition is treated exactly as if it is a separate mass storage device and can be formatted, and have a file system installed and mounted, if required. The partitions can be arranged so they either overlap or are totally separate. In both cases, an installed file system cannot exceed the partition size (the number of blocks allocated to it) and the lower boundaries of the file system and partition are the same. With non-overlapped partitions, the file system cannot be changed to overlap and destroy the data of an adjacent partition. With an overlapped arrangement, this is possible. Changing partition dimensions requires, at best, the reinstallation of the operating system or other software and, at worst, may need them to be completely rebuilt. Fortunately, this only usually concerns the system administrator who looks after the system. Users do not need to worry about these potential problems.

Partitioning provides several other advantages. It allows partitions to be used exclusively by Linux or another operating system, such as MS-DOS, and it reduces the amount of data backup needed to maintain a system's integrity. Most Linux implementations running on an IBM PC allocate partitions to either MS-DOS or Linux and the sizes of these partitions are usually decided when the system software is first installed. Some implementations use the same idea, but create large MS-DOS files, which are used as Linux partitions. In both cases, partitioning effectively divides the single physical hard disk into several smaller logical ones and allows the relatively easy transfer from Linux to MS-DOS, and vice versa.

Data caching

One method of increasing the speed of disk access is to keep copies of the most recently used data in memory so it can be fetched without having to keep accessing the slower electromechanical disk. The first time the data is needed, it is read from disk and is copied into the cache memory. The next time this data is required, it comes directly from cache memory — without using the disk. This access can be up to 1,000 times faster — which greatly improves system performance. The amount of improvement depends on the amount of cache m~   nd the quantity of data needed from disk. If cache
                      uired amount of data, the maximum performance
                      — all the data is read once and can be completely
                      The system frequently caches the new data — so the
                      nory. As this memory is volatile, if the machine is
                      t. If this information also includes *directory* changes,
the file system will have been corrupted and, at best, parts of it will have been destroyed. At worst, the whole file system can be lost by switching the power off without executing a power down sequence. Most times, an accidental loss of power will not cause any real damage — but it is playing Russian roulette with the system.

The user can force the system to update the disk by executing the *sync* command as required. This is a recommended practice.

Multitasking systems

Most operating systems used on PCs today, such as MS-DOS, can only execute one application at a time. This means that only one user can use the computer at any time, with the further limitation that only one application can run at a time. While a spreadsheet is executing, the PC can only wait for commands and data from the keyboard. This is a great waste of computer power because the PC could be executing other programs or applications or, alternately, allow other users to run their software on it. The ability to support multiple users running multiple applications is called multi-user multitasking. This is a feature of Linux — and is one of the reasons for its rapid adoption.

A multitasking operating system works by dividing the processor's time into discrete time slots. Each task (or process, as it is known within the Linux environment) requires a certain number of time slots to complete its execution. The operating system kernel decides which process can have the next slot, so instead of executing a process continuously until completion, its execution is interleaved with other processes. This sharing of processor time among processes gives each user the illusion that he or she is the only one using the system.

Such operating systems are based around a mu~~l~~ ~~ernel~~ s
the time slicing mechanisms. A time slice is the ti~~~~ r
execution before it is stopped and replaced ~~context switch~~ ;
periodically triggered by a hardware interru
interrupt may provide the system clock and sev ~~control blocks~~
and counted before a context switch is perforr

When a context switch is performed, the curr
processor's registers are saved in a special table ... that particular process, and
the process is placed back on the "ready" list to await another time slice. Special
tables, often called control blocks, store all the information the system requires
about the process, for example, its memory usage, its priority level within the
system and its error handling. It is this context information that is switched
when one process is replaced by another.

The "ready" list contains all the processes and their status and is used by the
scheduler to decide which process is allocated the next time slice. The scheduling algorithm determines the sequence and takes into account a process's
priority and present status. If a process is waiting for an I/O call to complete,
it will be held in limbo until the call is complete.

Once a process is selected, the processor registers and status at the time of its
last context switch are loaded back and the processor is started. The new
process carries on as if nothing had happened, until the next context switch
takes place. This is the basic method behind all multitasking operating systems,
including UNIX. One important characteristic to understand is that the computer system cannot magically maintain the same computation and processing
throughput if additional users and processes are added to its workload. As the
system is loaded, response times to commands depend on how much time the
scheduler within the kernel can allocate to each process. If the system is lightly
loaded, it may appear that the system has an instantaneous reaction. This is
caused because the system devotes all its processing power to perform a single
request. As the system becomes loaded, this amount of time decreases and the
same amount of work will take longer because it is regularly interrupted by
other processes. I have heard of systems which, when very heavily loaded,
have taken as long as 15 minutes to respond to a login command! In such
circumstances, the system does not have enough processing power to provide
a reasonable response. However, it will work through its workload, albeit
slowly, and is quite capable of accepting more work.

Multi-user systems

Given a multitasking operating system, it is easy to create a multi-user environment, where several users can share the same computer. This is done by taking

the special interface program that provides the command line and prompts, and running multiple copies of it as separate processes. When a user logs into the computer, a copy of the program is automatically started. In the Linux environment, this is called the *shell,* and there are several different versions available. The advantages of multi-user systems are obvious — powerful computer systems can be shared amongseveral users, rather than each having a separate system. With a shared system, it can also be easier to control access and data, which may be important for large workgroups.

With any multi-user system, it is important to prevent users from corrupting each other's work, or gaining access to sensitive data. To facilitate this, Linux allocates users password protected login names, which uniquely identifies them. Users are normally allocated their own directory within the file system and can configure their part of the system as needed. Users can be organized into groups and every file within the system is given access permissions controlling which user or group can read, write or execute it. When a file is accessed, the requesting user's identity (or ID) is checked against that of the file. If it matches, the associated permissions are checked against the request. The file may be defined as read only, in which case a request to modify it would not be allowed — even if the request came from the user who created it in the first place. If the user ID does not match, the group IDs are checked. If these match, the group permissions are used to judge the validity of the request. If neither IDs match, a third set of permissions, known as others, are checked.

These permissions can be changed as and when required by the system administrator, who must set up the Linux system and control how much or how little access each user has to the system and its facilities. This special user (or superuser) has unlimited access by being able to assume any user and/or group identity. This allows an organized structure to be easily implemented and controlled.

Linux software structure

The software structure used within Linux is very modular, despite its long development history. It consists of several layers starting with programming languages, command scripts and applications, and shells and utilities, which provide the interface software or application the user sees. In most cases, the only difference between the three types of software is their interaction and end product, although the more naive user may not perceive this.

The most common software used is the *shell,* with its commands and utilities. The *shell* is used to provide the basic login facilities and system control. It also enables the user to select application software, load it and then transfer control to it. Some of its commands are built into the software but most exist as applications, which are treated by the system in the same way as a database or other specialized application.

Programming languages, such as C and FORTRAN, and their related tools are also applications but are used to write new software to run on the system.

All these layers of software interface with the rest of the operating system via the system call interface. This provides a set of standard commands and services for the software above it and enables their access to the hardware, filing systems, terminals and processor. To read data from a file, a set of system calls are carried out that locate the file, open it and transfer the required data to the application needing it. To find out the time, another call is used, and so on. Having transferred the data, system calls are used to call the kernel and special software modules, known as device drivers, which actually perform the work required.

Processes and standard I/O

One problem facing multi-user operating systems is that of access to I/O devices such as printers and terminals. Probably the easiest method for the operating system is to address all peripherals by unique names and force application software to directly name them. The disadvantage of this for the application is that it could be difficult to find out which peripheral each user is using, especially if a user may log in via a number of different terminals. It would be far easier for the application to use some generic name and let the operating system translate these logical names to physical devices. This is the approach taken by Linux.

Processes have three standard files associated with them: *stdin, stdout* and *stderr*. These are the default input, output and error message files. Other files or devices can be reassigned to these files to either receive or provide data for the active process. A list of all files in the current directory can be displayed on the terminal by typing *ls<cr>* (where *<cr>* indicates pressing Return or Enter) because the terminal is automatically assigned to be *stdout*. To send the same data to a file, *ls > filelist<cr>* is entered instead. The extra *> filelist* redirects the output of the *ls* command. In the first case, *ls* uses the normal *stdout* file that is assigned to the terminal and the directory information appears on the terminal screen. In the second example, *stdout* is temporarily assigned to the file *filelist*. Nothing is sent to the terminal screen — the data is stored within the file instead.

Data can be fed from one process directly into another using a "pipe". A process to display a file on the screen can be piped into another process that converts all lowercase characters to uppercase. It can then pipe its data output into another process, which paginates it automatically before displaying it. This command line can be written as a data file or shell script, which provides the commands to the user interface or shell. Shell scripts form a programming language in their own right and allow complex commands to be constructed from simple ones. If the user does not like the particular way a process presents information, a shell script can be written which executes the process, edits and reformats the data and then presents it. There are two commonly used shell interfaces: the standard Bourne shell and the C shell. Many application programs provide their own shells that hide the Linux operating system completely from the user.

Executing commands

After a user has logged onto the system, Linux starts to run the shell program by assigning *stdin* to the terminal keyboard and *stdout* to the terminal display. It then prints a prompt and waits for a command to be entered. The shell takes the command line and deciphers it into a command with options, file names, and so on. It then looks in a few standard directories to find the right program to execute or, if the full path name is used, goes the directory specified and finds the file. If the file cannot be found, the shell returns an error message.

2 Installing Linux

Obtaining the software

The first obstacle in installing Linux is obtaining the system software and associated utilities in the first place. There is an ever-increasing amount of software available and new versions of the kernel appear almost every day as facilities are added and bugs fixed. With Linux distributed essentially as freeware under the GNU software license, most of the software is available from several sources

CD-ROM

CD-ROM is undoubtedly the easiest way of getting the software. It is possible to download it from other sources but the sheer size of the files means it takes a very long time and can cost a considerable amount in telephone charges. The CD-ROM delivers about 660 Mbytes of software for a few dollars. Since CD-ROMs are now nearly standard on PCs, it is the easiest way of getting started. This is why a CD-ROM has been included with this book — instead of having to download many megabytes, it has been done for you! See Appendix A for details.

CD-ROM distribution does have its problems: it can only provide a snapshot of the software, and as stated previously, Linux is developing rapidly and thus the latest software is often only available a few months or even a year after it appears on the Internet or on bulletin boards and on-line services. To combat this, some suppliers offer update services where for a suitable fee, update CD-ROMs are sent out between major releases. However, it is an ideal way to start with Linux.

There are several well-known packaged CD-ROM releases available. The most popular are:

Slackware This is probably the most well known. It is a relatively easy package to use and includes all the major software components and utilities. It comes as a multiple CD-ROM set and concentrates on one or two kernel releases chosen for their stability.

Plug and Play This is also a popular choice but I found it to be a bit more difficult to use and install the software. It again concentrates on a couple of stable kernels for its release.

The CD-ROM accompanying this book is slightly different from these offerings in that it contains the released versions of Linux 1.3 and 2.0 including all the interim updates, basic utilities and compilers with their associated documentation, to allow new kernels and drivers to be built and installed. The problem

I found with using a lot of the Linux software, was that inevitably a new device driver or application needed a later kernel release that I did not have. While downloading a couple of hundred Kbytes is not a daunting task, downloading the 5 Mbytes of kernel software that I also needed was a different matter entirely. By supplying as many of the updates and releases as possible, each release occupying over 5 Mbytes in compressed format, this not only saves time and money over downloading from the Internet but also provides almost any required kernel version that a driver or application may need instantly from the disk. The CD-ROM includes some standard builds to allow the reader to quickly install Linux on almost any modern PC that has a 80386 or better processor, a standard CD-ROM drive and hard disk.

Internet and FTP sites

If you have access to an Internet or FTP link, then the Linux software can be downloaded from several sites. The most popular is Walnut Creek's site (www.cdrom.com for web access, ftp.cdrom.com for FTP). The Linux software is located in the directory /pub/linux.

Other important repositories are the Sunsite locations. There is a mirror in almost every country and it is often faster to access one of these sites than try and get to the original Sunsite.

Bulletin boards and on-line services

Many on-line services such as CompuServe now provide access to the latest Linux software.

Selecting a host PC

Although Linux is available for many other processors and computer systems, including a PowerPC port for the Apple Macintosh, the predominant system is the IBM PC. Most IBM PCs that have a 80386 processor or better are capable of running Linux. Please note the term "most": the problem is that MS-DOS and Windows device drivers for add-on hardware are not compatible with Linux and cannot be used. As a result, some graphics adapters, tape drives and CD-ROM drives cannot be accessed with Linux. This means that some hardware may need replacing with Linux-compatible components. Such incompatible hardware includes:

- Philips LMS CD-ROM drives
- Sound cards that emulate SoundBlaster in software only
- Tape streamers that use the floppy interface
- Old Ethernet cards
- Devices that use proprietary interface cards

With most Linux software packs, there is a list of supported hardware and it is worth checking this list to ensure that your system is supported. There are also many additional drivers provided on the Internet that might support a more obscure device. While this part of an eventual solution, it can require overcoming a chicken-and-egg problem.

Take a Philips LMS CD-ROM drive for example. There are some drivers available to support some of the models — LMS206 for example but not the LMS205 — but the driver has not been built into any of the standard installation kernels. This means that as soon as Linux is booted, the CD-ROM drive is not accessible and the rest of the installation process cannot continue because it relies on CD-ROM access to get the files. Without the files, the new kernel with the CD-ROM driver cannot be built. Without the new kernel, the CD-ROM cannot be accessed.

One potential solution would be to transfer the files to the MS-DOS partition on the disk under MS-DOS where its driver can access the CD-ROM. The disadvantage of this method is that the Linux files inevitably use a 32-character file name that gets truncated when the files are moved to the MS-DOS environment. The truncated file name can then cause problems with the installation scripts. Some distributions like Slackware have already converted the file names of the source files to overcome this problem.

There are really only two practical solutions to this dilemma: the simplest is to replace the CD-ROM drive with one that is recognized and supported, such as an IDE, SoundBlaster, SCSI or ATAPI drive. Alternatively, the files can be accessed from another system using a network connection, but this does require a second working Linux system and assumes that the new system has a recognized Ethernet connection. The moral of this story is: if the CD-ROM or Ethernet board is not a recognized or supported standard, consider replacing it. It will save a lot of time and effort!

Processor choice

The minimum processor that is needed is a 80386SX or DX but in reality, a 80486 or Pentium class processor can speed up many computer intensive operations such as XFree86 and kernel rebuilds and compilations. It will not run on a 80286 or lower processor because the software relies on the 80386 facilities such as addressing modes and so on to execute. I have rebuilt kernels, tested drivers and so on quite happily on a simple 25 MHz 80486SX, for example.

The kernel can be optimized for 386/486 and Pentium processors through settings in the kernel make file. Hardware floating point is an advantage however, especially for graphics programs such as XFree86, and greatly improves the drawing and execution speed. For processors without a hardware floating point unit such as the 80486SX series, Linux comes with a software emulation that can provide compatibility, albeit at a greatly reduced rate. The software emulation tries to detect a hardware floating point unit on startup and if there is one present, disables itself in favor of the hardware. In this way, the software emulation can effectively be left installed in the kernel without the fear of poor software performance when hardware is available to perform the floating point calculations. The only disadvantage is the few kilobytes of memory that it takes up.

Disk space

There are two decisions to be made concerning disk space: how much to allocate and, whether it should be sourced from a file or from a disk partition.

The first decision is dependent on the type of system and its use. The second decision concerns the method used to provide the disk space. There are two methods available. The first creates a file within the existing MS-DOS file system on a disk that is used to act as the Linux file system. If a Linux file system with 50 Mbyte disk space is needed, a file is created during the installation process that is 50 Mbytes in size. The contents of this file is the Linux file system with its own directory structures and files.

It has several disadvantages:

- Older versions of MS-DOS have file size limits that can limit the size of the Linux file system. This can be worked around by creating multiple files and thus multiple Linux drives.
- The Linux file system is at the mercy of the MS-DOS and/or Windows system and can be deleted, moved or corrupted by a MS-DOS/Windows program or virus.
- It can be less reliable and slower. This is because the file system is accessed via the BIOS calls and effectively the Linux file system is accessed via a MS-DOS wrapper. To access Linux data within the file, the raw sectors are accessed using the MS-DOS file system and through its structures. As a result, each disk access is effectively a two-stage affair.
- It is, in my experience, less reliable and appears to be more prone to crashes and problems.

It has some advantages too:

- A Linux system can be quickly set up using available disk space without repartitioning.
- The system startup procedure can be left as normal.
- MS-DOS/Windows based utilities can be used to back-up the file and hence the Linux file system.

The alternative to using a file within the MS-DOS file system is to create partition(s) that are dedicated to Linux and are thus not part of the MS-DOS environment. A partitioned disk is logically separated into several partitions with each partition acting like its own disk drive. With MS-DOS, this is often done to create two drives on a single hard drive. One partition would form drive C and the other drive D and so on. Each partition is identified by a code that can tell the operating system exactly which type the partition is, and more importantly, what it is used for. A partition can be used by operating systems other than MS-DOS and Windows and this is where Linux can exploit the partition system. By creating a partition on a disk, it can be designated as a Linux partition and thus used to provide the filing system. The partition is not used or recognized by MS-DOS or Windows and therefore is not under threat from deletion and other related problems. The Linux system can be used in conjunction with the original operating system running on the other partition(s) and by using a startup program such as lilo, the system can be made to boot from a choice of operating systems — my own offers a choice of MS-DOS, Windows 95, Windows NT and Linux from a variety of different kernels and configurations.

The advantages of the partition method do not stop there: large disks (>540 Mbytes) thatthe older BIOS chips that do not recognize or size correctly can be used. This is done by creating a partition where the recognized disk size is used to define the first partition for use with MS-DOS and/or Windows. Then a Linux partition is created. This needs to take some of the recognized space for this technique to work. For example, a 1 Gbyte disk can be divided into a 400 Mbyte MS-DOS partition and a 600 Mbyte Linux partition.

A variation on this is to add a new disk drive and use it solely for Linux. The drive can be configured to be either a single Linux partition or a set of multiple ones with each partition acting as part of the filing system.

Existing MS-DOS based partitions can also be configured within the Linux installation to appear as a drive when either MS-DOS or Linux is used. In this way, the partition sharing provides a way of transferring large files from one environment to another. For example, updates or applications could be downloaded from a bulletin board or on-line service using a MS-DOS or Windows application such as Terminal and stored in a directory on the MS-DOS drive that corresponds with the shared partition. Linux could then be booted up and the files copied over into their final space within the Linux file system or used where they are. In practice, it is probably better to copy them into the Linux file system because of file name restrictions — more about that later on. The problem with partitions is creating them in the first place!

Memory

Linux will run in as little as 4 Mbyte of RAM but this limits the system to command line utilities and effectively precludes the use of an X-windows based interface. It would probably run but the response time would be very slow due to the swapping out to disk. In addition, very large compilations such as kernels may not run or again be very slow with such a small amount of RAM. If the user wants to get the experience of using Linux, then it is sufficient to get started, but don't expect to be able to support multiple users with lots of different devices and so on.

For more serious work, 8 Mbytes of RAM is more comfortable and is sufficient to rebuild kernels and install additional drivers. It is enough to run the X-windows interface albeit with a small screen size of VGA (640 x 480) or SVGA (800 x 600) and with some swapping out to memory.

For an X-windows based system, 16 Mbytes is probably the minimum RAM to use. It is large enough to support RAM-based buffers within X-windows, which speeds up the screen drawing and so on dramatically.

If the system is being used as a multi-user mode with other users logging in remotely across a network connection or through terminals attached to the serial ports, then it is prudent to increase the memory allocation by 1 Mbyte per user. Again, this is not mandatory but better system performance can be obtained by providing sufficient RAM to prevent disk swapping.

Please remember that the RAM sizes mentioned here are minimum values and Linux systems, like most computers, benefit from the maximum amount of memory that can be installed.

Screen support

In terms of screen support, Linux will support almost all the common screen configurations such as EGA, VGA, SVGA, CGA and so on for use within its text-based command line mode. For use with X-windows through XFree86, the VGA and SVGA screen sizes and supported color depths are the basic choices. It is possible to configure XFree86 to work with specific graphics controllers such as ATI and S3 and support different pixel resolutions and color depths but this can be quite involved as it involves the modification of some configuration files. To do this will require the video timing specifications such as refresh rate, dot clock and so on. For more information, refer to Chapter 9.

File systems

Several different types of file systems are supported including MS-DOS. These are explained in more detail later in this chapter.

Installation and configuration

The installation process is split into two segments: the preliminary process is to install all the hardware and test it out and the second part involves booting Linux and installing its components. This involves creating a bootable floppy disk that contains a stripped-down version of Linux along with the appropriate device drivers to access the hard disks, CD-ROMs and/or the network so that the rest of the software can be installed. Typically, this disk is made while running MS-DOS or Windows, but with some releases, a special boot up floppy disk is supplied. With the Linux CD-ROM supplied with this book, a range of different bootable floppies are stored on the disk with a utility that creates a bootable floppy disk. More about this process later.

The process follows this generic pattern:

- Identify and configure the PC hardware.
- Configure the hard disk to create a free partition(s).
- Use an MS-DOS utility such as *rawrite.exe* to create a bootable floppy disk. Some distributions use a single combined floppy disk, others such as Slackware use a separate boot disk and root disk. Depending on the hardware configuration (CD-ROM type and so on), a specific boot disk may need to be selected from a set.
- Boot up the PC using the floppy disk to start the stripped-down version of Linux.
- Assign the spare partition for use with Linux.
- Install a file system on the partition.
- Install the applications and utilities that make up Linux.
- Configure Linux for your use.

The next sections within this chapter will go through both the hard and easy ways of installing Linux. The hard way goes through the steps in detail and is useful in not only understanding the process but when going alone and reconfiguring a Linux system. The easy way is based on the Slackware release that is on the companion CD-ROM.

Preliminary hardware configuration

The first part of the process is to identify all the hardware that is in the system and obtain the associated interrupt, DMA and I/O address information. This data is needed to further configure the Linux boot sequence. Most Linux kernels are built to support many different CD-ROM drives, Ethernet boards, and so on and will automatically detect the presence of this hardware within the system. This autodetect process can take some time and it is possible to override it and speed up the booting process by telling Linux which cards are present and their hardware details.

Interrupt, DMA and I/O addresses

This information is essential to configure Linux and without it, you will have to rely on the autodetection process which is slow and prone to making mistakes. There are several ways of getting this information: the first way is to run MS-DOS version 5.x or greater and then run the *MSD* command. This will display a window that will give a lot of this information for the standard peripherals.

For other cards such as SCSI controllers, Ethernet boards, SoundBlaster cards and associated CD-ROM drivers, the required information can sometimes be obtained by looking at the CONFIG.SYS and AUTOEXEC.BAT files to see the driver entries and how they have been set up. Options such as /I5 and /220 are good clues: an "I" option followed by a number normally indicates the interrupt level, a "d" followed by a number is often used for the DMA channel and a three digit number often represents the I/O address.

The hardware itself can also prove useful with jumper and switch settings defining exactly the hardware details. This is not always the case, especially with boards that are software programmable such as the N2000 clone Ethernet boards. With these, the diagnostic software supplied with the boards is used to either reveal the hardware settings or change them.

With multifunction boards such as SoundBlaster cards with CD-ROM interfaces, there are several sets of hardware settings to be obtained: those for the audio part of the card, and those for the CD-ROM. Most cards allow the audio settings to be changed but can treat the CD-ROM interface in one of two ways: the common method is to locate it at a fixed address and the second method is to locate it at an offset from the audio address. If the SoundBlaster is configured at 0x220 (220 hex), then the CD-ROM interface would be at an offset of 0x020 and be located at 0x260. This offset can vary from card to card and may require delving into the depths of the user manual. In my experience, Linux is more accurate in its requirements for correct addresses compared to MS-DOS drivers and installation programs, which are quite happy to work out offsets automatically. An easy mistake to make with Linux is to force it to look for the CD-ROM at the SoundBlaster audio address — it is often the procedure when installing an MS-DOS driver, so why shouldn't it work with Linux? Trust me, it doesn't... and you either have to specify the exact address or leave it alone and let the autodetect to find the CD-ROM and take note of the address for use next time.

Testing with MS-DOS, Windows, diagnostic software

Armed with the hardware settings, the next process is to test that the hardware works together. It is easier to test the hardware configuration to make sure all the devices work together under MS-DOS or Windows rather than simply start installing Linux and not know if the failure to recognize the CD-ROM is a hardware fault, a software fault or in some cases both!

If Linux is being installed on an existing PC, then the chances are that the system is already correctly configured. With a new machine, it is best to install MS-DOS and/or Windows to ensure that there are no address, interrupt level or DMA channel conflicts that can cause problems. The first thing to do is check the list of settings for duplication or conflict. If there is, then the conflict must be resolved by changing the settings appropriately.

Some boards come with diagnostic software that will test the board and make sure that there are no other conflicts. I strongly recommend that this is done.

Creating a Linux disk preparation

This section describes the process of creating partitions. The process is simple if a spare partition is available in the first place. If this is not the case, and when installing Linux on an existing and working PC, this is often the situation, space must be created on the disk to allow a partition to be defined. The quickest way of doing this is to add a new disk drive, providing that there is a drive connection free. Linux supports the extended IDE interface as well as the normal IDE one and thus supports up to three disk drives and a CD-ROM interface connected to the extended IDE interface. With the standard IDE interface, only two drives or one hard disk and a CD-ROM can be supported. Fortunately, extended IDE cards are inexpensive and upgrading is a low-cost way of having multiple hard disks and CD-ROMs connected to the PC.

The MS-DOS utility that does this is called *FDISK* and unfortunately, its method of reallocating disk space to create a new partition involves deleting an existing partition and then creating a new one with the right size. Deleting a partition will destroy all the data that is stored on it and this is not the desired process.

There are two solutions to this dilemma:

- Backup all the data from the partition before deleting it and creating the new partitions. With the new partitions defined, the data can be copied back to restore the original system.

This assumes that the backup program can copy and restore all the hidden system files that make an IBM PC start MS-DOS/Windows in the first place and second, that there is sufficient free disk space in the original partition to allow two partitions to be derived. The first partition must be big enough to hold the restored data and provide some additional storage for temporary and swap files.

- The second solution is to use the MS-DOS *FIPS* utility which will move files to create the required free space and then adjust the partition information to reduce the size of the original partition and free space to create the new partition.

This is a far neater solution but before use, all data should be backed up in case the utility encounters a problem or the system experiences a power cut. The repartitioning process involves defragmenting the files and moving them around to create the free space as a contiguous set of sectors. If something goes wrong during this process, then the data will be corrupted and irretrievably lost.

The process of assigning partitions for Linux use is performed during the installation process using the Linux *fdisk* utility and is covered in detail later in this chapter.

Creating boot disks

The boot disks are normally supplied either as floppy disks or as disk images stored on the CD-ROM or supplied with the distribution. There are essentially two types:

- A single bootable disk that contains all the files needed to get the system up and running. This is normally created using the *syslinux* command which replaces the MS-DOS boot information with a Linux equivalent.
- A pair of disks with a bootable disk known as boot and a second disk that contains the basic file system and utilities. The bootable disk is like the previous version in that it boots up Linux and gets it started. It typically uses a RAM disk, where some of the system memory is used as a replacement disk drive to provide a temporary file system. This is necessary because the main hard disk drive has not yet been configured.

The bootable disk contains a compressed Linux kernel with all the drivers for a particular system configuration. As a result, there are frequently many to choose from. It is important that the correct one is used, that is, one where the hardware matches the installed drivers. This is particularly important when installing from a CD-ROM or across a network. If the drivers are not there, the hardware cannot be accessed and the software installation will fail.

If the floppy disks are not supplied, then they must be created. This is done by using a MS-DOS utility called *rawwrite.exe* which will transfer an image to a formatted floppy disk. This procedure is shown below. Many distributions including the one supplied with this book, have small batch files that tell you the driver configuration for a particular kernel contained within the image. This allows a final check before the batch file copies the image file across. Any previous contents on the floppy will be destroyed during this operation, so please be careful!

```
J:\BOOTDSKS.12>bare.bat

This option makes the BARE bootdisk.  This disk (in conjunction with
one of the rootdisks in the rootdsks directory) will allow you to
install Linux from floppy disk, floppy tape, or an IDE hard drive.

IT WILL NOT ALLOW YOU TO INSTALL DIRECTLY FROM THE CD-ROM — USE ONE OF
THESE FOR THAT: AZTECH, CDU31A, OLD31A, CDU535, IDECD, MITSUMI, SBPCD,
SCSI.

Insert formatted disk in drive A: and hit a key to continue or CTRL-C
to abort...

Press any key to continue . . .

Number of sectors per track for this disk is 18
Writing image to drive A:.  Press ^C to abort.
Track: 03  Head:  1 Sector:  7
```

Creating a boot disk

Booting Linux for the first time

There are several techniques available to boot Linux. The actual method will depend on the Linux distribution used. The common method, especially when booting for the first time, is to use a boot and root disk. The boot floppy disk contains a compressed kernel that has the drivers for the PC hardware. Typically this would include the drivers to access a CD-ROM or create a network connection via an Ethernet link so that the rest of the software can be loaded from these sources (from the CD-ROM or from another PC running Linux).

The root disk contains the root partition and sufficient software in terms of utilities to allow the rest of the system installation to proceed. While there may be many boot disk images to choose from, the root images are normally limited to a partition or MS-DOS file based contents.

The procedure with the two disk system is to insert the boot disk and reset or restart the PC using CONTROL-ALT-DELETE or by powering off and on. This will display the standard "Linux booting" type of messages and start to install the drivers. At some point during this process, the system will prompt for the insertion of the root disk. Typically the boot disk will create a RAM disk which is used as temporary storage to contain the file system — at this point, the hard disk has not been prepared for use by Linux and is unavailable. Using a RAM disk prevents unnecessary floppy disk swapping and speeds up the process.

With the system up and running, a login prompt will appear. Log in as *root* and, when or if asked for the password, simply press the Return or Enter key. At this point, you are now logged into the system and are ready to start preparing the disk drives by partitioning them and allocating them to Linux.

Making Linux partitions

Linux typically requires a minimum of two partitions: one acts as the file system and the second is used as the swap area for the virtual memory system. These partitions are created and defined using the Linux *fdisk* command — yes, it is the same name as the MS-DOS command! And yes, you can set up the partitions beforehand using the MS-DOS command but will not be able to assign the system IDs. To do this, you will need to use the Linux version. Because of this, it is probably easier to do the partition definition and system ID assignment with the Linux *fdisk* utility, rather than split the tasks.

It is fairly easy to use and allows the many changes to be made to create the partitioning information before it is written to disk to update the configuration.

fdisk

fdisk [device name]

The device name is optional and if not specified, the first drive is used. To specify a specific hard disk drive, the device name is added. For an IDE, ESDI or MFM system, the names are:

/dev/hda   First IDE device
/dev/hdb   Second IDE device
/dev/hdc   Third IDE device
/dev/hdd   Fourth IDE device

The command is an interpreter, that is, it requires additional commands to be entered just like entering commands at the Linux prompt. The commands are:

Standard command set

a   Toggle a bootable flag.
c   Toggle the MS-DOS compatibility flag.

d Delete a partition.

l List known partition types. These are the codes, known as system IDs, that are used to identify the partition type.

m Print this menu — also known as the help command.

n Add a new partition.

p Print the partition table.

q Quit without saving changes. The partition settings revert to the values prior to using the *fdisk* command.

t Change a partition's system ID.

u Change display/entry units.

v Verify the partition table.

w Write table to disk and exit.

x Extra functionality (experts only). This is used to access the expert command set.

Expert command set

b Move beginning of data in a partition. This is used to create holes within the partition table to allow other partitions to be created. This command will destroy any data within the partition.

c Change number of cylinders. This will change the number of cylinders associated with the drive and can be used to override the disk details that are automatically detected.

d Print the raw data in the partition table. This shows the raw data and is useful with unknown partitioning schemes.

e List extended partitions.

h Change number of heads. This will change the number of heads associated with the drive and can be used to override the disk details that are automatically detected.

m Print this menu — also known as the help command.

p Print the partition table.

q Quit without saving changes. The partition settings revert to the values prior to using the *fdisk* command.

r Return to main menu — standard commands.

s Change number of sectors. This will change the number of cylinders associated with the drive and can be used to override the disk details that are automatically detected.

v Verify the partition table.

w Write table to disk and exit.

When installing Linux, this utility is used to define a disk partition for the Linux file system and a partition for the swap area to support the virtual memory system. These two partitions are created by first defining the partition and then assigning the appropriate system ID to it. Examples of creating both partition types are shown in the screen shots. The size of the partitions have been defined by using the number of cylinders but as the prompt shows, the size can be defined in megabytes if necessary. Typically the swap size should be 2-3 times the size of the physical RAM installed in the PC. In this case, the PC has 48 Mbytes of RAM and a swap area of about 90 Mbytes has been used.

In the following examples, the first partition — denoted by a 1 suffix to the drive name — is used for MS-DOS and is not touched. The new partitions — denoted by the 2 and 3 suffixes — are added to create space for the Linux file system and swap area. Access to the MS-DOS partition is not denied and can be set up by making an appropriate entry in the *letc/fstab* file.

```
Command (m for help): p

Disk /dev/hda: 64 heads, 63 sectors, 525 cylinders
Units = cylinders of 4032 * 512 bytes

   Device Boot  Begin   Start    End  Blocks   Id  System
/dev/hda1    *     1      1     204  409720+   6  DOS 16-bit >=32M
Partition 1 does not end on cylinder boundary:
     phys=(203, 15, 63) should be (203, 63, 63)

Command (m for help): n
Command action
   e   extended
   p   primary partition (1-4)
p
Partition number (1-4): 2
First cylinder (204-525):
First cylinder (204-525): 204
Last cylinder or +size or +sizeM or +sizeK ([204]-525): 500

Command (m for help): t
Partition number (1-4): 2
Hex code (type L to list codes): l

  0   Empty            9  AIX bootable    75  PC/IX          b7  BSDI fs
  1   DOS 12-bit FAT   a  OS/2 Boot Manag 80  Old MINIX      b8  BSDI swap
  2   XENIX root      40  Venix 80286     81  Linux/MINIX    c7  Syrinx
  3   XENIX usr       51  Novell?         82  Linux swap     db  CP/M
  4   DOS 16-bit <32M 52  Microport       83  Linux native   e1  DOS access
  5   Extended        63  GNU HURD        93  Amoeba         e3  DOS R/O
  6   DOS 16-bit >=32 64  Novell Netware  94  Amoeba BBT     f2  DOS sec-
ondary
  7   OS/2 HPFS       65  Novell Netware  a5  BSD/386        ff  BBT
  8   AIX
Hex code (type L to list codes): 83
```

Creating a disk partition

```
Command (m for help): n
Command action
   e    extended
   p    primary partition (1-4)
p
Partition number (1-4): 3
First cylinder (501-525): 501
Last cylinder or +size or +sizeM or +sizeK ([501]-525): 525

Command (m for help): t
Partition number (1-4): 3
Hex code (type L to list codes): 82
Changed system type of partition 3 to 82 (Linux swap)

Command (m for help): p

Disk /dev/hda: 64 heads, 63 sectors, 525 cylinders
Units = cylinders of 4032 * 512 bytes

    Device Boot  Begin   Start     End   Blocks   Id  System
/dev/hda1    *       1       1     204  409720+    6  DOS 16-bit >=32M
Partition 1 does not end on cylinder boundary:
     phys=(203, 15, 63) should be (203, 63, 63)
/dev/hda2          204     204     500  598248    83  Linux native
/dev/hda3          501     501     525   50400    82  Linux swap

Command (m for help): q
```

Creating a swap area

There are several points about using the Linux *fdisk* command:

- It is like the MS-DOS *fdisk* command in that changing a partition will destroy any data that is stored on it.
- To see the partition details, use the p (print) command. This will "print" the information on the screen and not on a printer.
- Do not forget to write any changes to the disk using the w command. The changes are not automatically written and therefore do not take effect until this command is used.
- If a mistake has been made and you need to start again or alternatively restore the original settings, use the q command.

The partitioning must be done for all drives in the system before they can be used.

Drives and partition names

The *fdisk* command will use the first drive it encounters but with systems with multiple drives or those that use SCSI instead of or as well as IDE, the drive name must be specified. The problem that is usually encountered is... What are their names? A good clue can be obtained by watching the startup messages in some, but not all, cases. To help overcome this problem, the common names for disk drives on IDE and SCSI controllers use a consistent pattern as follows:

Name	Description
/dev/fd0	The first floppy disk drive (A:).
/dev/fd1	The second floppy disk drive (B:).
/dev/hda	The *whole* first disk drive (IDE or BIOS compatible disk drive e.g. ESDI, ST506 and so on).
/dev/hda1	The first primary partition on the first drive.
/dev/hda2	The second primary partition on the first drive.
/dev/hda3	The third primary partition on the first drive.
/dev/hda4	The fourth primary partition on the first drive.
/dev/hdb	The *whole* second disk drive.
/dev/hdb1	The first primary partition on the second drive.
/dev/hdb2	The second primary partition on the second drive.
/dev/hdb3	The third primary partition on the second drive.
/dev/hdb4	The fourth primary partition on the second drive.
/dev/hdc	The *whole* third disk drive.
/dev/hdc1	The first primary partition on the third drive.
/dev/hdc2	The second primary partition on the third drive.
/dev/hdc3	The third primary partition on the third drive.
/dev/hdc4	The fourth primary partition on the third drive.
/dev/hdd	The *whole* fourth disk drive.
/dev/hdd1	The first primary partition on the fourth drive.
/dev/hdd2	The second primary partition on the fourth drive.
/dev/hdd3	The third primary partition on the fourth drive.
/dev/hdd4	The fourth primary partition on the fourth drive.
/dev/sda	The *whole* first disk drive (LUN 0) on the first SCSI controller.
/dev/sda1	The first primary partition on the first drive.
	And so on...

With the partitions created, the next job is to create the file systems on the partitions.

Installing the Slackware release

The easiest way of installing Linux is to use the automated facility provided with the Slackware release. It is this release that is provided on the companion CD-ROM. To access it, enter the command *setup*. This will display a menu driven interface with a set of commands, as shown in the figure below. These commands will automatically set up the system and transfer the software into its correct location.

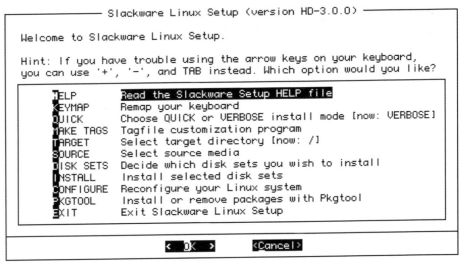

The setup main menu

Keymap

This command allows the keyboard nationality to be set up. The default is US. The resulting menu lists a number of country command files. These are identified by the suffix at the end of each file name. After selecting one, it can be tested to ensure that it is correct. This is a self-contained command that returns to the main menu.

Quick

This describes the method for selecting the installed software. This should be set to *QUICK*. If it is not, use this command to change it. Again, this is a self contained command that returns to the main menu.

Make Tags

This is an advanced command that can be ignored in most cases. It allows the software selections to be changed.

Target

This sets up the Linux partition(s) and allows them to be formatted and a file system created for each one. It works by displaying a list of partitions and then asking which one will be used for the root directory and so on. It can also check the disk integrity for bad blocks. This command is not self contained. On completion, you can either go to the next command or back to the main menu.

Source

This command selects the software source. It can be floppy based, from a CD-ROM, from a local hard disk or from another machine on a network. The easiest way is from a CD-ROM. This assumes that the boot kernel has the appropriate CD-ROM driver installed. The command will ask for the CD-ROM drive type to be chosen and will mount the CD-ROM as part of the file system so that it can be used. Make sure that the disc is installed. On completion, you can either go to the next command or back to the main menu.

There are a couple of further options to consider: when installing from a CD-ROM, the software can be installed onto the hard disk, which is the faster and most common option or alternatively, the software can be linked to the hard disk. This means that links are created on the hard disk that refer back to the actual files on the CD-ROM. The advantageof this is that it dramatically reduces the amount of hard disk space that is needed. The disadvantage is that the performance can be slower because of the CD-ROM's slower access time and data rates. ***This option is not supported on the companion CD-ROM***. The files were removed to install the kernel libraries and other information. If you want to use this method, you will need to get the Slackware CD-ROM from Walnut Creek. This will give you a lot more additional software as well as the latest releases.

Installing from a floppy disk is possible but requires transferring the different disk sets to floppy disk prior to installation. This can be done but it does take a lot of disks and is slow and cumbersome. If you don't have a CD-ROM on the target machine, then this can be a good but time-consuming method.

It is also possible to install across a network. This requires that you have a machine already running Linux with the networking support for NFS already installed. This is described in Chapter 8. The trick is to make the CD-ROM mountable by creating an appropriate NFS entry. This will allow the other system to mount it remotely across the network and thus use it to get the software transferred and installed. The target system must be booted with a kernel that has the network software and drivers for the target Ethernet card. If this is not available, you cannot use this method. The problems arise when the network cannot make a connection: is it a problem with the target system kernel or hardware? If so, how do you resolve it? I have done it using a standard NE2000 card at a "standard" I/O address with a "standard" interrupt setting but I believe I was lucky, having talked to several others who have failed!

If the network option is selected, the script will ask for the IP address of the other system and the directory as well. The target system will need its IP address to be set up so that the remote server will recognize it. An alternative is to set up the remote to accept any access. The script will then try and mount the remote directory. If this is successful, all well and good. If not, then either the fault must be traced and rectified or an alternative method used to install the software. All in all, if it goes wrong, it makes buying a CD-ROM drive and installing it a very sound investment indeed.

Disk sets

This command allows the installer to define which software components should be added. I would install the base system only first to make sure that the system runs correctly before proceeding to install the rest. The rest of the components can be installed at a later date by running setup and selecting this command directly. If a disk set has been installed and is not selected when installing additional software, it is not deleted but remains intact. On completion, you can either go to the next command or back to the main menu.

Install

This command will install the software as defined by the disk sets. It will prompt for choices on each set and will mark the recommended selections by a cross. Use the up and down cursor keys to make a selection and then press the space bar to select or deselect. When the choices have been made, highlight the OK button and press Enter. The software will then be installed. Simply using the default selections will be enough to get the system software installed and up and running. There is one exception to this and this concerns the choice of kernel. Only one should be chosen and this should include the drivers for your system (CD-ROM, IDE, SCSI drives and so on). If the wrong kernel is chosen, then the system may boot up but not recognize the system hardware. If this is the case, boot the system using the original root floppy disk and use setup again to select the right kernel. For IDE-based PCs with SoundBlaster CD-ROM drives, the *sbpcd1* kernel is the right choice. On completion, you can either go to the next command or back to the main menu.

Configure

This command will configure the system and setup the mouse, networking names and IP addresses (see Chapter 8 for more on networking). This is a self contained command that returns to the main menu. Configure can also be run later to overwrite and change the settings. If you do this, all the settings need to be re-entered to ensure that they are correctly configured.

Pkgtool

> This tool is used to install or remove additional software selections. This is a self-contained command that returns to the main menu.

Exit

> This command exits the *setup* command and returns to the prompt.

Installing the swap file manually

> If you have used the *setup* command, then this is done when the TARGET command is selected. Linux will then as part of its startup turn the swapping on and there is no need to perform this manually. For completeness, I have included the manual procedure here.

> There are times in trying to rescue a system, when you need to install the swap file manually. This is done in three stages: the first requires the creation of the swap partition as previously explained. The second uses the *mkswap* command to create the swap area on the partition. The final step is to switch the swapping on using the *swapon* command.

mkswap

> mkswap -c [partition] [size]

> The device name is optional and if not specified, the first drive is used. To specify a specific hard disk drive, the device name is added. The file names are the same as the detailed in the previous section.

swapon

> swapon -c [partition] [size]

> The device name is optional and if not specified, the first drive is used. To specify a specific hard disk drive, the device name is added — refer to the list prior to this section for actual names.

Installing the file system manually

> This is also done through the TARGET command from the Slackware setup menu and providing no other changes have been made, the system will automatically check the file systems and mount them.

> If a new disk drive has been added, then it must have a file system installed. The first step is to partition it using the *fdisk* command and thus create partitions with a type "Linux native." The second stage is to install the file system using the *mke2fs* command.

mke2fs

mke2fs -c partition size

The device name is optional and if not specified, the first drive is used. To specify a specific hard disk drive, the device name is added. For an IDE system, refer to the list earlier in this chapter. This command assumes that the file system type is the ext2 type, which is the standard file system used on floppy disks. There are alternative systems available and these can be used instead by using the *mkfs* command instead.

mkfs

mkfs -c partition size type

This is almost like the MS-DOS format command in that it installs the directory structure onto a partition prior to its use. Linux supports several different file systems as shown in the following table, but the most commonly used are MS-DOS format to allow the ability to transfer files between an MS-DOS/Windows environment and Linux and the ext2 format which supports long file names (256 characters) and is the predominant format in use.

Type name	Description
ext2	Second extended file system. This is the normally used file format.
ext	Extended file system. This has been superseded by ext2 but is occasionally seen with older releases of Linux.
minix	Minix file system. This is a historical artifact from the origins of Linux that was based on the minix operating system.
xia	Xia file system. Similar to ext2 but rarely used.
uMS-DOS	UMS-DOS file system. This is used to create a Linux file system by using a MS-DOS file instead of a disk partition.
MS-DOS	MS-DOS file system. This provides compatibility and access to MS-DOS systems. It is not used for Linux systems in general because of its limited 8+3 character file names.
proc	/proc file system. This is not a true file system as such. It is used to access process and other system performance and configuration information.
iso9660	ISO 9660 format. This is used to access CD-ROMs.
xenix	Xenix file system format. This is used to access Xenix files.
sysv	System V file format. This is used to access Unix System V files.
coherent	Coherent file system. This is used to access files from Coherent Unix based systems.
hpfs	HPFS files system for double space drives — read only access.

With the files systems created, entries must now be made in a couple of files so that the new files systems / disks can be mounted and made available. The files in question are */etc/mtab* and */etc/fstab*. The commands to mount and unmount the file systems are *mount* and *umount*. They can be used with explicit names for the partitions, as outlined in Chapter 3, but the easy way to use them is to create entries in these tables. Entries in the */etc/mtab* table have the benefit of automatically mounting when the system starts.

To create an entry, the following data is needed: the name of the physical device, the target directory that the device will be mounted as, the file system type, the read write access and a couple of optional numbers that may be used by the file system.

```
hosts1:/etc# cat mtab
/dev/hda2 / ext2 rw 1 1
/dev/hda1 /MS-DOS MS-DOS rw 1 1
none /proc proc rw 1 1
/dev/hdc /cdrom iso9660 ro 0 0
hosts1:/etc#
hosts1:/etc# cat fstab
/dev/hda3          swap          swap          defaults    1    1
/dev/hda2          /             ext2          defaults    1    1
/dev/hda1          /MS-DOS       MS-DOS         defaults    1     1
none               /proc         proc          defaults    1    1
hosts1:/etc#
```

To use these tables, use the *mount* command with the target directory. To mount a CD-ROM, type *mount /cdrom*. To unmount it, type *umount /cdrom*. To add new entries to the tables, use an editor like vi or append a new line directly from the keyboard. Whitespace is used to separate the data. The example shown allows the A: floppy disk to be mounted as the directory */flopA*.

```
hosts1:/etc# echo "/dev/fd0    /flopA    MS-DOS    defaults    1    1" >>fstab
hosts1:/etc# cat fstab
/dev/hda3          swap          swap          defaults    1    1
/dev/hda2          /             ext2          defaults    1    1
/dev/hda1          /MS-DOS       MS-DOS         defaults    1     1
none               /proc         proc          defaults    1    1
/dev/fd0           /flopA        MS-DOS         defaults    1    1
hosts1:/etc#
```

Rebuilding the kernel

It is important when installing the source of new kernels to ensure that they go in the right location along with the correct links. It can be very frustrating when a silly mistake can result in a wasted recompilation.

The source code is normally stored in */usr/src* in a special directory which is normally called *linux*. Unfortunately, this is not quite as straightforward as you would imagine. The directory *linux* is actually a symbolic link to the actual directory that contains the kernel source. This means that the normal practice when you have multiple kernels is to place each set of source files into their own directory and then change the link so */usr/src/linux* points to the required directory.

To confuse matters, this procedure is not strictly necessary and I have successfully recompiled kernels by simply going into the directory and issuing the *make* commands from that directory. However, this falls down with some drivers that require a kernel recompile to not only include the driver but also generate other files such as headers and library files so that related applications can be generated. The application *make* files may assume that */usr/src/linux* contains the source files and if the kernel and driver havebeen built elsewhere, the *make* scripts will fail.

Installing the source files

The kernel source is normally stored in */usr/src/linux* where *Linux* is actually a link to the directory that actually contains the source. Depending on the distribution, there may be several directories within the */usr/src* location that contain various releases or versions of the kernel. The Linux link can be found by using the *ls -alsi* command. Typically the kernel source is stored in a separate directory and a link is then made to */usr/src/linux*. For example, the kernel source for version 2.0.20 may be stored in a directory */usr/src/v2.0.20*. A symbolic link is then made linking */usr/src/linux* to */usr/src/v2.0.20/linux*. If there are other directories with different kernels, this link should be changed as needed. If it is not, then there is a possibility that a kernel rebuild or associated application compilation might file. I must admit that I don't change this link and in general it has not been a problem. However, I did not do it once and it cost me a day finding why a utility would not compile!

Decompressing

Most Linux software, including kernels and patches, is available in a compressed tar format and have the suffix .gz. The command to install the files is:

tar -xzvf kernel.gz

```
sodom:/usr/src# mkdir v2.0.20
sodom:/usr/src# dir /home/ftp/incoming
linux-2.0.20.tar.gz
sodom:/usr/src#
sodom:/usr/src# cp /home/ftp/incoming/* v2.0.20
sodom:/usr/src# dir v2.0.20
linux-2.0.20.tar.gz
sodom:/usr/src# cd v2.0.20
```

```
sodom:/usr/src/v2.0.20# tar -xzvf linux-2.0.20.tar.gz
```

- •
- • A list of the files appears here as they are decompressed and installed.
- •

```
Linux/Documentation/ide.txt
Linux/Documentation/logo.gif
Linux/Documentation/logo.txt
Linux/Documentation/xterm-linux.xpm
sodom:/usr/src/v2.0.20# dir
Linux/                   linux-2.0.20.tar.gz
sodom:/usr/src/v2.0.20#ln -s /usr/src/v2.0.20/linux /usr/src/linux/
```

Symbolic links

The Linux system assumes some links especially when applications use files that are produced from the kernel compilation. Without these links, some of the application *make* files can fail. This is similar to the symbolic link */usr/src/linux* that was described earlier. The required links are shown below.

```
root>cd /usr/include
root>rm -rf Linux
root>rm -rf asm
root>ln -s /usr/src/linux/include/linux Linux
root>ln -s /usr/src/linux/include/asm-i386 asm
```

The *make* procedure(s)

To build a new kernel, it is necessary to use a combination of *make* commands that will either clean out files from previous versions or create a new kernel immediately. The commands are actually scripts that are used by the *make* utility to control the build process. The *make* utility is very sophisticated, but fortunately knowledge of how it is used and perhaps more important, how the scripts are created, is not needed. The kernel source comes with several pre-defined scripts and commands. If new drivers are added to the kernel source, the act of patching the original source will modify the scripts so that they work as before, but this time include the additional commands to include the new software.

make depend   Cleans out dependencies. This is often used with *make clean* to clear out old versions prior to a rebuild. This particular utility removes dependencies so that old files are not used.

make clean   Cleans out all files by deleting object files and so on and thus forcing the compilation of the different modules prior to their use in building up the kernel.

make mrproper   Cleans out all files and does a better job!

make config	Sets up the configuration information that switches drivers in and out.
make menuconfig	Performs the same function as *make config* except that it uses a pretty menu-based interface.
make xconfig	Performs the same function as *make config* except that it uses a X-windows based interface.
make zImage	Creates a new kernel based on the configuration information created by the *make* command. The kernel file is called *zImage* and is in */usr/src/linux/arch/i386/boot*.
make zdisk	This also creates a new kernel but will write it to a floppy disk inserted into drive A at the end of the operation, using the *dd* command. The floppy disk should be formatted to prevent a transfer error. If it is not, then the transfer can be done manually without having to rebuild the kernel.

To use these commands, you will need to be in the Linux directory of the kernel source. This is created automatically when the .gz file is decompressed. The next stage is to clean out the files so that past versions are not used by mistake. This is very important to prevent errors. This can be done on three levels using the *make dep, make clean* and *make mrproper* commands.

```
sodom:/usr/src# pwd
/usr/src
sodom:/usr/src# dir
atm/                linux-1.3.20/      sendmail/        v2.0.20/
atm07.tar*          linux-1.3.53/      snd-util.tar*    xview/
ftape-2.03b.tar.gz  linux1.3.53.tar*   sndkit/
ghostscript-2.6.2/  linuxelf-1.2.13/   term-2.3.5/
Linux/              ncurses-1.9.4/     v2/
sodom:/usr/src# cd v2.0.20
sodom:/usr/src/v2.0.20# dir
Linux/              linux-2.0.20.tar.gz
sodom:/usr/src/v2.0.20# cd Linux
sodom:/usr/src/v2.0.20/linux# make dep
```

-
- A list of the files and directories appears here
- as they are cleansed.
-

```
make[1]: Leaving directory '/usr/src/v2.0.20/linux/arch/i386/mm'
make[1]: Entering directory '/usr/src/v2.0.20/linux/arch/i386/lib'
if [ -n "checksum.c semaphore.S" ]; then \
gawk -f /usr/src/v2.0.20/linux/scripts/depend.awk *.[chS] > .depend; fi
make[1]: Leaving directory '/usr/src/v2.0.20/linux/arch/i386/lib'
mv .tmpdepend .depend
sodom:/usr/src/v2.0.20/linux#
```

Configuring the kernel

With the kernel source installed, the next stage is to configure all the build parameters so that the recompilation builds the kernel with all the required drivers that are needed. As mentioned previously, there are three *make* commands that can do this: *config, menuconfig* and *xconfig*. *Config* is line based, *menuconfig* is menu based and *xconfig* uses X windows. When using either *menuconfig* or *xconfig*, it is not uncommon for the utilities to be compiled before they are executed. If you see some strange commands appear — don't panic! Allthat you are seeing is this process.

The rest of the section shows how the *make config* command is used. This is the text based version and easy to use, albeit a little long-winded at times!

It works by displaying a question about the system and prompting a response from the user. This can consist of one of five characters followed by a Return or Enter key. The choices are:

N   No! This option is not required.

Y   Yes! This option is required.

?   Help required. This will normally print a detailed help file and recommend some suggestions for making a choice.

M   Yes, this option is required but install as a module. This is sometimes available as an option but not always.

<Return>   Pressing Return or the Enter key will select the default option. The default selection is normally shown as the first letter within the square brackets and is typically in capitals where the other options are lowercase. When responding to the prompt either upper or lowercase characters are recognized.

```
make config
rm -f include/asm
( cd include ; ln -sf asm-i386 asm)
/bin/sh scripts/Configure arch/i386/config.in
#
# Using defaults found in .config
#
*
* Code maturity level options
*
Prompt for development and/or incomplete code/drivers
(CONFIG_EXPERIMENTAL) [N/y/?] ?

This option is for experienced users only. If N is selected then experi-
mental i.e. software that is known to have bugs can be configued and
selected. The recommended response for most users is N.
```

```
•
• A list of the options appears here
•

*
* Kernel hacking
*
Kernel profiling support (CONFIG_PROFILE) [N/y/?] ?

This is for kernel hackers who want to know how much time the kernel
spends in the various procedures. Most people do not select it and enter
N.


The Linux kernel is now hopefully configured for your setup.
Check the top-level Makefile for additional configuration,
and do a 'make dep ; make clean' if you want to be sure all
the files are correctly re-made

sodom:/usr/src/v2/linux#
```

Compiling the kernel

With the kernel configured, it is time to compile the kernel. There are two commands that will do this: *make zImage* and *make zdisk*. The *zImage* version will create the new kernel as a file called zImage in the directory */usr/src/v2/linux/ arch/i386/boot/* and this can then be transferred to its final destination or directly used by the *lilo* command (see the next section).

The *zdisk* command also compiles the kernel but writes the file onto a formatted floppy disk ready for testing. It is important that a blank formatted floppy disk is available before executing this instruction. If it is not, it will be overwritten

```
sodom:/usr/src/v2.0.20/linux# make zDisk

•
• A list of the files appears here as they are compiled
•

make[2]: Leaving directory '/usr/src/v2/linux/arch/i386/boot/compressed'
objdump -k -q  -o 0x1000 compressed/vmlinux > compressed/vmlinux.out
tools/build bootsect setup compressed/vmlinux.out CURRENT > zImage
Root device is (3, 2)
Boot sector 512 bytes.
Setup is 4332 bytes.
System is 355 kB
sync

sodom:/usr/src/v2/linux#
```

If an error occurs during the compilation, it can be cured by cleaning out the files by using the *make dep; make clean; make proper* command to ensure that everything is correct and old corrupt files are not used by mistake. In some cases, I have even found deleting all the files and reinstalling the source will cure any build problems. Other problems can be caused if a driver is not used with a particular version of the kernel. It should not be assumed that a driver that asks for version 1.3.54 of the kernel will work with earlier revisions. It might but there is probably a good reason why the author has asked for a particular version — it doesn't work with anything earlier! Later versions are usually fine but if an error is encountered, it may be worth using the exact version that the author specifies to prove that it works.

Testing the new kernel

Direct from a disk

To do this, the rebuilt kernel is transferred to a floppy disk and the system booted using the floppy disk instead of the hard disk. The advantage this offers is that the original kernel is left alone and if the rebuilt kernel crashes, the system can be rebooted as normal using the hard disk.

There are two simple ways of transferring the image to the floppy disk: the first uses the facility incorporated in the *make zDisk* command. The second method uses the *make zImage* command and then transfers the *zImage* file to the floppy disk.

```
dd bs=8192 if=/dev/fd0
dd: /dev/fd0: No such device or address
make[1]: *** [zdisk] Error 1
make[1]: Leaving directory '/usr/src/v2/linux/arch/i386/boot'
make: *** [zdisk] Error 2
sodom:/usr/src/v2/linux#
sodom:/usr/src/v2/linux# cd /usr/src/v2/linux/arch/i386/boot
sodom:/usr/src/v2/linux/arch/i386/boot# dd bs=8192 if=/dev/fd0
dd: /dev/fd0: No such file or directory
1+0 records in
0+1 records out
sodom:/usr/src/v2/linux/arch/i386/boot#
```

The second method uses the Lilo loader as described in the next section.

Lilo configuration

The *lilo* utility is the most commonly used Linux loader and it uses a configuration file to control and define how and which kernel is booted up. The configuration file is used by the Linux command */sbin/lilo* to configure the loader software and install it on the hard disk that is used to boot from. The file works by defining a label and associating with it the location of the Linux kernel that should be booted.

It is in fact a replacement for the MS-DOS boot program thatresides on sector 0 of a bootable disk or floppy. It replaces this with a utility that knows where various Linux kernels are located and provides a simple text-based menu to allow the user to select them. In addition, it can relocate the original MS-DOS (or Windows, Windows '95 or Windows NT) boot software to a different location so that the original Microsoft boot procedure can be followed. This facility, coupled with the use of separate partitions, allows a PC to run multiple operating systems. *lilo* can be configured either manually or through the Slackware setup routines. In either case, the configuration information is stored in a file called */etc/lilo.conf.*

/etc/lilo.conf

The configuration file consists of several parts: the first part contains information thatis common to the booting of any Linux kernel and effectively defines the default settings that will be used. The second part is the settings that allow the standard MS-DOS boot to occur. This is given a specific name and can be called from the *lilo* prompt to boot any MS-DOS or Windows-based operating system. This is done by referring *lilo* to the MS-DOS boot information instead of a kernel. The third part contains the references for the Linux kernel(s) and is where additional entries are stored to support multiple different kernels. By using this facility, different kernel versions or versions with different driver sets can be stored on the disk and simply selected at boot time.

Please note that comments can be added to the file by prefixing them with a hash (#). It is a good idea to comment the different kernels and have names that convey some idea of the kernel's capabilities. In the examples shown, this has been done by adding the version number or a description of the kernel's capabilities.

```
sodom:~# cat /etc/lilo.conf
# LILO configuration file
# generated by 'liloconfig'
#
# Start LILO global section
append="eth0=0x300,0x0b  sbpcd=0x230,SoundBlaster"
boot = /dev/hda
#compact         # faster, but won't work on all systems.
prompt
vga = normal     # force sane state
ramdisk = 0      # paranoia setting
# End LILO global section
# DOS bootable partition config begins
```

```
other = /dev/hda1
  label = WIN95
  table = /dev/hda
# DOS bootable partition config ends
# Linux bootable partition config begins
# This is version 1.2.13 with SoundBlaster support.
image = /linux-1.2.13
  root = /dev/hda2
  label = linux-1.2.13
  read-only # Non-UMS-DOS filesystems should be mounted read-only for
checking
# Linux bootable partition config ends
# This is version 1.3.20 with SoundBlaster support.
image = /linux-1.3.20
   root = /dev/hda2
   label = linux-1.3.20
   read-only
# Entry for experimental ATM kernel
# This is version 1.3.53 with ATM support.
 image = /linux-ATM
   root = /dev/hda2
   label = linux-ATM
   read-only
# Entry for experimental kernel
# This is an experimental kernel.
image = /zImage
  root = /dev/hda2
  label = test-linux
  read-only
# Linux bootable partition config begins
image = /linux-v2
  root = /dev/hda2
  label = linux-v2
  read-only # Non-UMS-DOS filesystems should be mounted read-only for
checking
# Linux bootable partition config ends
# End of real config file
sodom:~# /sbin/lilo
Added WIN95 *
Added linux-1.2.13
Added linux-1.3.20
Added linux-ATM
Added test-linux
Added linux-v2
sodom:~#
```

Configuring lilo using liloconfig

This is a menu driven tool for creating an initial *lilo.conf* file. The word "initial" is used advisedly because it does not allow the creation of multiple entries for Linux kernels. For inexperienced users, this is easier than worrying about how to use *vi* and editing the file directly.

```
sodom:~# liloconfig

LILO INSTALLATION

LILO (the Linux Loader) is the program that allows booting Linux directly
from
the hard drive. To install, you make a new LILO configuration file by
creating
a new header and then adding at least one bootable partition to the file.
Once
you've done this, you can select the install option. Alternately, if you
already have an /etc/lilo.conf, you may reinstall using that. If you make
a
mistake, just select (1) to start over.

1 - Start LILO configuration with a new LILO header
2 - Add a Linux partition to the LILO config file
3 - Add an OS/2 partition to the LILO config file
4 - Add a DOS partition to the LILO config file
5 - Install LILO
6 - Reinstall LILO using the existing lilo.conf
7 - Skip LILO installation and exit this menu
8 - View your current /etc/lilo.conf
9 - Read the Linux Loader HELP file

Which option would you like (1 - 9)? 2
```

Configuring lilo manually

To manually update the configuration, the file is edited using an editor like *vi* or *emacs* and the entries changed accordingly.

Using Lilo with existing operating systems

By using Lilo carefully, it is possible to arrange for multiple operating systems to be loaded and available on a single PC. The trick is to load the Lilo program onto the master boot record (MBR) of the startup hard disk and then create a Lilo entry for that disk. By doing this, Lilo will pass control over to the original Microsoft MBR software and the system can boot up MS-DOS and the Windows or even go into another loader program like that supplied with Windows NT. In this case, the system offers Windows NT as well.

The key is to create a Lilo entry for the MS-DOS startup disk like this:

```
# DOS bootable partition config begins
other = /dev/hda1
  label = WIN95
  table = /dev/hda
# DOS bootable partition config ends
```

The */dev/hda1* is the Linux name for the MS-DOS partition. WIN95 is the name that has been assigned to it and is used at the *lilo* prompt. The */dev/hda* entry refers to the Linux name for the whole disk drive that contains the MS-DOS partition. This entry can be used as a template and inserted into the *lilo.conf* file. With most PCs that use standard drives such as IDE where the first partition is used for MS-DOS, the */dev/hda* and */dev/hda1* entries are the correct ones. All that is needed is to change the name if required.

Booting with lilo

When the PC is started, *lilo* will run and it will present a prompt and wait for a choice to be made. By pressing the Tab key, it will list all the possibilities. By simply pressing theReturn key, the first entry will be selected. To select any others, the name must be entered followed by pressing the Return key. The system will then boot up and display a list of status information. This is useful when checking any modifications. The data can be retrieved by using the *dmesg* command once logged in. It will print to the screen the same bootup status information.

```
LILO boot:
LILO boot: WIN95  linux-1.2.13  linux-1.3.20  linux-ATM  test-linux linux-
v2
LILO boot: linux-v2
Linux booting......
Uncompressing kernel......
Console: 16 point font, 400 scans
Console: colour VGA+ 80x25, 1 virtual console (max 63)
Calibrating delay loop.. ok - 31.85 BogoMIPS
Memory: 14884k/16384k available (620k kernel code, 384k reserved, 496k
data)
This processor honours the WP bit even when in supervisor mode. Good.
Swansea University Computer Society NET3.035 for Linux 2.0
NET3: Unix domain sockets 0.12 for Linux NET3.035.
Swansea University Computer Society TCP/IP for NET3.034
IP Protocols: ICMP, UDP, TCP
Checking 386/387 coupling... Ok, fpu using exception 16 error reporting.
Checking 'hlt' instruction... Ok.
Linux version 2.0.0 (root@sodom) (gcc version 2.7.0) #1 Tue Oct 1 16:17:24
GMT 1
996
Serial driver version 4.13 with no serial options enabled
tty00 at 0x03f8 (irq = 4) is a 16450
tty01 at 0x02f8 (irq = 3) is a 16450
hda: ST51080A, 1033MB w/128kB Cache, LBA, CHS=2100/16/63
ide0 at 0x1f0-0x1f7,0x3f6 on irq 14
Floppy drive(s): fd0 is 1.44M
Started kswapd v 1.4.2.2
FDC 0 is an 8272A
```

```
sbpcd-0 [01]:  sbpcd.c v4.4 Eberhard Moenkeberg <emoenke@gwdg.de>
sbpcd-0 [02]:  Scanning 0x230 (SoundBlaster)...
sbpcd-0 [03]:  Drive 0 (ID=0): CR-562 (0.76) at 0x230 (type 1)
ne.c:v1.10 9/23/94 Donald Becker (becker@cesdis.gsfc.nasa.gov)
NE*000 ethercard probe at 0x300: 00 c0 f6 20 11 9c
eth0: NE2000 found at 0x300, using IRQ 11.
Partition check:
 hda: hda1 hda2 hda3 hda4
VFS: Mounted root (ext2 filesystem) readonly.
Adding Swap: 93236k swap-space
sbpcd-0 [04]:  sbpcd_open: no disk in drive.
VFS: Disk change detected on device 02:00
end_request: I/O error, dev 02:00, sector 0
sbpcd-0 [05]:  sbpcd_open: no disk in drive.
Unable to identify CD-ROM format.


Welcome to Linux v2.0.0

Sodom login:
```

Testing kernels

A good trick is to have an entry in the *lilo.conf* file for a generic kernel such as */test/zImage* with a suitable name such as test-linux. A new kernel can be copied into this location and the */sbin/lilo* utility executed. The system is rebooted and the test-linux kernel entered in response to the *lilo* prompt. If it crashes or does not do what is expected, the system can be booted using a different kernel by entering a different name.

If */sbin/lilo* is not run, then the boot process is likely to halt with an error. The reason is that *lilo* uses the physical kernel location and by overwriting without updating, the data can be corrupted. The system will start to boot but fail with a buffer error of some kind.

Patching kernels

New drivers are typically added by patching the kernel source using a patch file and the patch command. The procedure is as follows. The patch file is decompressed and placed in the kernel source directory. This will use the *tar* command in the same way that it is used to decompress and install the original kernel: *tar -xzvf patchfile.gz*. This should then patch the kernel source and add configuration information to the config file if necessary.

The next stage is to compile the kernel so that the drivers are included. After this has been completed, the new patched kernel complete with new drivers/ bug fixes and so on can be tested. These stages follow the methods previously described in this chapter.

The CD-ROM has the kernel patch files for the intermediate versions of the kernel and each one must be run on the base level kernel to create the new version. For example to create a kernel version 1.3.54, install the source for kernel version 1.3.50 and then patch it with *patch.1.3.51, patch.1.3.52, patch1.3.53,* and finally *patch1.3.54* to create the kernel source 1.3.54. The kernel can now be recompiled to create the 1.3.54 version. It is not necessary to compile the intermediate versions unless these are specifically required as well.

The */proc* file system

Linux has a special file system called /proc. This is not a file system in the true sense of the term but a simple method of getting information about the system using the normal tools and utilities. As will be shown, this is not always the case and there is at least one special utility commonly used with this file system. It is useful in making sure that all the drivers and other system components you expected to be installed are actually there.

To access the */proc* file system, it must be built into the kernel. Most, if not all, standard kernels do this to provide debugging information at the very least. If you are running a special kernel make sure that it is selected in the configuration file.

The simple method of accessing the contents of */proc* is to go to that directory and display the contents of the files using the *cat* command. The commonly used files will show the following system data:

ioports   This file will display the I/O cards and devices installed and recognized within the system. Please note that only recognized devices are listed here. If you have a card installed without the relevant driver built into the Linux kernel, the card will not appear in this list. This list is useful in making sure installed cards are recognized and located correctly.

```
sodom:/proc# cat ioports
0000-001f : dma1
0020-003f : pic1
0040-005f : timer
0060-006f : keyboard
0080-009f : dma page reg
00a0-00bf : pic2
00c0-00df : dma2
00f0-00ff : npu
01f0-01f7 : ide0
0230-0233 : sbpcd
02f8-02ff : serial(auto)
```

```
0300-031f : NE2000
03c0-03df : vga+
03f0-03f5 : floppy
03f6-03f6 : ide0
03f7-03f7 : floppy DIR
03f8-03ff : serial(auto)
sodom:/proc#
```

mounts This file lists the file systems that have been mounted. It shows the partitions, their file system names, their file system types and read/write permissions followed by major and minor numbers.

```
sodom:/proc# cat mounts
rootfs / ext2 rw 0 0
/dev/hda3 /usr ext2 rw 0 0
/dev/hda1 /WIN95 MS-DOS rw 0 0
none /proc proc rw 0 0
```

kcore Do not use *cat* to display this file. It is a binary file and will only send strange characters to the screen and potentially lock up the terminal and its connection.

net/ This is a directory that contains several files that have information on the network and can be used to display transmission statistics. These files are really for the advanced user.

cmdline This displays the command line that was used to boot the kernel. It can be used to check both that the right parameters were used and that the *lilo* configuration is correct.

```
sodom:/proc# cat cmdline
BOOT_IMAGE=linux-v2  ro  root=302  ramdisk=0
eth0=0x300,0x0b sbpcd=0x230,SoundBlaster
sodom:/proc#
```

kmsg This is another binary file — do not use cat to display this file. It is used with a command *dmesg* to display the messages that appear on the screen when Linux boots up. This allows the user to see exactly how the kernel booted and any error messages without having to take down notes during the boot process itself.

scsi/ This directory is empty because this kernel has no SCSI drivers installed. If there were, it would contain a set of files describing the SCSI devices connected to the adapter.

cpuinfo This file contains information on the processor type. The example below is for an SGS-Thomson 80486DX2-80.

```
sodom:/proc# cat cpuinfo
processor      : 0
cpu            : 486
```

```
model           : unknown
vendor_id       : unknown
stepping        : unknown
fdiv_bug        : no
hlt_bug         : no
fpu             : yes
fpu_exception   : yes
cpuid           : no
wp              : yes
flags           :
bogomips        : 31.84
sodom:/proc#
```

ksyms   This file contains a rather long list of the kernel symbols and their respective addresses. It is essentially for advanced users.

devices   This file contains a list of device types that the kernel/system supports. They are divided into character and block devices. The terminal connections are ttyp.

```
sodom:/proc# cat devices
Character devices:
  1 mem
  2 pty
  3 ttyp
  4 ttyp
  5 cua
  7 vcs

Block devices:
  2 fd
  3 ide0
 25 sbpcd
```

dma   This file contains the number of DMA (direct memory access) channels that the kernel and system has. For a AT class PC, this will inevitably be four.

sys/   This directory contains files that contain the parameters of the system such as the Linux version number and date it was compiled, the host and domain name of the system and so on. The contents of these files can be used within scripts to check the system before performing certain operations. By reading the contents of */proc/sys/kernel/hostname*, a script can check that the system has been assigned one.

filesystems This displays the file systems that the kernel supports. If the term *nodev* preceded the entry it means that no devices are currently using it. With the */proc* file system, this is always the case because of its special nature. With the NFS entry, it is because no remote file systems have been mounted and made available.

```
sodom:/proc# cat filesystems
        ext2
        minix
        MS-DOS
nodev   proc
nodev   nfs
        iso9660
```

meminfo   This file contains information about the amount of RAM and swap space that the system has available.

```
sodom:/proc# cat meminfo
        total:      used:       free:     shared: buffers:
cached:
Mem:  15241216   7704576   7536640   5341184    925696
3362816
Swap: 95473664          0 95473664
MemTotal:     14884 kB
MemFree:       7360 kB
MemShared:     5216 kB
Buffers:        904 kB
Cached:        3284 kB
SwapTotal:    93236 kB
SwapFree:     93236 kB
sodom:/proc#
```

interrupts   This will display the interrupt level allocation for the system. With a AT class PC, there are 15 available interrupt levels. The file will only display those that can be reassigned and does not display a complete list.

```
sodom:/proc# cat interrupts
 0:   2116804    timer
 1:         2    keyboard
 2:         0    cascade
11:     58497    NE2000
13:         1    math error
14:     13340 +  ide0
sodom:/proc#
```

modules   This file contains a list of any installed modules.

version   This file contains the version information for the kernel.

3 Linux commands

The biggest criticisms levelled against UNIX and thus Linux are that its commands are not intuitive and the fact that it seems to have multiple commands that appear to do the same job. These pose difficulties to both novice and occasional users, who find it infuriating when they cannot find or remember how to perform some simple operation or when a command works in some cases, but not in others. The normal procedure for UNIX documentation is to list the commands in alphabetical order because this make its easier for someone to find them. This is fine — but it does not help those who do not know the Linux commands in the first place. As a result, I have arranged the commands in this chapter according to their use and not alphanumeric position. Commands associated with transferring data from disk to disk are grouped together and so on.

Login shells

The programs the user interfaces to are called shells. The standard shell for Linux is called *bash* and is similar to the *Bourne shell*. There are alternatives such as *tcsh* which are similar to the *C shell*. Although they provide the same basic facilities, they are different and shell scripts (batch files) written for one will not necessarily run on another. The commands described in this chapter are identified if they are specific to one shell or another. However, the detailed operations of the shells are so different that they are covered in separate chapters. The system administrator decides which shell the users see by specifying it in the user's entry in */etc/passwd*.

Logging in

The first encounter with the Linux shell occurs when the user logs in to the computer. This is achieved, as far as the user is concerned, by pressing the Return or ^D (Ctrl-D) keys a few times until a login prompt appears, entering a valid user name and then, if necessary, a password. If all is well, the system welcomes the user, provides a prompt and waits for commands to be entered. When the user has finished, entering *logout* or *exit* logs out of the system and the session is completed. Commands are entered on the command line and are executed when the Return (or Enter) key is pressed. The actual user interface is controlled by a shell program, of which there are two in common use. Multiple commands can be entered on the command line, providing they are separated by a semicolon.

There are four special keys used to perform special functions:

ERASE   #   Rub out the last character typed.

CANCEL   @   Cancel the current line.

INTERRUPT   **DEL** Interrupt any currently executing command.

EOF   **^D**   End of file (also known as EOT).

The DEL key is normally ^DELETE, although this depends on the terminal or keyboard. These key functions can be redefined either by assigning a terminal type or through the use of *stty* (see later in this chapter). Most systems will change ERASE to ^H and CANCEL to ^X so that the default # and @ characters can be used normally. The INTERRUPT key is also known as the KILL key — but this should not be confused with the command of the same name. The *stty* command is used to change the ERASE and other characters.

The prompt Returned depends on the user's status, the shell that is running and if it has been changed by a *.profile* file. Linux uses two profile files: */etc/profile* which executes by all users on logon and a *.profile* in the home directory which is specific to that user. By default, any user with the same ID as root has superuser status — and is assumed to be experienced in Linux. With any other ID, normal user status is assumed. The standard superuser prompt for the bash/Bourne shell is #, while that for a user is $. A second prompt, >, may appear by default if the command entered on the command line needs more data. In many cases, such as processing input directly from the keyboard, pressing Return does not complete the command — it simply results in another prompt. If this happens, ^D will terminate the prompts (abort the current command). For those systems that use a tcsh or C shell, the user and superuser prompts are replaced by a number of alternatives, including %, ?, and a number in brackets.

The *.profile* is normally supplied by the system administrator but can be changed by the user. It is a shell script file thatexecutes its text as commands and is used to customize the user's environment. Special characters can be defined, path names changed and so on. For users running the tcsh or C shell, this file is called *.login* and it performs the same function.

```
$cat .profile
$
#ident  "@(#)sadmin:etc/stdprofile    1.2"
#       This is the default standard profile provided to a user.
#       They are expected to edit it to meet their own needs.
$
```

If a password is forgotten, the only way to gain access to the system is for the superuser to remove the original password from the user name entry in */etc/ passwd* and replace it with a known one using the *passwd* command.

login

login *username*

This command allows the user to log in to the system again without logging out. If a user *username* is specified, the command logs the user in as that user. If the user then logs out, he is Returned to his original shell and not logged off the system.

logout

logout

This command is the only way of logging out (except for using *login* to logout and *login* again) if the environment variable *ingnoreeof* is set. If it is, the EOF character is ignored and typing ^D displays a message suggesting the use of the command.

su

su [- [name [arg ...]]

It is not necessary for a user to log off a system and log in again as superuser to gain the appropriate powers to perform some form of system administration. Instead, the *su* command can be executed which allows any user to become the superuser. Needless to say, if the superuser is password protected, the command's first response is to ask for the password. If the correct password is not entered, it is aborted. To return to the original user status, type ^D. If the first argument is a hyphen, the shell environment is changed to that which the superuser would have had, had he or she actually logged in. A program name, together with any associated arguments, can be given as well.

```
Linux 1.3.20 (ess2.tvr.com) (ttyp0)

ess2 login: powermac
Last login: Sun Nov 17 09:00:47 from 200.200.200.200
Linux 1.3.20.
ess2:~$ su
ess2:~#
```

Navigating the file system

Linux has a hierarchical filing system that contains all the data files, programs, commands and special files that allow access to the physical computer system. The files are usually grouped into directories and subdirectories. The file system starts with a root directory and divides it into subdirectories. At each level, there can be further subdirectories that continue the file system onto further levels. There can also be files that contain data. A directory can contain both file types, although if no more directories are present, the file system will stop at that level for that path. A file name describes its location in the hierarchy by a combination of the path taken to locate it, starting at the top and working down. The splitting of the file structure makes it look like that of a tree and branches, where the trunk is represented by the root directory and branches by the subdirectories. Not surprisingly, this type of structure is frequently referred to as a tree structure. If turned upside down, it resembles a tree by starting at a single root directory — the trunk — and branching out.

The full name, or path name, for the file *steve* located at the bottom of the tree would be */etc/usr/steve*. The / character at the beginning is the symbol used for the starting point and is known as root or the root directory. Subsequent use within the path name indicates that the preceding file name is a directory and that the path as followed down that route. The / character is the opposite to that used in MS-DOS systems: a tongue-in-cheek way to remember which slash to use is that MS-DOS is "backward" compared to UNIX and thus, its slash character points backward.

cd

cd [directory]

This is probably the most used Linux command. It changes the current directory to that specified by the directory file name thataccompanies it. Unlike many other Linux commands, which exist as separate executable files, *cd* is built into the shell itself. If no directory is specified, *cd* starts to look at various shell variables to decide which directory to go to. Without a specified directory, the directory specified in the $HOME shell parameter is used. If the specified directory does not exist in the current level, *cd* searches for it using the paths specified in the shell parameter $CDPATH. If the directory starts with / or . (one period) or .. (two periods), the directory path is taken from root, from the current directory or from the level above the current working directory.

For example, if the current directory is */user/steve/book* :

cd /user   will change the current directory to */user*
cd ..   will change it to */user/steve*
cd .   will change it to */user/steve/book*
cd ../letters will change it to */user/steve/letter*

If the current directory is / and *CDPATH=/user/steve*

cd book   will change the current directory to */user/steve/book*

These shortcuts can also be used to define file names for other commands. For example, if the current directory is */steve/book*, then *cat ./chap1* would print the file */steve/book/chap1* on the terminal screen.

echo

echo [arg] ...

echo writes the associated arguments to standard output and is frequently used to display messages on the terminal screen in shell scripts, or to put data in the beginning of a pipe. By default, the command terminates the output with a new- line character and interprets the following C-like structures to allow special characters to be printed:

\b	Backspace
\c	Print line without new-line
\f	Form-feed
\n	New-line
\r	Carriage Return
\t	Tab
\v	Vertical tab
\	Backslash
\0n	Where *n* is the 8-bit character whose ASCII code is the 1, 2 or 3-digit octal number for that character.
\07	Sound the terminal bell

When using these special characters, the backslash must be escaped (by enclosing it in quotes) to prevent its incorrect interpretation by the *shell* instead of *echo*. To display the word WARNING and sound a bell on a terminal, the command would be written as *echo "WARNING\07"*.

find

find path name expressions

find is one of those infuriating yet extremely useful commands. It recursively searches the files and directories given on the command line comparing each file with the command line expressions. These expressions perform an operation if the file matches a particular characteristic or, in some cases, with every file without exception. If the expression is true, the operation is performed and if not, it does not.

Why is it frustrating? The main reason is that the command can take a very long time if the path name is / and it is searching the whole file system. The second reason is that, unlike its MS-DOS counterpart, it does not display any information unless explicitly told to do so. If this is forgotten, a long search may apparently reveal no files or matches when, in reality, they are there — but their presence has not been displayed! The path name can be any normal path name, such as used with *ls* or *cd*. The expressions supported are:

-name *file*   True if the current file matches *file*. The normal file name wildcards can be used, providing they are escaped or quoted correctly.

-perm *-onum*   True if the file permissions exactly match those of *onum* where *onum* contains the settings in octal. If *onum* is negative, the comparison is slightly changed: only set bits in *onum* are used for comparison.

-type c   True if the file type is of type c, where c is one of the following characters:

b	block special file
c	character special file
d	directory
p	pipe or fifo
f	plain, ordinary file

-links *n*   True if the file has *n* links.

-user *usr*   True if the file belongs to the user *usr*.

-group *grp*   True if the file belongs to the group *grp*.

-size n[c]   True if the file is *n* blocks long or, if followed by a c, the size is in characters.

-atime n   True if the file has been accessed in *n* days.

-mtime n   True if the file has been modified in *n* days.

-ctime n   True if the file has been changed in *n* days.

In these three commands, *n* can be prefixed by + or - and have slightly different meanings:

+n	greater than *n* days.
n	*n* days exactly.
-n	less than *n* days.

-exec *cmd*   True if the executed *cmd* Returns 0 as an indication of a successful completion. To use the current file name, {} is used as a command argument and \; must be used to indicate the end of the command.

-ok *cmd*   Like *-exec*, except that the generated command line is printed followed by a question mark. Typing *y* will continue the execution.

-print   Prints the current path name.

-cpio *device*   Writes the current file onto *device* using *cpio* format. *device* is a physical device name for a tape or disk drive. See *cpio* for details.

-newer *file*   True if the current file has been modified more recently than *file*.

-depth   Acts on all the files within a directory before the directory itself.

(*expr* **)**   True if *expr* is true. This is used to OR options together using *-o*. The parentheses must be escaped. ! is used as the symbol for logical NOT.

Using *find* can be a little tricky. The first example shows how to use the time options. It uses *-mtime* to test the time of modification. With an argument of 0, it selects the files that have been modified in the last day or 24 hours. With the -2 argument, the test is for any files that have been modified in the last two days — obviously a superset of the results from the first command. The third argument, +2, selects files that were last modified more than two days ago.

```
$ find . -mtime 0 -print
.
./stest
./test4
$ find . -mtime -2 -print
.
./test2
./test3
./stest
./test4
./test5
./test
$ find . -mtime +2 -print
././.profile
./script
./script1
./data
./ed.hup
./6
$
```

The next example uses *-exec* to execute the *cat* command with every selected file and prints the files *stest*, *test4*, *test5* and *local*.

```
$ find . -mtime 0 -exec cat {} \;
```

The next example demonstrates how to look for particular files. The first command selects files beginning with *t* or *littlea* and prints their name. The second command prints out the name of any file that does NOT begin with a *t*.

```
$ find . \( -name 't*' -o -name 'littlea?' \) -print
./testfile
./testfile2
./littleab
./littleac
./test4
$ find . \( ! -name 't*' \) -print
.
././.profile
./ed.hup
./6
./stest
./littleab
./littleac
./local
$
```

ls

ls -RadCxmnlogrtucpFbqisf [files]

For such a small command, *ls* has a very large list of options! The command lists the files and directories within a specified directory, together with related information, if requested. This can include file size and type; read, write and execution permissions; date of creation and last modification, and so on. It is the equivalent of the DOS *dir* command. Linux will normally create a script that lets you type *dir* and run *ls*. If no file names are specified, the current directory is listed. The output is normally sorted into alphabetical order.

Two environment variables are used by *ls* to format the output with the -*C*, -*x* or -*m* options. COLUMNS stores the maximum number of characters on a line. If this variable is not set, *ls* uses the variable TERM to find it from the terminal type. If neither is set, it defaults to 80 characters.

-R   Search recursively through any subdirectories.

```
$ ls -Rx
prose   test

./test:
dd1         dd2     ddresult    ddresult2   ddtest      file1       file2
file3       filea   target1     target2     target3     test        xx02
$
```

-a   List all entries — will also include "hidden" entries whose name begins with a full stop, such as *.profile*.

-d   Lists directories.

-C   Multicolumn output with entries sorted down the columns

-x   Multicolumn output with entries across the page.

```
$ ls -x
dd1         dd2         ddresult    ddresult2   ddtest      file1       file2
file3       filea       target1     target2     target3 test          xx02
$
```

-m   Stream output format.

-l   List in long format, giving mode, number of links, owner, group, size in bytes and time of last modification for each file. If the file is a special file, the size field contains the major and minor device numbers instead.

-n   The same as -*l*, except that the owner's ID and group's ID numbers are printed, rather than the associated character strings.

```
$ ls -l
total 2
-rw-r—r—   1 root other 52 Mar 13 02:05 prose
$ ls -n
total 2
-rw-r—r—   1 0     1   52 Mar 13 02:05 prose
$
```

-o   The same as *-l*, except that the group ID number is not printed.

```
$ ls -o
total 2
-rw-r-r-    1 root 152 Mar 13 02:05 prose
$
```

-g   The same as *-l*, except that the owner UID number is not printed.

```
$ ls -g
total 2
-rw-r-r-    1 other 152 Mar 13 02:05 prose
```

-r   Reverse the order of sort to get reverse alphabetic or oldest first.

-t   Sort by time of last modification (latest first) instead of by name.

-u   Use time of last access instead of last modification for sorting or printing.

-c   Use time of last modification of the *inode* i.e. file created, mode changed.

-p   Identifies directories by putting a slash after the file name such as: *book/*

-F   Identifies directories by putting a slash after the file name, and executable files by an asterisk such as: *book/cut**

-b   Forces nonprinting characters to be displayed using the octal notation. This is extremely useful to see if any hidden control characters are present in a file name.

-i   Print the *i* number for each file.

-s   Gives the size in blocks, including indirect blocks, for each file.

-f   Forces each argument to be interpreted as a directory and lists the name found in each slot. This option turns off *-t*, *-s*, and *-r*, and turns on *-a*; the order is the order in which entries appear in the directory.

The *-l* option gives a complete line of information for each file in the directory.

```
$ ls -l /dev
total 3
crw——    1 root sys 15,176 Apr 6 1989 X11.c
crw——    1 root sys 15,160 Apr 6 1989 X11.m
br——     1 root sys 0, 0   Apr 6 1989 boot
$
```

The first character is in the lefthand group of ten characters describes the file type as follows:

d   If the entry is a directory.

b   If the entry is a block special file.

c   If the entry is a character special file.

p   If the entry is a fifo (aka "named pipe") special file.

-   If the entry is an ordinary file.

The next 9 characters are three sets of three bits each, and are similar in format to the bits used in the *chmod* command. The first set describes the owner's permissions, the second the permissions of others in the user group of the file and the third the permissions for all others. The three characters indicate, respectively, permission to read, write and execute the file as a program. If a directory is described as executable, it means that it can be searched to find a file. The permissions are indicated as follows:

r   Read permission.

w   Write permission.

x   Execute permission.

t   Sticky bit and execution are on.

T   The sticky bit is on, but execution is off!

s   User or group set ID and execution are on.

S   Set user ID is on, but user execution is off!

l   The file is locked during access to all others.

-   If the indicated permission is not granted.

The next column gives the number of links that the file may have. Each link is effectively another file that shares the same data but may have a different name and/or directory. After that, the login name of the file owner is shown, followed by the group name. In the */dev* directory example on the previous page, all the files belong to the user, root. The information that follows depends on the file type. If it is a standard file, its size is displayed in bytes or characters. If the file is a directory, the total number of blocks is printed. If it is a special file, such as a terminal or peripheral, two numbers are given — the major numbers and minor numbers — which identify the file and the hardware it controls. The date of last modification appears next, followed by the file name.

passwd

passwd login-name

This command allows the current password for a user to be changed. If no login name is given, the current one is assumed. It asks for the new password to be entered twice to verify the change. A valid password must have at least six characters.The superuser can change any password and can even change a password to null (a simple Return). To remove a password completely, the appropriate password field in */etc/passwd* is cleared. If this is done, the system will not even prompt for a password when logging in. Passwords never actually appear on the screen.

```
$ passwd steve
Old password:
New password:
Password is too short - must be at least 6 digits
```

```
New password:
Password must contain at least two alphabetic characters and
at least one numeric or special character.
New password:
Reenter new password:
$
```

pwd

pwd

Probably the easiest command in Linux, *pwd* prints the path name of the working (current) directory. Any error messages usually indicate data corruption within the file system.

```
$ pwd
/user/author/steve
$
```

Redirecting output and input

Processes have three standard files associated with them: *stdin*, *stdout* and *stderr*, which are the default input, output and error message files. Other files or devices can be reassigned to these files to either receive or provide data for the active process. The syntax for both the Bourne shell and C shell is straightforward:

Bourne shell (bash) redirection

command > output file	redirect *stdout* to output file
command >> output file	append *stdout* to output file
command < input file	take commands from input file
command 2> error file	redirect *stderr* to output file
command 2>> error file	append *stderr* to output file

C shell (tcsh) redirection

command > output file	redirect *stdout* to output file
command >> output file	append *stdout* to output file
command < input file	take commands from input file
command >&file	redirect both *stdout* and *stderr* to file
command >>&file	append both *stdout* and *sterr* to file

A pipe connects the *stdout* of one command to the *stdin* of another. It differs from redirection in that it transfers output to the input of another command and not to a data file.

```
$ls -l | cat
total 5
-rwxr-xr-x 1 root other 6   Aug 3 16:39 DIR
-rwxr-xr-x 1 root other 160 Aug 4 19:49 life
$
```

Linux provides a special file called */dev/null* that contains nothing and stores nothing. Redirecting output to it simply discards the data. Appending data from it to a file effectively clears the file. These techniques are frequently used in shell scripts where a command is executed but no data is required.

tee

tee [-i] [-a] [file] ...

tee is a very useful command that takes data for *stdout* and displays it as normal, as well as making a copy in a file. Its name comes from a tee junction in a water pipe, which takes a single output and splits it into two. There are two options:

-i   Ignores interrupts.

-a   Causes the output to be appended to the files rather than overwriting them.

One use of *tee* is to log a shell session to record the output from shell to a file. This is done by invoking another copy of the shell and piping its output into *tee* as shown. If this is done, Return must be pressed to restore the prompt.

```
$sh | tee session
$ ls -x
DIR   _elif  _until  background   backup
brk   cflop  demo    dos_mode$    format
$ pwd
$ /sh

$ $cat session
DIR   _elif  _until  background   backup
brk   cflop  demo    dos_mode$    format
/sh
$
```

This technique is also useful for debugging shell scripts. A new shell is set up as shown, is set to print out shell script commands as they are executed. The data will be displayed on the screen and saved in a file for further inspection. It is possible to pipe the output of the *tee* command to another command, or even another *tee* if needed.

```
$ls -x |tee sess1 | tee sess2
DIR   _elif  _until  background   backup
brk   cflop  demo    dos_mode$    format
$cat sess1
DIR   _elif  _until  background   backup
brk   cflop  demo    dos_mode$    format
$cat sess2
DIR   _elif  _until  background   backup
brk   cflop  demo    dos_mode$    format
$
```

File name generation

Many Linux commands require a file name to be provided and, to provide greater flexibility, there are some special characters that can be used to replace parts of a file name and act as wildcards. These should not be confused with the metacharacters that replace all or part of the path name (./ ../ and so on). File name generation is similar but NOT identical to the pattern matching used within *ed, ex* and *vi*:

*   Matches any sequence of characters (including none).

?   Matches any single character.

[abc] Matches any one of a, b or c.

[a-d] Matches any one of a, b, c or d.

~   Refers to the user's home directory and is shorthand for *$home* (C shell only).

If a file name uses both metacharacters and wildcard characters, the metanotation is evaluated first followed by the file name generation.

```
$ls -x
dd1     dd2     ddresult ddresult2 ddtest     exdemofile1     file2       file3
filea target1         target2     target3     test  xx02
$ls -x *
dd1     dd2     ddresult ddresult2 ddtest     exdemofile1     file2       file3
filea target1         target2     target3     test  xx02
$ls -x dd*
dd1     dd2     ddresult  ddresult2 ddtest
$ls -x dd?
dd1   dd2
$ls -x [aeiou]*
exdemo
$ls -x [aeiou]
[aeiou]: No such file or directory
$ls -x ???
dd1   dd2
$ls -x ../[mp]*
../prose
../mode:
crontab.list  testfile      timer
$
```

The square bracket notation and question mark only replace a single character and, unless other characters or an asterisk are included in the file name, the command looks for file names with single characters — which is unlikely to be what is needed. The last example shows what happens when two directories are identified by the file name with a *ls* command: each directory's contents is displayed. Note the use of the metanotation in the file path name — the two full stops in front of the forward slash.

The shell environment

date

date [mmddhhmm[yy]]

date [+format]

date performs two functions: using it, the *superuser* can change the system time and date and any user can print out the current values in any format. If the argument starts with a +, it is interpreted as formatting information. If it does not, the argument is interpreted as a date and time. The system normally works in GMT. The command prints the current time and date and, by supplying a format string, this information can be formatted in different ways:

n	Insert a new-line character.
t	Insert a tab character.
m	Month of year — 01 to 12.
d	Day of month — 01 to 31.
y	Last 2 digits of year — 00 to 99.
D	Date as mm/dd/yy.
H	Hour — 00 to 23.
M	Minute — 00 to 59.
S	Second — 00 to 59.
T	Time as HH:MM:SS.
w	Day of week — Sunday = 0.
a	Abbreviated weekday — Sun to Sat.
h	Abbreviated month — Jan to Dec.
r	Time in AM/PM notation. For example:

```
date '+DATE: %m/%d/%y%nTlME: %H:%M:%S'
```
will give this output:
DATE: 08/01/96
TIME: 14:45:05

To change to a different time zone, the *TZ* variable can be altered. It normally takes the format *GMT*, followed by the number of hours difference between Greenwich mean time and the required time zone. A negative difference indicates that the time zone is ahead of *GMT*, while a positive value is used if the time zone is behind *GMT*.

```
$ TZ=GMT1;export TZ
$ date
Wed Oct 29 11:48:16 GMT 1996
$ TZ=GMT0
```

```
$ date
Wed Oct 29 12:48:36 GMT 1996
$ TZ=GMT-1
$ date
Wed Oct 29 13:48:49 GMT 1996
$
date; sleep 10 ;date

Wed Oct 29 03:51:34 GMT 1996
Wed Oct 29 03:51:44 GMT 1996
$
```

File access permissions

chmod

chmod mode file ...

chmod mode directory ...

Each file or directory within UNIX has certain permissions that control who can access it and whether they can execute or modify it. *chmod* is the utility thatallows these permissions to be changed and is frequently used when creating shell scripts, when it must be run to change the shell script permission to execute, to allow the script to be run. The file mode is split into four levels of permissions, with a level allocated to the owner of the file, another to the other users within the owners group and a third level for anyone else. The fourth level is associated with additional permissions, such as the sticky bit and file locking. When a file is created, its default permissions are obtained from a variable called *umask* thatcan be changed. As standard, it is set to 0022, which allows read and write access to the owner and read access to anyone else. There is no permission to execute the file for anyone. The superuser has unlimited access to any file, irrespective of its mode.

The permissions of the named files or directories are changed according to a mode, which may be symbolic or absolute. Absolute changes to permissions are stated using octal (base 8) numbers, although symbols can be used and are easier to remember. For example:

chmod nnnn file(s)

where *n* is an octal number from 0 to 7.

chmod a operator b flle(s)

where *a* is one or more characters corresponding to *user, group,* or both, an operator is +, -, or =, signifying granting or denying of permission and where *b* is one or more characters corresponding to the permission.

An absolute mode is given as an octal number constructed from the logical OR of the following modes (if the bit is already set it stays set):

4000 Set user ID on execution.

20x0 Set group ID on execution if x is 7, 5, 3, or 1.
          Enable mandatory locking if x is 6, 4, 2, or 0.

1000 Sticky bit is turned on.

0400 Read by owner.

0200 Write by owner.

0100 Execute (search in directory) by owner.

0070 Read, write, execute (search) by group.

0007 Read, write, execute (search) by others.

A symbolic mode is constructed from the following options:

u User permissions.

g Group permissions.

o Others' permissions.

a All — this is equivalent to *ugo*.

+ Add permission.

- Remove permission.

= Add permission but remove all other permissions. This effectively resets all the other bits.

r Read permission.

w Write permission.

x Execute permission.

t Set sticky bit — can only be done by the superuser.

s User or group set ID is on.

l The file be locked during access to all others.

User or group set ID means that the user assumes the ID of the owner or group while executing it. This is useful in enabling access to other files on a temporary basis.

The *l* option is used to control mandatory file locking and is not supported on many early UNIX implementations. It prevents other users from accessing a file if another user is using it. This is essential to prevent the file from being corrupted by two or more users updating it at the same time. However, the option is mutually exclusive with group execution and the set group ID permissions. The setting of group permissions to execute and file locking or set group ID and file locking are illegal combinations and give error messages.

The sticky bit can be set by the superuser and, if set, keeps a copy of the file in the page swap area on the hard disk. This seems a little strange but the advantage is one of speed. If the file is frequently used, it is quicker to fetch it from the swap area than the file system on disk because the data will be sequential and not fragmented. The down side of this is that the available swap area is reduced in size and this may impact performance of some programs or, in some severe cases, actually prevent them from running. This is why only the superuser has the authority to set this bit. The examples show how the symbolic options can be used to change the permissions as necessary. The *ls -l* command shows the result of the previous *chmod* command.

```
$umask
0022
$echo "echo Hello world" > testf
$ls -l
total 1
-rw-r—r—  1 root other 17 Aug 10 16:38 testf
$chmod g=rwx testf
$ls -l
total 1
-rw-rwxr— 1 root other 17 Aug 10 16:38 testf
$chmod g=x testf
$ls -l
total 1
-rw—xr—   1 root other 17 Aug 10 16:38 testf
$chmod g+r,u+r,o+x testf
$ls -l
total 1
-rw-r-xr-x1 root other 17 Aug 10 16:38 testf
$chmod u-w testf
$ls -l
total 1
-r—r-xr-x 1 root other 17 Aug 10 16:38 testf
$chmod -x,-r,-w testf
$ls -l
total 1
————        1 root other 17 Aug 10 16:38 testf
$chmod +x testf
$ls -l
total 1
—x—x—x    1 root other 17 Aug 10 16:38 testf
$chmod +x,g+r,u+rw testf
$ls -l
total 1
-rwxr-x—x 1 root other 17 Aug 10 16:38 testf
$
```

chown,
chgrp

chown owner file ...

chown owner directory ...

chgrp group file ...

chgrp group directory ...

The *chown* command changes the owner of the files or directories. The owner may be either a decimal user ID or a login name found in the password file

/etc/passwd. The *chgrp* command is similar to *chown* but changes the group ID of the files or directories instead. The group may be either a decimal group ID or a group name found in the group file, */etc/group*.

If either command is invoked by other than the superuser, the set-user-ID and set-group-ID bits of the file mode are cleared. This is necessary to prevent users other than the owner or superuser from changing ownership. If the bits are set, any user will assume the group or user ID and automatically have permission to change ownership. On some early UNIX implementations, these bits were not cleared, creating a loophole in the security and access control system.

```
$ls -l
total 1
-rwxr-x—x 1 root other 17 Aug 10 16:38 testf
$chown sys testf
$ls -l
total 1
-rwxr-x—x 1 sys  other 17 Aug 10 16:38 testf
$chown root testf
$ls -l
total 1
-rwxr-x—x 1 root other 17 Aug 10 16:38 testf
$chgrp sys testf
$ls -l
total 1
-rwxr-x—x 1 root sys   17 Aug 10 16:38 testf
$chgrp other testf
$ls -l
total 1
-rwxr-x—x 1 root other 17 Aug 10 16:38 testf
$
```

umask

This changes the standard octal value used to assign read, write and execute permissions. *umask*, when used on its own, displays the standard setting of octal 0022, which gives read and write permission to the owner and read only permission to the group and others. To change this, the new octal value is added. Any files subsequently created will automatically have the new permissions.

```
$umask
0022
$echo this is a test > newfile
$ls -l newfile
-rw-r—r— 1 root other 15 Aug 8 00:58 newfile
$umask 0055
$echo this is another test > newfile2
$ls -l newfile?
-rw—w—w- 1 root other 21 Aug 8 00:59 newfile2
$
```

Files and directories

basename,

dirname   *basename* and its associated command *dirname* take a file path name and remove the upper levels or the lowest level respectively. They are frequently used in shell scripts to control file and directory copying or movement.

```
$ basename /user/steve/bench
bench
$ dirname /user/steve/bench
/user/steve
$
```

cat

cat [-u] [-s] [-v [-t] [-e]] file

cat reads each file in sequence and writes its contents to the standard output, that is the terminal screen. It is used to display the contents of a file in a similar way to the *type* command in MS-DOS. Like the *type* command, there is virtually no control over how the data is printed and once started, *cat* will continue until terminated or it has reached the end of the file(s). It can take a list of file names as an input and by redirecting the standard output, several files can be combined or concatenated into a larger single file. If no file is specified, input is taken from the standard input,(the keyboard), until an end of file character is typed. This is frequently used to create small data files rather than using an editor.

cat has the following options:

-v   Causes nonprinting characters (with the exception of tabs, new-lines and form-feeds) to be printed visibly. Control characters are printed ^X (Control-x), the DEL character (octal 0177) is printed ?, and so on. Non-ASCII characters (with the high bit set) are printed as M-x, where x is the character specified by the seven low order bits.

-u   The output is not buffered. (The default is buffered output.)

-s   *cat* ignores non-existent files and does not display any error messages.

When used with the -v option, the following additional options may be used.

-t   Causes each tab to be printed as ^I.

-e   Causes a $ character to be printed at the end of each line (prior to the new-line).

This command can be a little misleading and unforgiving. The command *cat filel file2 >file1* will join the files *file1* and *file2* and store the combined data in *file1*. However, because *file1* already exists, it is overwritten and the original data lost. Needless to say, no warning is given. In addition, *cat* will print any file — text, binary, core dump and so on, and can cause a lot of problems when the standard output cannot cope with the data. If a binary file is printed to a printer or screen, it will invariably contain nonprinting and control characters thatwill not be handled correctly. Such commands cause rubbish to be displayed, the terminal display to change settings or, in some cases, lock up completely. If this happens, it is sometimes possible to kill the *cat* command directly from the keyboard by typing ^X. If this is ignored, the superuser may be able to kill it from another terminal by using *ps* to discover the process ID and stop it using the *kill* command. It is not a good idea to type ^D from the keyboard in the vain hope of stopping *cat*. The command will be buffered and not acted on until *cat* finishes, when the shell will log the user off!

mkdir

mkdir -m mode -p directory name

mkdir is like its MS-DOS namesake. It creates a new directory as defined by the full directory name. There are two options, of which -*p* is probably the most useful. This option automatically creates all the non-existent parent directories in the path name and is a more efficient method than creating the directory level by level. The new directory will assume the user and group identities. To change the permissions, the -m option can be used, followed by the mode as defined by the *chmod* command. The command assumes that the user has write permission in the parent directory.

rmdir

rmdir -p -s directory name

rmdir is similar to *rm* except that it removes empty directories only and is usually used after *rm* has deleted all the files within the directory. The current working directory is not classed as empty, and to remove it, *cd* must be used to move up at least one level or to another branch of the file system. The -*p* option removes all the directories within a file name as they become empty. The -*s* option suppresses any messages.

touch

touch [-amc] [mmddhhnn[yy]] files

touch updates the access and modification times of each file that is passed to it as an argument. The current time is used unless a time is specified using the field descriptors below:

mm   Month of year — 01 to 12.

dd   Day of month — 01 to 31.

hh   Hour — 00 to 23.

nn   Minutes — 00 to 59.

yy   Last 2 digits of year — 00 to 99.

The *-a* and-*m* options cause *touch* to update only the access or modification times respectively (default is *-am*). The *-c* option silently prevents *touch* from creating the file if it did not previously exist. The Return code from *touch* is the number of files for which the times could not be successfully modified (including files that did not exist and were not created).

Copying and deleting files

There are many ways of copying files within Linux, depending on the source and destination and how the data is to be transferred. Some of the commands, *cpio, tar,* and *dd,* use physical device names and these differ from system to system. It is essential to consult the system documentation to determine the names thatmust be used to make the commands work correctly.

cp, ln, mv

cp filel [file2 ...] target
ln [-f] filel [file2 ...] target
mv [-f] filel [file2 ...] target

These three commands copy a file or list of files to a destination file or device and provide similar facilities to the MS-DOS *copy* utility. They are normally used with files, but standard input and output or physical devices, like terminals, can be specified. Although *cp, ln* and *mv* copy data or files, each does it in a slightly different way. *cp* carries out the standard file copy — the files specified in the argument are read and transferred to the destination specified as the last argument. For example:

cp file1 file2	copies *file1* and calls the new version *file2*.
cp filel file2 target	copies *file1* and *file2* to the file *target*.
cp file1 /dev/tty	copies the contents of *file1* to the terminal *tty*.

The important characteristic of *cp* is that it makes a new and separate copy of the input data and, at the command completion, two versions of the same data will exist within the file system.

ln performs a similar function, except that the new file is linked to the original and simply shares the original data. Linking creates a new directory entry for the target file, but uses same data that the original file uses. No additional copy of the data is made, but each file exists in the filing system. The advantage over *cp* is the reduction in file space needed to store both the original and the new versions. *mv* effectively copies the source file to a new target and then deletes the original. In reality, the data is not copied — all that is changed are the directory references. This command is used to move a file from one directory location to another.

There are several restrictions when using these commands:

- Under no circumstance can the source and destination files be the same.
- If *target* already exists, its contents are destroyed.
- Only *mv* allows the source to be a directory, in which case, it must have the same parent as the destination.
- *ln* will not link across file systems (i.e. networked systems, floppy disks), because they can be added and removed at will. Removing the data source for linked files is dangerous!
- If *target* forbids writing, the current mode is printed out. The user is then expected to confirm the write operation by entering a response whose first character is a *y*. If the response starts with any other letter, the operation aborts. The *-f* option will force the command to complete as is also the case if the standard input is not a terminal.
- When *cp* is used to create a new file, it will have the same mode as the original file except that the sticky bit will not be set. This bit can only be set if the operation is performed by the superuser. Other information, such as modification and last access time, are set using the time of operation and not that of the original file.
- If *file1* and *target* are on different file systems, the file is moved by copying *file1* to *target* and then deleting *file1*. In such cases, any links with other files are lost.

cpio

cpio -o[acBv]

cpio -i[BcdmrtuvfsSb6] [patterns]

cpio -p[adlmuv] directory

This is a very important command because it transfers files to and from the file system or more importantly, to and from floppy disk or tape. It is frequently used to back up and restore the file system and to move files from one system to another. The command is a little strange because its syntax and operation are not intuitive. The *cpio -o* (copy out) command reads the standard input to obtain a list of files and copies these files onto the standard output, complete with full path name and status information. The file is always transferred in 512 byte segments and padded out if necessary. The *cpio -i* (copy in) command extracts files from the standard input, which is assumed to be the product of a previous *cpio -o*. In both cases, the standard input can be redirected to a formatted floppy disk or tape by using the appropriate */dev/ file*. This the main use of this utility.

With the *cpio -i* command, a regular expression or expressions can be used to define a name pattern used to select which files are copied across. The default is * and selects all. Files are copied into the current directory and the file permissions archived with the original *cpio -o* operation.

The *cpio -p* (pass) command reads the standard input to obtain a list of file names that are conditionally created and copied into the directory that follows the options on the command line. Using this command, it is possible to copy files and directories from one part of the file system to another — something that *mv* does not do easily. The originals can then be deleted using *rm* to free up disk space. Files archived using *cpio* can usually be transferred from one set of hardware to another, providing the machines are running the same Linux or UNIX implementation.

In all cases, the easiest way of generating a file list is to use either the *ls* or *find* command and pipe itsoutput into *cpio*.

Available options for *cpio* are:

a   Reset access times of input files after they have been copied. These times are not reset for linked files when *cpio -pla* is specified.

B   Input/output is to be blocked 5,120 bytes to the record (does not apply to the pass option! It is meant to be used only with data directed from a character-special device, such as */dev/rmt/Om*).

d   Directories are to be created as needed.

c   Write header information in ASCII character format for portability. Always use this option when origin and destination computers are different.

t   Print a table of contents of the input. No files are created.

r   Interactively rename files. If the user types a Return on its own, the file is skipped and not copied. (Not available with *cpio -p*.)

u   Copy unconditionally — overwrite newer versions if they exist.

v   Verbose: causes a list of file names to be printed. When combined with the *t* option, the output is similar to that of the *ls -l* command.

l   Link files whenever possible (valid with the *-p* option only).

m   Retain previous file modification time. This option is ineffective on directories that are being copied.

f   Copy in all files except those in patterns.

s   Swap bytes within each half word. Use only with the *-i* option.

S   Swap halfwords within each word. Use only with the *-i* option.

b   Reverses the order of the bytes within each word. Use only with *-i* option.

6   Process an old (UNIX System Sixth Edition format) file. Only useful with *-i* (copy in).

If *cpio -o* reaches the end of a disk or tape, it prompts for another. For systems with multiple disk drives or tape streamers, this allows them to be alternated. While one is being read by *cpio*, the other can be loaded. The device name must be entered — if the Return key is pressed on its own, the transfer will terminate.

If *cpio -i* reaches the end of a disk or tape and needs another to complete the transfer, it prompts for the next one in the series. If the wrong one is inserted, the transfer will terminate. Typing *q* also aborts the transfer. If the transfer was aborted by mistake, it cannot be restarted where it left off and a message saying that there is a bad header will appear if this is attempted. The only solution is to restart with the first disk or tape in the series and include the *-u* option to ensure that the files that were transferred previously are overwritten. This is especially important with large files: *cpio* will split them and, if the transfer aborts in mid-file, the file state may be indeterminate and corrupt. It is safer to completely restart and overwrite.

```
/CPU/sim/src/chip/proc/put_fust.c
/CPU/sim/src/chip/proc/ref_sat.c
Reached end of medium on input.
Change to part 2 and press RETURN key. [q]
/CPU/sim/src/chip/proc/reg_mgr.c
/CPU/sim/src/chip/proc/resetchp.c
```

Here are some examples of its use.

cd /user/steve

find . -print | cpio -ocvB /dev/rflpa

This takes all the files and directories in */user/steve*, the current directory, and copies them to the raw floppy disk device */dev/rflpa*. It is frequently used to back up directories and files to floppy disk or tape. *find . - print* generates a list of all the files in */user/steve*, which is piped into *cpio*.

cd /user/john
cpio -icvdumB /dev/rflpa

In this example, all the files from the raw device */dev/rflpa* are copied into the current directory, */user/john*. This is the equivalent restore version of *cpio* to complement the previous backup. If the raw device was a disk with the file system archived from the previous example, the file system in */user/steve* would have been copied into */user/john*. This is what the *-p* option would do without having to go via a floppy disk or tape.

cpio -itvc /dev/rflpa

This command will simply print the list of files that are archived on */dev/rflpa*. No copying is performed and this is an equivalent directory command for *cpio* format disks and tapes.

cpio -icvdumB /dev/rflpa read.me

This restores a single file called *read.me*. The filename can be replaced with a regular expression to restore a group of files, if required.

When exchanging media, please remember these points:

- Always label the medium with the command that was used to copy the files onto it, the number of disks and tapes that comprise the complete set and their sequence number.

- *cpio* Returns the number of blocks that have been transferred. Again, it is a good idea to include this on the label so the recipient can check that the number of blocks that are read back is the same as that written.

- If the files need to be transferred to a specific directory, specify it on the label so that the directory can be created before installation. One set of software I installed told me to read a file to find out where the files should reside. The file was on the tape, so I had to extract it, read it and then install the files, which was a tedious job! The tape took 15 minutes to rewind after each *cpio* operation.

dd

dd [option=value] ...

The *dd* command copies the specified input file to the specified output with possible conversions. The standard input and output are used by default. The input and output block size may be specified to take advantage of raw devices. It is frequently used to perform "sector copy" disk copying, where the raw data is taken from a source disk and copied to a destination disk. The command appears to be very complicated but it is fairly straightforward, providing the idea of block transfers is understood. In a block transfer, instead of moving the data file by file, data is moved by taking it directly from the file system — with no regard for the file structure. It is like copying a set of office files by duplicating the contents of a filing cabinet, rather than extracting the individual files, copying them and Returning the originals. The advantage of *dd* over *cpio* or *cp* is seen when copying disks or in some form of file conversion, where you need to know how many blocks to move, which block to start and end with, or the relevant block size. It is usually this information, or the lack of it, that causes most problems. These are the options:

if=file	Input file name; standard input is default.
of=file	Output file name; standard output is default.
ibs=n	Input block size *n* bytes (default 512).
obs=n	Output block size *n* bytes (default 512).
bs=n	Set both input and output block size, replacing any value specified by *-ibs* or *-obs*; also, if no conversion is specified, it is particularly efficient since no in-core copy need be done.
cbs=n	Conversion buffer size. This option is only used if character conversions to ASCII or EBCDIC are performed.
skip=n	Skip *n* input blocks before starting copy.

seek=n   Seek *n* blocks from beginning of output file before copying.
count=n   Copy only *n* input blocks.
conv=ascii   Convert EBCDIC to ASCII.
conv=ebcdic   Convert ASCII to EBCDIC.
conv=ibm   Slightly different map of ASCII to EBCDIC.
conv=lcase   Map alphabetic characters to lowercase.
conv=ucase   Map alphabetic characters to uppercase.
conv=swab   Swap every pair of bytes.
conv=noerror Do not stop processing on an error.
conv=sync   Pad every input block to *ibs*. Note: multiple *conv* options are specified by separating by commas: *conv=ascii,swab, noerror*.

Where a size is specified, the expected number defines the number of bytes to be used. If the number ends in a *k*, it is multiplied by 1,024 to convert it to bytes. If the suffix is *b*, the number is multiplied by 512 to convert blocks to bytes. The suffix *w* multiplies the number by 2 to convert words to bytes. Alternatively, expressions such as 12x50 are also permitted, which in this example, would result in a size of 600 bytes.

The example below shows the results of some file conversions. The first *dd* command takes the file *ddtest*, converts it to uppercase characters, swaps the pairs of bytes and stores the results in *ddresult*. Note that in this case, *dd* uses the file names to work out all the relevant block information automatically. Printing the two files to the screen shows the effect — the lowercase characters have been changed to uppercase and each pair of characters has been swapped around. This byte swapping is very useful when moving data from one computer to another that disagrees on the byte ordering within a word. The second *dd* command also swaps bytes and converts the characters to EBCDIC format. Printing the resultant file gives rubbish. EBCDIC formats are not normally used in the UNIX environment, which normally expects ASCII characters. Its attempt at interpretation causes the data to be seen as rubbish. The ability to convert is useful when receiving or sending data from an EBCDIC- based computer.

```
$ dd if=ddtest of=ddresult conv=ucase,swab
0+1 records in
0+1 records out
$ cat ddtest
abcdefghijklmnop
$ cat ddresult
BADCFEHGJILKNMPO
$ dd if=ddtest of=ddresult2 conv=swab,ebcdic
0+1 records in
0+1 records out
$ cat ddresult2
```

```
       %?#
$ dd if=/dev/rflpA of=/tmp/floppy bs=720k
0+1 records in
0+1 records out
$
```

The last part of the example above shows how to use the *dd* command to read sectors from a device and transfer it to a file. This example specifies block information rather than files. By doing so, it gets around the problem of foreign file systems and allows the Linux system to copy any floppy disk or media — without needing to know how the data is structured. Providing the physical data format is the same; any floppy disk, tape or hard disk can be duplicated using this method. Switching the input and output files in a command would copy the file onto the disk.

rm

rm [-fri] file...

rm has been responsible for more wasted time than any other command. It removes files and directories from the file system and is a very necessary command — but there are some options that change it from a relatively safe utility to an uncontrollable monster that simply devours all the files on disk! It works by first removing links and if the directory entry is the last link to the file, the file is destroyed. Removal of a file requires write permission in its directory but neither read nor write permission on the file itself.

If a file has no write permission and the standard input is a terminal, its permissions are printed and a line is read from the standard input. At this point, the user can either confirm, with a reply beginning with a *y*, that the file is to be deleted. Any other first character is treated as a no and the file remains untouched. There are several options with *rm*:

-f   Inhibits any questions.

-i   Forces the interactive mode where *rm* asks in turn whether to delete a file. Typing a reply confirms the deletion, otherwise the file is left.

-r   Searches recursively down through the directories. In this case, empty directories below the starting point are deleted. This is the only instance in which *rm* will delete a directory. If the starting file name is a directory and *-r* is not specified, an error message appears.

rm can appear to be a little strange but its actions follow a few golden rules. If it is asked to delete a directory and the current working directory is a subdirectory of that directory, it deletes any further subdirectories below the current working directory but leaves everything above alone. The example shows how the location of the current working directory stops the removal and also how the *-r* option must be used to remove a directory:

```
$cd /
$mkdir /rem
$mkdir /rem/rem1
$mkdir /rem/rem1/rem2
$mkdir /rem/rem1/rem2/rem3
$rm /rem
rm: /rem directory
$cd /rem/rem1/rem2
$rm -r /rem
$dir
/rem/rem1/rem2:
$cd /
$rm -r /rem
$dir /rem
/rem: No such file or directory
$
```

It is possible to use regular expressions to define which files must be removed and this is where *rm* has caused much pain. If *rm -r ** or *rm -r *.** is typed when in the root directory, it will delete all the files in the file system — with disastrous results! Other dangerous versions are *rm -r */bin/**, which deletes most of the commands, utilities and other files — and virtually renders Linux dead. If a user tries to do this, *rm* starts to question the access permissions and will probably prevent damage — but if the superuser executes the command, there is nothing to be done as the superuser has total access to all files. This is one very good reason why access to supervisor status should be password protected — it prevents inexperienced users from inadvertently wiping the file system.

sum

sum [-r] file

sum calculates and prints a 16-bit checksum and prints the number of blocks of the named file. It is typically used to look for bad spots or to validate a file communicated over a transmission line. The option *-r* causes an alternate algorithm to be used in computing the checksum.

A read error experienced during file access is indistinguishable from end of file on most devices and gives an incorrect checksum. To confirm a correct calculation, check the printed block count against that for the file shown by the command *ls - l*.

sync

sync

sync executes the sync system primitive, which forces all unwritten file system data to be written out to disk, thus ensuring that the system does not lose its integrity. In a multi-user system, *sync* operations are repeatedly carried out in background, but it is good practice for users to sync the system occasionally. If the lights start to dim or there is some other indication of a potential power failure, execute a *sync* immediately! If power is lost and data has not been written to disk, it is like playing Russian Roulette with the file system. Nine times out of ten, there will be no damage — but it is possible to lose the entire file system! I know, I have been there!

tar

tar [key] [files]

tar stands for Tape ARchive. It is used to dump and restore files and directories to and from magnetic tape. Its origins are from the days when data was archived onto nine track magnetic tape drives, although it can be used with any output device and will even move data from one part of the file system to another. One important difference between it and other commands, is that the options are not necessarily preceded by a - and are now called keys. The list of file arguments can specify files and directories. If a directory is specified, *tar* recursively searches all the subdirectories below it and includes all files and subdirectories it finds.

The data is written to and read from the tape or device in blocks and, as such, the device is accessed directly. There is no need to mount the device to use *tar*. With the data stored in this way, it is possible, through another key, to append other files or more recent versions to the same tape or device. In such cases, where there are multiple versions of the same file on the tape or device, the last version to be written will be the version that is used when the files are restored from tape. Although the others are restored, each new version overwrites its predecessor. Valid keys are:

r   The named files are written on the end of the tape. The *c* function implies this function.

x   The named files are extracted from the tape. If a named file matches a directory whose contents had been written onto the tape, this directory is (recursively) extracted. If a named file on tape does not exist on the system, it is created with the same mode as the one on tape — except that the set-user-ID and set-group-ID bits are not set unless the superuser is carrying out the operation. This can cause immense problems, as discussed later. If the files exist, their modes are not changed, except for the bits described above. The owner, modification time and mode are restored, if possible. If no file arguments are given, the entire content of the tape is extracted.

t   The names of all the files on the tape are displayed. This effectively provides a directory listing and is useful in checking the tape or device before committing to a restore.

u   Performs an update and *should* be considerably quicker than performing a full backup. Unfortunately, it is not and a full backup is probably quicker! The named files are added to the tape if they are not already there, or have been modified since last written on that tape.

c   A new tape is created and writing begins at the beginning of the tape, instead of after the last file. This command implies the *r* function.

z   Compress or decompress the file using the *gzip* utility. This is frequently used as the most common form of compressed file is a *gzip* compressed *tar* file. The kernel distributions use this format for instance.

The following characters may be used in addition to the letter that selects the desired function:

$s   The $ is a tape drive number (0,...,7) and s is the density: l — low (800 bpi), m — medium (1600 bpi), or h — high (6250 bpi). This modifier selects the drive on which the tape is mounted. The default is 0m (drive 0 using 1600 bpi). Please note that 0m is not the same as m0.

v   Normally, *tar* does its work silently. The *v* (verbose) option causes it to type the name of each file it treats. With the *t* function, *v* gives more information about the tape entries than just the name.

w   Forces an interactive mode, where *tar* prints the action to be taken, followed by the name of the file and waits for the user's confirmation. If a word beginning with *y* is given, the transfer is performed. Any other input is interpreted as "no".

f *arg*   The argument after *f* is the name of the device *tar* is to use instead of /*dev*/ *mt*. As most systems do not use ninetrack tape for backup and their device names are rarely /*dev*/*mt*, this option becomes almost mandatory. It can be used with floppy disks or virtually anything else. If the name of the file is -, *tar* writes to the standard output or reads from the standard input.

b *arg*   Causes *tar* to use the next argument as the blocking factor for tape records. The default is 1, the maximum 20. This option should only be used with raw magnetic tape archives. The block size is determined automatically when reading tapes. The blocking factor is the number of blocks of data that are read or written to the tape at a time. The higher the block factor, usually the faster the transfer. Do not use if the archive is to be updated (*u* option), as *tar* cannot cope and may corrupt the tape, the file system or both!

l   Forces tar to complain if it cannot resolve all of the links to the files being dumped. The default is not to print error messages in the event of an error.

m   Tells *tar* not to restore the modification times. The modification time of the file is then taken as the time of extraction.

o   Instructs *tar* to change user and group identifiers of extracted files to that of the user running the program, rather than those on the tape.

Here are some typical commands:

tar xvf /dev/rmt0 will copy the files on tape device */dev/rmt0* and transfer them to the current directory.

tar tv /dev/rmt0 will display information about the files stored on the tape device */dev/rmt0*.

Printing

Most Linux systems offer two methods of printing documents. The first simply redirects the standard output of a command, like *cat* or *pr*, to the printer directly and the second uses a spooling facility. The redirection method is very similar to that used in many personal computer systems. It is easy to use and implement — but it does have some drawbacks. The user cannot continue working while the file is being printed and, if two or more users send files to the printer at the same time, the data will become intermixed as there is no scheduling! The spooling system solves these problems by making a copy of each document and printing each copy, in its entirety, in the background. This frees up the user's terminal to carry on working and prevents multiple print requests from corrupting each other.

The printer device name is usually */dev/lp* but it may vary from system to system. It is necessary to consult the system documentation to determine which names to use to make the commands work correctly. The spooling system and associated commands require the system administrator to set up the system before they can be used correctly. This procedure is complex and is described in detail in the HOWTO documents on the CD-ROM.

pr

pr [options][files]

This command is similar to *cat* in that it takes one or more files and prints their contents on standard output unless redirected. If no file is specified or - appears in its place, the standard input is used. Its advantage over *cat* is that it can control the page format without having to alter the original files. The options may be used singly or combined:

+*n*   Begin printing with page *n* (default is 1).

- *n*   Produce *n*-column output (default is 1).

-**a**   Print multicolumn output across the page.

-**e***cn*   Change tabs to character positions *n+1, 2n+1* and so on. Spaces are used to replace tabs in the output. *c* is any non-digit character and is interpreted as the tab character. If not present, the default tab is used.

-m   Merge and print all files simultaneously, one per column.

-d   Double-space the output.

-i*cn*   This is the reverse of the *-e* option, where white space is replaced by tab characters at positions *n+1, 2n+1* and so on. Again, *c* is any non-digit character and is interpreted as the tab character. If not present, the default tab is assumed.

-n*ck*   Number the lines at *k* intervals (the default is 1) and use the non-digit character, *c*, to separate the number from the start of each line.

-w*k*   Set the width of a line to *k* character positions (default is 72).

-o*k*   Offset each line by *k* character positions (default is 0).

-l*k*   Set the length of a page to *k* lines (default is 66).

-h   Use the next argument as the printed header instead of the file name.

-p   Pause before beginning each page if the output is directed to a terminal. The bell rings and *pr* waits for a Return before continuing.

These two examples show how the command works. No redirection has been used and so the command's output appears on the screen. It must be redirected to the printer to print out the data.

```
$pr -110 -2 data
This is line 1                      This is line 3
This is line 2                      This is the
last line
$pr -110 -2 data > /dev/lp
$
```

Printer spooler commands

As previously stated, the spooling system and associated commands require the system administrator to set up the system before they can be used correctly. The printers are either referred to by name or, if they are organized in groups called classes, by class.

lprm

lprm jobid

This is the equivalent of the *cancel* command and is used to remove jobs from the printer. The *jobid* can be found by using *lpq*. If a hyphen is used, all the user's current print jobs will be cancelled.

lpq

lpq [option]

This is the equivalent command to *lpstat* and provides information about the number of print jobs that a printer is handling. Again, there are two common options:

-P *printid*	Displays information about printer *printid*.
+*n*	Displays information every *n* seconds until the printer has no outstanding jobs to do.

lpr

lpr [options] files

To print out a file, *lp* is used. It is normally used without any options and assumes the default printer that has been assigned by the system administrator. It Returns a request ID (identity) if the request has been accepted but may Return an error message if the printer is unavailable. Its options may appear in any order and may be intermingled with file names:

-c	Make copies of the files and use these instead of the originals. If this option is not given, the user must not remove the files before they are printed and any modifications to the file after the request but before its actual printing will be printed.
-d*dest*	Allows a particular printer or class of printers to be used instead of the default. If not specified, the command uses the default printer.
-m	Send mail after the files have been printed. The default is not to send any.
-n*number*	Print *number* copies (default 1) of the output.
-o*option*	Passes the *option* to the printer model driver. Several options can be passed by repeating the structure, e.g. *-o12pt -obold -o45lines.*
-s	Suppresses any messages, including the Returned request ID.
-t*title*	Prints *title* on the banner page.
-w	Sends a message to the user's terminal after the files have been printed. If the user is not logged on, mail message is sent instead.
-# *n*	Print *n* copies of the file.
-P *printid*	Use the printer *printid.*

Text formatting

cmp

cmp [-l] [-s] file1 file2

This command compares two files and gives an indication if they differ. With no options, *cmp* prints a message with the first occurrence of a difference, giving the line and character number of the discrepancy. If there is no difference, nothing is printed and the normal prompt appears. It Returns various codes indicating the results of its testing. Code 0 means the files were identical, 1 for different files and 2 for missing or incorrect arguments. Its options are:

-l   Prints the byte number (decimal) and the differing bytes (octal) for each difference.

-s   Prints nothing for differing files and only Returns codes.

```
$cat file1
This is line 1.
This is line 2.
$cat file2
This is line a.
This is line b.
$ cmp file1 file2
file1 file2 differ: char 14, line 1
$ cmp -l file1 file2
    14   61 141
    30   62 142
    46   63 143
$ cmp -s file1 file2
$
```

col

col [-b] [-f] [-x]

col reads from the standard input and writes onto the standard output and is used to provide the line overlays. It is capable of complete line overlays and forward and reverse half-line overlays. and is usually used with the *nroff* text formatter. Control characters are used to indicate when to perform these operations — esc7 for a complete line, esc8 and esc9 for reverse and forward line feeds. The options are fairly simple:

-b   Assume that the output device is incapable of backspacing. *col* will calculate the last character for each character location and print that.

-f   Enable fine positioning.

-x   Use whitespace instead of tabs (the default is tabs).

banner

banner strings

banner takes the following string(s) and prints it in very large letters. It is frequently used to create banners — hence its name. Other uses include headings for printouts and other hard copy. The effect it creates relies on monospaced typefaces — which are normal for most dot matrix printers but not for laser printers.

comm

comm [- [123]] file1 file2

This command compares *file1* and *file2* and prints out their lines in three columns. The first column contains those that appear only in *file1*, the second column only in *file2* and the third column lines that are common to both files.

In the example below, *dog* is unique to *file1*, *fox* is unique to *file2* and *cat* and *hen* are common to both files. It is recommended that both files are sorted into ASCII order to ensure that this utility functions correctly. This can be done using the *sort* command.

```
$ comm file1 file2
                cat
dog
        fox
                hen
$
```

The *-[123]* options suppresses the printing of the first, second and third columns respectively. To print out common lines in the previous example, the command line is *comm -12 file1 file2*.

csplit

csplit [-s] [-k] [-f prefix] file argl [... argn]

The *csplit* command reads *file* and separates it into n+1 sections, defined by the arguments *argl. . . argn*. It has many uses, such as splitting large files into smaller sections so other utilities can process the data without error, or to extract a section for modification. It can also be used when the original file is too large to go on a floppy disk. The file is split into disk-sized sections and then copied onto the disks. By default, the sections are placed in files called *xx00 - . . .xxn*, where *n* may not exceed 99. The sections are defined by the arguments in the command line and can be line references, character strings or other regular expressions. The original file can be recreated by using the *cat* command: *cat xx00 xx01 xx02 >file*.

The options to *csplit* are

-s   *csplit* normally prints the character counts for each file created. This option stops this.

-k   *csplit* normally removes created files if an error occurs. This option preserves such files.

-f *prefix*   Normally the split files are named *xx00...xxn* where *n* is the number of the last section. The *-f prefix* option changes the default names to *prefix00...prefixn*.

The arguments (argl . . . argn) to *csplit* can be a combination of the following:

00   The file start to (but not including) the line referenced by arg1.

01   From the line referenced by arg1 up to the line referenced by arg2.

n+1   From the line referenced by arg*n* to the end of file. If the file argument is a -, standard input is used.

/rexp/   The section includes the current and subsequent lines, up to the first line containing the regular expression *rexp*. The line containing the expression is used as the current line for the next section.

This argument may be followed by an optional + or - some number of lines (e.g. */Page/-5*).

```
$ csplit file3 /line2/
15
45
$ cat xx00
This is line1.
$ cat xx01
This is line2.
This is line3.
This is line4.
$
```

%rexp%   This argument is the same as */rexp/*, except that no file is created for the section.

lnno   A file is to be created from the current line up to (but not including) *lnno*. The current line then becomes *lnno*.

{num}   If it follows a *rexp* type argument, that argument is applied *num* more times. If it follows *lnno*, the file is split into *num* sections, each *lnno* lines in length.

```
$ csplit file3 01 03
0
30
30
$ cat xx00
$ cat xx01
This is line1.
This is line2.
$ cat xx02
This is line3.
This is line4.
$
```

cut

cut -clist [file ...]
cut -f list [-d char] [-s] [file]

cut is used to cut out columns of data from a file. Each line is read in turn and the command line arguments used to specify which fields or characters are to be removed. The fields can either be character positions or defined by delimiting characters such as tabs. This utility is often used as a filter to ensure that data matches a certain format before processing it. If another utility can only handle lines of length 40 characters or less, *cut* can be used to filter the standard input in case more than 40 characters are input. The extra characters would be ignored. The meaning of the options are:

list   A comma-separated list of integer field numbers (in increasing order), with optional - to indicate ranges [e.g. *1,4,7*; *1-3,8*; *-5,10* (short for *1-5,10*); or *3-* (short for third through last field)].

-c*list*   The *list* following -c (remember no space!) specifies the absolute character positions. e.g. *-c1-56* would pass the first 56 characters of each line. *-c9-20* would pass 12 characters starting with the ninth character in the line.

-f*list*   The *list* following *-f* is a list of fields assumed to be separated in the file by a delimiter character. *-f1,7* copies the first and seventh fields only.

          If a line does not have any delimiters (and therefore has no fields defined), the line is passed through without any changes unless the -s option is specified. This is useful for preserving headings and titles within data tables.

-d*char*   The character *char* following *-d* is the field delimiter (*-f* option only) which is used to define the end of each field. The default is a tab character but spaces, colons and other punctuation marks can be used. Remember that space or other characters with special meaning to the shell must be quoted.

-s   Suppresses lines with no delimiter characters in case of *-f* option. Unless specified, lines with no delimiters are passed through untouched. Either the *-c* or *-f* option must be specified.

If no files are given or a file name of "-" is used, the standard input is used. There is a line length limitation of 1,023 characters and *cut* does not like multiple adjacent backspaces.

```
$ cut -c1-9 | cat
1234567890abcdef
123456789
$

$ cat test
field1:field2:field3:field4:field5
$ cut -d: -f2,4 test | cat
field2:field4
$
```

diff

diff [-efbh] file1 file2

diff compares two files, *file1* and *file2*, and displays what changes are needed to convert *file1* into *file2*. If either file is a directory, the other file name is assumed to refer to a file in that directory. Depending on selected options, the changes can be shown as a set of lines where those affected in *file1* are flagged by < and all the lines that are affected in the second file are flagged by >, or as a set of *ed* commands.

-b   Ignores trailing blanks (spaces and tabs). If there are strings of blanks at the same location within the files, these are treated as the same.

-e   Produces a script of a, c, and d commands for the editor which will recreate *file2* from *filel*.

-f   Produces a similar list but in the opposite order.

-h   Does a fast, half-hearted job. It works only when changes are small and widely spread, but it does work on files of unlimited length. Options *-e* and *-f* are unavailable with *-h*.

```
$ diff filea file2
2c2
< This is line2.
—
> This line2.
$ diff -e filea file2
2c
This line2.
.
$
```

diff3

diff3 [-ex3] filel file2 flle3

diff3 is similar to the *diff* utility, except that it compares three versions of a file and marks disagreeing ranges of text flagged with these codes:

====   All three files differ

====1   Filel is different

====2   File2 is different

====3   File3 is different

-e   Produces a script of a, c, and d commands for the editor which will recreate *file2* from *filel*.

-x   Only incorporate changes that are flagged ====.

-3   Only incorporate changes that are flagged ====3.

```
$ diff3 filea file1 file2
====
1:1,4c
  This is line1.
  This is line2.
  This is line7.
  This is line4.
2:1,4c
  cat
  dog
  hen

3:1,4c
  This is line1.
  This line2.
  This is line7.
  This is line4.
$
```

nl

nl [options] file

nl is a line numbering utility that adds line numbers to a file. Its format is to take a file, number it and print the results on standard output. To create a new file, the output must be redirected to a file. It can cope with logical pages where various text sections, such as a header, a footer and body text make up a logical page. The headers and footers are text that is printed at the top and bottom of every page, while the logical pages are formed from the lines that are in the middle of each page. The headers and footers are not numbered by default. The start of the various sections are defined by line contents as follows:

\:\:\:	start of header
\:\:	start of body text in logical page
\:	start of a footer.

There are two sets of options that control the numbering and which sections within each logical page are numbered.

-v*start*	Use *start* as the first line number. The default is 1.
-i*adder*	Increment the line numbers by *adder*. The default is 1.
-p	Do not reset the line numbering with every new page.
-l*number*	Determines the *number* of blank lines to be considered worthy of a single line number. This option only works if all lines are numbered e.g. *-ba, -ha* or *-fa*.
-s*string*	Changes the default tab character to *string* that is used to separate the line number from the rest of the data on each numbered line.
-w*width*	Changes the number of characters used for the line number from the default of 6 to *width*.
-n*format*	Changes the format used for the line number, where *format* is:

	ln	left justified and leading zeros suppressed.
	rn	right justified and leading zeros suppressed(default).
	rz	right justified with leading zeros.

-d*xx*	Changes the delimiter characters, normally \:, to *xx* to signify the start of a logical page.
-b*type*	Specifies which body text lines are numbered.
-h*type*	Specifies which header lines are numbered.
-f*type*	Specifies which footer lines are numbered.

In the above three options *type* is one of the following:

a	number all lines
t	number lines with printable text (default)
n	no line numbering
p*str*	number only lines that contain the regular expression *str*.

```
$ cat test
     1   6
     2   data
     3   ed.hup
$ nl test
     1            1  6
     2            2  data
     3            3  ed.hup
$ nl -i10 test
     1            1  6
    11            2  data
    21            3  ed.hup
$ nl -v567 -i20 test
   567            1  6
   587            2  data
   607            3  ed.hup
$ nl -v567 -i20 -nln -sline test
567    line     1         6
587    line     2         data
607    line     3         ed.hup
$
```

paste

paste -s -d string file1 file2

paste is the horizontal version of *cat* in that it takes two files and joins them by combining their lines so that the two files appear side by side. There are two options:

-s   Merges subsequent lines rather than use the default of a line from each file.

-d *string*   Replaces the default tab character which is inserted between the joined data by the character or characters in *string*. The special escape sequence characters can be used.

\n	new line
\t	tab character
**\ **	backslash
\0	null character — nothing at all

In the following example, *diff* is used to confirm that the files *test3* and *test4* are identical. *paste* is then used to create test5 from these two files.

```
$ cat test4
     1   6
     2   data
     3   ed.hup
     4   script
     5   script1
$ diff test3 test4
$ paste test3 test4 >test5
```

```
$ cat test5
      1   6               1   6
      2   data            2   data
      3   ed.hup          3   ed.hup
      4   script          4   script
      5   script1         5   script1
$
```

spell

spell -v -b -x -l +local_file files

spell performs a spelling check on the files passed to it via the command line. Words that are either spelled incorrectly or missing from its dictionary are printed. The dictionary is usually stored in a file called */usr/lib/spell/hlist* and there may be versions to support both American and British spelling. The five basic options are straightforward:

-v   Prints all words that are not in the dictionary and suggests alternatives.

-x   Prints out all the partial words that are plausible using a = to indicate them. This is helpful in identifying which part of a word is causing an error.

-l   Searches any other files that are referenced within the file using *troff* syntax.

-b   Uses British spelling instead of American.

+*local_file***   Use *local_file* as an effective additional dictionary.

more, less

more filename   less filename

The BSD equivalent to *pg* is the command *more*. It works in a similar manner and many systems make a copy of *more* and call it *pg* and vice versa to provide both commands to users. The Linux version is called *less* but most other UNIX systems call it *more*.

split

split -n file name

This is very similar to *csplit*, in that it also splits a file into several smaller sections. It takes *file* and splits it into smaller files, starting with *name* and using the suffix *aa...ab...ac* through to *zz*. Each new file contains *n* lines. If *n* is not specified, it defaults to 1,000. The alphabetical suffix allows a single file to be split into 676 smaller ones! Again like *csplit*, the files can be joined together by using the *cat* command as shown. The *diff* command at the end demonstrates a successful concatenation.

```
$ cat test3
     1   6
     2   data
     3   ed.hup
     4   script
     5   script1
     6   test2
$ split -3 test3 little
.$ dir little*
littleaa     littleab     littleac
$ cat little[a-z][a-z] > test4
$ cat test4
     1   6
     2   data
     3   ed.hup
     4   script
     5   script1
     6   test2
$ diff test3 test4
$
```

tail

tail [options] file

This copies the end part of the file to standard output starting at a particular line, block or character. The options are:

±*number*l   Start at line *number*. If the *number* is negative, start counting backward from the last line. If positive, count forward from the front. If no *number* is given, the value of 10 is assumed.

±*number*b   Start at block *number*. If the *number* is negative, start counting backward from the end of the file. If positive, count forward from the front. If no *number* is given, the value of 10 is assumed.

±*number*c   Start at character *number*. If the *number* is negative, start counting backward from the end of the file. If positive, count forward from the front. If no *number* is given, the value of 10 is assumed.

-f   Use the follow mode. This option causes *tail* to go into an endless loop where it prints data from the file as instructed, sleeps for a second and then repeats. This is extremely useful in monitoring a file for any changes.

tr

tr [cds] [string1 [string2]]

tr copies the standard input to the standard output with substitution or deletion of selected characters. Input characters in *string1* are mapped into the corresponding characters of *string2*. Any combination of options may be used:

-c   Complements the set of characters in *string1* with respect to those characters with ASCII codes 001 through 377 octal.

-d   Deletes all input characters in string1.

-s   Squeezes all strings of repeated output characters that are in *string2* to single characters.

The following abbreviation conventions may be used to introduce ranges of characters or repeated characters into the strings:

[a-z]   Stands for the string of characters whose ASCII codes run from character a to character z, inclusive.

[a*n]   Stands for *n* repetitions of a. If the first digit of n is 0, n is considered octal; otherwise, n is taken to be decimal. A zero or missing n is taken to be huge. This facility is useful for padding *string2*.

nnn   Use ASCII character *nnn*. For example, a new-line is *nnn*=012

The following example creates a list of all the words in *file1*, one per line, in *file2*. A word is taken to be a maximal string of alphabetic characters. The strings are quoted to protect the special characters from interpretation by the shell; \\012 is the ASCII code for new line.

tr -cs "[A-Z][a-z]" "[\\012*]" <file1>file2

sort

sort -cmu -ooutput -ykmem -zrecsz -dfiMnr -btx +pos1 -pos2 files

sort sorts lines of all the files together and writes the result on the standard output. If no files or - are specified, the command takes input from the standard input, the terminal keyboard. Comparisons are made using either each line or selected parts of each line called keys. The default is to use the whole line as a key and sort using the ASCII character ordering. All characters, including control characters, are considered. There are several groups of options.

Changing the default behavior:

-c   Check that the input files are already sorted correctly. If so, do not proceed further.

-m   Merge the files together. It is assumed that the files are already sorted.

-u   Unique. Removes any duplicated lines that have the same keys. If the key is specified as the whole line, this removes duplicate lines. If the key is specified as part of the line, the removed lines will have identical keys but may be unique. Use this option with caution.

-o *output*   Use the file *output* instead of the standard output.

-y*kmem*   Instructs the command to use *kmem* kilobytes of RAM. If *kmem* is not specified, the maximum amount of memory is used. This is used to control memory usage when memory is at a premium.

-**z***recsz*   Specifies the longest line size for merge only (*-m* option) execution. If not specified, the system default is used which, if exceeded causes an error. Specifying *recsz* as number of bytes in the longest line stops the problem.

Changing the default ordering rules:

-**d**   "Dictionary" order: only letters, digits, and blanks (spaces and tabs) are used in comparisons.

-**f**   Treat lower and upper case as the same.

-**i**   Ignore characters with an ASCII number below 40 and greater than 176 in text comparisons.

-**r**   Reverse the comparison order.

-**n**   Sort text strings that represent numbers by arithmetic value.

-**M**   Compare as months. The first three nonblank characters of the field are converted to uppercase and are compared with JAN, FEB, MAR, and so on up to DEC. Any other text is treated as lower than JAN. This option ignores leading blanks and implies the *-b* option.

Defining sort keys:

+*pos1* -*pos2*   Define a key using *pos1* and *pos2*. The starting point is specified by +*pos1* and the ending point by -*pos2*. They both have the form of *m.n* but differ slightly in its interpretation: with a + prefix, the *m* is the the *m*+1st field and *n* is the *n*+1st character. With a - suffix, *m* refers to the *m*th field and *n* to the *n*th character after the last character in that field. They can then be followed by any of the options for changing the default ordering rules. If *.n* is missing, the default value of 0 is used to find the first character. For example:

+3.6   start key with the 7th character in field 4.

+3.6b   start key with the 7th non-blank character in field 4.

+4   start key with the 1st character in field 4.

- 3.6   end key with the 6th character after field 3.

- 3.6b end key with the 6th nonblank character after field 3.

-**4**   end key with the 0th character after field 4 (the last character in field 4).

-**t***x*   Use *x* as the field separator character. *x* is not considered to be part of a field and each occurrence of *x* is recognized — *xx* would be interpreted as an empty field.

-**b**   Ignore leading blanks determining the start and ending positions of fields.

sort is extremely powerful and useful. The way to get the most out of it is to play around with the command. Here are some examples(overleaf).

```
$ cat sort1
Field1 :   Field 2: Field 3 :
apple :   pear : orange:
disk : cup          :   knife : sink
Spanner : hammer::Screwdriver
$ sort sort1
Field1 :   Field 2: Field 3 :
Spanner : hammer::Screwdriver
apple :   pear : orange:
disk : cup          :   knife : sink
$ sort -f sort1
apple :   pear : orange:
disk : cup          :   knife : sink
Field1 :   Field 2: Field 3 :
Spanner : hammer::Screwdriver
$ sort -f -r sort1
Spanner : hammer::Screwdriver
Field1 :   Field 2: Field 3 :
disk : cup          :   knife : sink
apple :   pear : orange:
$
```

In the next set, the first command specifies the key as field three using a colon as the field separator and treats uppercase and lowercase letters as the same. However, the output is not quite what was expected. The command takes into account any spaces, and this changes the expected alphabetical order. The "spanner" line has nothing in that field and is therefore always first. The second command is similar to the first but uses the *b* option to ignore blanks and this generates the expected order. The third example further defines the key as starting with the third character in the field and again, this changes the ordering. Note that the fields do not have to be the same size in any of the lines.

```
$ sort -f -t: +2 -3 sort1
Spanner : hammer::Screwdriver
disk : cup          :   knife : sink
Field1 :   Field 2: Field 3 :
apple :   pear : orange:
$ sort -f -t: +2b -3b sort1
Spanner : hammer::Screwdriver
Field1 :   Field 2: Field 3 :
disk : cup          :   knife : sink
apple :   pear : orange:
$ sort -f -t: +2.2b -3b sort1
Spanner : hammer::Screwdriver
apple :   pear : orange:
Field1 :   Field 2: Field 3 :
disk : cup          :   knife : sink
$
```

uniq

uniq -udc +n -n input output

uniq searches through a file and removes repeated copies of any lines. The repeated lines must be adjacent to each other for this operation to work correctly and the *sort* command is often used to prepare the file before *uniq* is used. In addition, the input and output files must be different. The options are:

-n   Ignore the first *n* fields where each field is separated by tabs or spaces.

+n   Ignore the first *n* characters.

-u   Only the lines that are unique are transferred to the output file.

-d   One copy of any repeated line is sent to the output file.

-c   Each line is preceded by a repeat count.

The default is a combination of options *u* and *d*.

Background processing

at

at time

This takes commands and executes them later, at a given time. Users are only permitted to use this command if their name appears in the file */usr/lib/cron/ at.allow* or does not appear in the file */usr/lib/cron.at.deny*. If the latter is empty, any user can invoke the command. If neither file is present, only *root* is allowed to use the command. Its use is a little strange. The commands that are to be executed later are piped into the *at* command. The results are not immediately displayed on the screen, but are available by typing the *mail* command. This displays the standard output and error data from the *at* command.

```
$ echo "ls -alsi" | at now +1 minute
job 669444240.a at Wed Mar 20 04:44:00 1991
$ date
Wed Mar 20 04:47:03 GMT 1991
$ mail
From root Wed Mar 20 04:44 GMT 1991
total 36
204   1 drwxr-xr-x 2 root sys 2 Mar 20 04:18 .
201   3 drwxr-xr-x 23 root sys 1440 Feb 5 04:23 ..
577   1 -rw-r-r—  1 bin bin 56 Apr  6 1989 .proto
1532 0 prw——     1 root root 0 Mar 20 04:43 FIFO
578   1 -rw-r-r—  1 bin bin 18 Apr6 1989 at.allow
579   1 -rw-r-r—  1 bin bin 18 Apr 6  1989 cron.h

**************************************************
Cron: The previous message is the standard output and standard error of one
of your cron commands.
```

crontab

crontab [file]

crontab -d

crontab -l

crontab allows the user to execute commands automatically by scheduling their execution at a certain time and date, or on a regular time interval. The commands are supplied either as a file or through *stdin* and replace the user's *crontab* file. The file containing the commands is a single line with five fields, followed by the command and any arguments. The *crontab* file can be listed by typing *crontab -l* as shown. The command is similar to *at*, which also uses *cron* to execute the command at a specific time. The difference is that *at* is a one time execution, while *crontab* can execute on a regular basis. The *-d* option removes the user's *crontab* file.

```
$crontab -l
#ident @(#)adm:root    1.1.1.1
#
# The root crontab should be used to perform
accounting data collection.
#
# NOTE: cron is intolerant of blank lines
# IMPORTANT: there must be one active entry in the crontabs directory for cron
00   00   1   1   0   sleep 1
41,11 * * * * /usr/lib/uucp/uudemon.hour
>/dev/null
45 23 * * * ulimit 5000;/bin/su uucp -c
"$instROOT/usr/lib/uucp/uudemon.cleanup"
> /dev/null 2>&1
1,30 * * * * /usr/lib/uucp/uudemon.poll >/dev/null
20 01 * * * /etc/init.d/acct cksize > /dev/null
$
```

Access to this facility is controlled by two files, */usr/lib/cron/cron.allow* and */usr/lib/cron/cron.deny*. If *cron.allow* contains the names of a requesting user, *crontab* will execute correctly; if not, access is denied. If the file does not exist, *cron.deny* is checked to see if the name is present. If so, access is denied. If not, the user can use *crontab*. If neither file exists, only *root* can use *crontab*. If *cron.deny* exists but is empty then any user has permission.

```
$cat /usr/lib/cron/cron.allow
root
sys
adm
uucp
$cat /usr/lib/cron/cron.deny
cat: cannot open /usr/lib/cron/cron.deny
$
```

Most systems only have a valid *cron.allow* file as default. The superuser must make any changes if they are needed. The first five fields are integer patterns that specify the following:

Minute (0 – 59),

Hour (0 – 23),

Day of the month (1 – 31),

Month of the year (1 – 12),

Day of the week (0 – 6 with 0=Sunday).

The pattern can consist of an asterisk, which is effectively a match all, an integer or a group of integers separated by commas. For example, *0 0 1,3,5 10,12 1 command* would execute command on the first, third and fifth of October and December as well as every Monday. The zeros used in the minutes and hours field force the execution at the stroke of midnight. Replacing the hours field with an asterisk would make the command execute every hour. Similarly, with the minutes field, an asterisk would force execution every minute. To add to the file list, copy the current *crontab* to a file, edit it and execute *crontab* with the new edited file name as shown. The *echo* command was used to append the new line, but the file could have been edited with *ed*, *ex* or *vi*. To remove an entry, repeat the procedure but delete the line from the file. To change, repeat and edit the fields as necessary.

```
$crontab -l > new_cron
$echo "1,2,3 * * * * echo countdown" >> new_cron
$cat new_cron
#ident  @(#)adm:root    1.1.1.1
#
# The root crontab should be used to perform
accounting data collection.
#
# NOTE: cron is intolerant of blank lines
# IMPORTANT: there must be one active entry in the crontabs directory for cron
00    00    1    1    0    sleep 1
41,11 * * * * /usr/lib/uucp/uudemon.hour
>/dev/null
45 23 * * * ulimit 5000;/bin/su uucp -c
"$instROOT/usr/lib/uucp/uudemon.cleanup"
> /dev/null 2>&1
1,30 * * * * /usr/lib/uucp/uudemon.poll >/dev/null
20 01 * * * /etc/init.d/acct cksize > /dev/null
1,2,3 * * * * echo countdown
$crontab new_cron
$crontab -l
#ident  @(#)adm:root    1.1.1.1
#
```

```
# The root crontab should be used to perform
accounting data collection.
#
# NOTE: cron is intolerant of blank lines
# IMPORTANT: there must be one active entry in the crontabs directory for cron
00    00    1    1    0    sleep 1
41,11 * * * * /usr/lib/uucp/uudemon.hour
>/dev/null
45 23 * * * ulimit 5000;/bin/su uucp -c
"$instROOT/usr/lib/uucp/uudemon.cleanup"
> /dev/null 2>&1
1,30 * * * * /usr/lib/uucp/uudemon.poll > /dev/null
20 01 * * * /etc/init.d/acct cksize > /dev/null
1,2,3 * * * * echo countdown
$
```

The new command outputs the word "countdown" every first, second and third minute of the hour on *stdout*. However, if the command is not redirected, the output and any error messages are mailed instead.

```
$mail
From root Sat Aug 10 18:03 GMT 1991
countdown


**************************************************
Cron: The previous message is the standard output
    and standard error of one of your cron commands.
? n
From root Sat Aug 10 18:02 GMT 1991
countdown


**************************************************
Cron: The previous message is the standard output
    and standard error of one of your cron commands.

? n
From root Sat Aug 10 18:01 GMT 1991
countdown


**************************************************
Cron: The previous message is the standard output
    and standard error of one of your cron commands.

? n
$
```

The *crontab* command can be used for many different activities, from periodic synchronization of the computer and files system backup to sending birthday messages to users. It is often used to change access permissions on any system games so they cannot be executed during office hours.

WARNING

If you inadvertently type *crontab* without a file name or *-l* option, it prompts for the command line from the terminal. DO NOT use ^D to get out as this will delete all the entries in the *crontab* file. Use DEL instead. It is good sense to keep a copy of the *crontab* file elsewhere in case of emergencies. The command *crontab -l > crontab.spare* will create a copy called *crontab.spare*.

wait

wait [process ID]

This forces the script to wait for either all associated background processes or, if a process ID is given as an argument, to wait for that specific process to complete. When waiting for all processes, a Return code of zero is given, while waiting for a specific process will Return the code from that process. In the example, *waitdemo* displays the current data and time and then starts another script called *snore* in the background which simply sleeps for 20 seconds. The *wait* command forces it to wait until *snore* has completed and this causes the 20 second difference in the times. *wait* is most frequently used in shell scripts.

```
$cat snore
sleep 20
$cat waitdemo
date
echo Now starting snore in the background
snore&
wait
date
$waitdemo
Thu Aug  8 01:19:58 GMT 1991
Now starting snore in the background
Thu Aug  8 01:20:18 GMT 1991
$
```

sleep

sleep n

sleep suspends execution for *n* seconds and can be combined with a command or just used to delay further commands, usually within a shell script.

System activity

df

df [-lt] [-f] file-system

df shows the number of free blocks and free inodes of any mounted file system, directory or mounted resource. It is similar to the MS-DOS *chkdsk* command. It examines the data stored in the superblocks. The file system may be specified either by device name (*/dev/dsk/cld0s2*) or by a direct directory name (*/usr*). It uses the following options:

-l   Only report on local file systems.

-t   Causes the figures for total allocated blocks and inodes to be reported as well as the free blocks and inodes.

-f   An actual count of the blocks in the free list is made, rather than taking the figure from the superblock (free inodes are not reported). This option does not print any information about mounted remote resources and can take some time to execute.

If multiple remote resources are listed that reside on the same file system or a remote machine, each listing after the first one is marked with an asterisk.

```
$ df
/   (/dev/dsk/c1d0s0 ):    35480 blocks     7785 i-nodes
$ df -t
/   (/dev/dsk/c1d0s0 ):    35480 blocks     7785 i-nodes
                 total:    74684 blocks     9328 i-nodes
$ df -f
/   (/dev/dsk/c1d0s0 ):    35480 blocks
$
```

du

du [-sar] [names]

du reports the number of blocks contained in all files and directories within the *names* argument. It recursively searches down all the directory paths. If *names* is not specified, the current directory is used. Files with two or more links are only counted once, providing the links do not go across different branches of the file system. If a link is to a file on a floppy disk and the other onto a hard disk, each link would be treated as a separate file. The block count includes any indirect blocks associated with a file, but the count may be incorrect if the file is non-contiguous and has "holes" in it. The optional arguments are as follows:

-s   Causes only the grand total (for each of the specified names) to be shown.

-a   Causes an output line to be generated for each file.

      If neither *-s* or *-a* is specified, an output line is generated for each directory only.

-r   Causes *du* to generate messages about directories that cannot read, files that cannot be opened and so on, rather than being silent (default).

```
$ du -a /user/book
1          /user/book/prose
1          /user/book/test/file1
1          /user/book/test/target3
1          /user/book/test/target1
1          /user/book/test/target2
1          /user/book/test/dd1
1          /user/book/test/dd2
1          /user/book/test/xx02
1          /user/book/test/ddtest
1          /user/book/test/ddresult
1          /user/book/test/ddresult2
1          /user/book/test/file2
1          /user/book/test/filea
13         /user/book/test
15         /user/book
$
```

nohup

nohup command arguments

This strangely named utility executes the command with its arguments without taking any notice of interrupts or quits. In other words, the command executes until completed, irrespective of hangups and logoffs. If the output has not been redirected, it is written to a file called *nohup.out* either in the current directory, providing write permission is given, or the home directory if not. In the example, an *ls* command is executed in the background using *nohup* and the user tries to log out. Normally, all processes associated with the user would be aborted but, because the command was invoked with *nohup*, this particular process was not aborted and allowed to complete. As a result, the logout was not executed because the *nohup* command was still running.

```
ess2:~# nohup ls -l&
[3] 206
ess2:~# nohup: appending output to `nohup.out'
logout
There are stopped jobs.
[3]   Done                    nohup ls -l
ess2:~#
ess2:~# cat nohup.out
ddtest      file2      nohup.out    target3     ddresult     exdemo
ess2:~#
```

The reason for this command is partly historical. Many users logged onto their UNIX computers via telephone lines and modems which were extremely expensive and prone to disconnection and noise. The advantage *nohup* gave was that processes could be started and completed without having to remain logged in all the time. If the process took a long time to run, the user could log off and save money. If the connection broke, the process would not be aborted and waste all the previous processing power.

kill

kill [-signo] process ID

kill is used to send a signal 15 (a software abort) to the process whose ID is given in the argument. This effectively terminates the process and stops any further execution. It is possible to send other signals to the process by preceding them with a hyphen. Of these, -9 is probably the most common and useful because it guarantees that the process is killed.

Process IDs or PIDs are Returned by the shell when commands are executed in the background or can be obtained by the *ps* command. *kill* only works on processes owned by the user — except for the superuser, who can *kill* anything.

kill is useful when a binary file is displayed by mistake and the binary data has locked up the terminal, so it fails to respond to any commands. The superuser can *kill* the shell associated with that terminal and effectively forcibly log the user off. If the terminal is then reset, the user can log in again. This technique can also be applied to shell scripts and programs that go into continuous loops and ignore the user. Again, the superuser or user can log on to another terminal, use *ps* to identify the PID and *kill* the offending process.

nice

nice [- increment] command arguments

nice executes commands with their arguments at a lower priority than normal. The increment defaults to 10 but can be any value between 1 and 19. With a lower priority, other processes appear to run faster, at the expense of this particular one. The superuser can increase the priority using a negative increment such as - -10. The double negative equates to a positive increase in the priority level.

ps

ps [-ealf] [-c corefile] [-n namelist] [-t tlist] [-p plist] [-u ulist] [-g glist]

ps interrogates the system and displays the currently active processes and their associated data, such as process ID and so on. It is frequently used to identify processes and their IDs before terminating them with the *kill* command.

-e	Print information on all processes.
-d	Print information on all processes, except process group leaders.
-a	Print information about all processes, except process group leaders and processes not associated with a terminal.
-f	Generate a full listing. Normally, a short listing containing only process ID, terminal ("tty") identifier, cumulative execution time and the command name is printed.

-1   Generate a long listing.

-c *corefile*   Use the file *corefile* in place of */dev/mem*.

-s *swapdev*   Use the file *swapdev* in place of */dev/swap*.

-n *namelist* The argument is taken as the name of an alternate namelist (*/unix* is the default).

-t *termlist* Restrict listing to data about the processes associated with the terminals given in termlist. Terminal identifiers may be specified in one of two forms: the device file name tty04 or, if the device file name starts with *tty*, just the digit identifier (04).

-p *proclist* Restrict listing to data about processes whose process ID numbers are given in *proclist*.

-u *uidlist*   Restrict listing to data about processes whose user ID numbers or login names are given in *uidlist*. In the listing, the numerical user ID is printed unless the *-f* option is used, in which case the login name is printed.

-g *grplist*   Restrict listing to data about processes whose process groups are given in *grplist*.

The column headings and the meaning of the columns in a listing are given below. The letters *f* and *l* indicate the option (full or long) that causes the corresponding heading to appear. *All* means that the heading always appears. Note that these two options only determine what information is provided for a process — they do not determine which processes are to be listed.

F (l)   Flags (octal and additive) associated with the process:

        01   In core

        02   System process

        04   Locked in core (physical I/O)

        08   Currently in primary memory

        10   Being swapped

        40   Another tracing flag

S (l)   The state of the process:

        O   Non-existent

        S   Sleeping

        W   Waiting

        R   Running

        I   Idle

        Z   Terminated

        T   Stopped

        X   Growing

UID (fl)   The user ID number of the process owner; the login name is printed under the *-f* option.

PID (all)   The process ID of the process; it is possible to kill a process if you know the PID.

PPID (fl)   The process ID of the parent process.

C (fl)   Processor utilization for scheduling.

STIME (f)   Starting time of the process.

PRI (1)   The priority of the process; higher numbers mean lower priority.

Nl (l)   Nice value; used in priority computation.

ADDR (l)   The memory address of the process if resident; otherwise, the disk address.

SZ (l)   The size in blocks of the core image of the process.

WCHAN(l)   The event for which the process is waiting or sleeping; if blank, the process is running.

TTY (all)   The controlling terminal for the process.

TIME (all)   The cumulative execution time for the process.

CMD (all)   The command name; the full command name and its arguments are printed under the *-f* option.

A process that has exited and has a parent but has not yet been waited for by the parent, is marked <defunct>. Under the *-f* option, *ps* tries to determine the command name and arguments given when the process was created by examining memory or the swap area. If it cannot get this information, the command name is printed in square brackets.

time

time *command* [arguments]

time measures time in seconds but it uses *stderr* for its output rather than *stdout* It is frequently used to measure the time it takes to perform a command or task. The measurement's resolution is one-tenth of a second and its timings are made by calculating the number of time slices or context switches that it experiences during its execution. For very small commands, the time it will Return can often be zero seconds. The *real* time is the total time elapsed, the *user* time is the proportion spent executing the process, and *sys* time is a measurement of the time the kernel spent in providing other services. In the example shown, the time to perform a *ls* command is measured.

```
$time ls -l > /dev/null

real       0.1
user       0.0
sys        0.1
$
```

Utilities

wc

wc -lwc files

This command counts the total number of lines, words and characters in either a single or multiple files. The *-lwc* option is the default and counts all lines, words and characters. To count only words, add *-w* and so on.

```
$ wc test2
      12     123     792 test2
$ wc *
       4      21      91 6
       4      17      70 data
       4      21      90 ed.hup
       3      14      81 script
      12     123     792 test2
      27     186    1124 total
$ wc -w t*
     123 test2
       1 testfile
       1 testfile2
     125 total
$
```

cal

cal date

cal is a calendar that displays for any particular month or day. The example below is not a misprint — the lost days happened when the United Kingdom switched calendars. There were many riots at the time with people complaining about the eleven days that the government had taken from them!

```
$ cal 9 1752
   September 1752
 S  M Tu  W Th  F  S
       1  2 14 15 16
17 18 19 20 21 22 23
24 25 26 27 28 29 30


$
```

Terminal configurations

stty

stty [-ag] [options]

stty is the command that is normally used to either display the current terminal settings or change them. It only works on the terminal that is assigned as the current standard input. Entering *stty* with no arguments displays the more important settings. With the -*a* option, a complete list is provided. The -*g* option provides the data in a format that can be passed to another *stty* command. No sanity checking is performed and it is therefore quite possible to set up conflicting settings! A very important option is *sane*, which resets the terminal options to a reasonable setting, should things go very wrong. The problem facing most people with this command is the sheer number of options and their meanings. Before going into the options, it is worthwhile to look at what control *stty* gives over the terminal settings and which options are the most important.

The terminal interface can be divided into several areas. The first concerns the serial interface, which is used to transfer data between the terminal and computer. It is important to get these settings right, as they form the basis of all future communication. The second area is the definition of certain character sequences that are specially interpreted to perform some other function —such as backspace, end of file, and so on. The third area controls the flow of information between the terminal and computer so that neither is swamped with data it cannot handle. The final area describes the sequences that are necessary to output data correctly.

Many *stty* options assume that the terminal is communicating with the computer via a modem, which dates back to the times when many users rented time on UNIX machines and connected to them via telephone links, or when the telephone system was used as a wide area network.

When a user presses a key at a terminal, quite a lengthy procedure is carried out before the character is seen on the display. The pressed key generates a specific code, which represents the letter or character. This is converted to a bit pattern for transmission down the serial line to the serial port on the computer system. The converted bit pattern may contain a number of start bits, a number of bits (5, 6, 7 or 8) which represent the data, a parity bit for error checking, followed by a number of stop bits. These are sent down the serial line by a UART (universal asynchronous receiver transmitter) in the terminal at a predetermined speed or baud rate.

Both the terminal and the computer must use the same baud rate and the same combination of start, stop, data and parity bits to ensure correct communication. If different combinations are used, bits will be wrongly interpreted. The result is garbage on the screen and an extremely confused UNIX computer! Up to this point, there is no visual confirmation on the terminal display that the key pressed has resulted in the transmission of a character. If the terminal UART is configured in half duplex mode, it echoes the transmitted character so it can be seen on the screen. Once the data is received at the computer end, it is read in by another UART and, if this UART is set up to echo the character, it sends it back to the terminal. If both UARTs are set up to echo, double characters appear on the screen! The character is then checked by the UNIX software against a list of special characters that perform operations such as backspace, clearing command lines and interrupting commands during their execution. If it is not a special character or a Return, the character is placed in a buffer where it stays until a Return is received. The advantage of buffered input is that the user can type commands ahead while waiting for the current command to complete. Once the Return character is received, the characters in the buffer are flushed out and passed to the shell or application to process. The buffer is thus emptied.

If the terminal is remote from the computer, the serial line may include a modem link where the terminal is connected to a modem and a telephone line and a modem at the other end is linked to the computer. The modem is frequently controlled by the serial line — so if the terminal is switched off, the modem effectively hangs up and disconnects the telephone line. Modems can also echo characters and it is possible to get four characters on the terminal screen in response to a single keystroke. In addition, the link has two methods of flow control. Flow control is necessary to prevent either the terminal or the computer from sending more data than the other can cope with. If too much is sent, it either results in missing characters or a data overrun error message. The first flow control method is hardware handshaking, where hardware in the UART detects a potential overrun and asserts a handshake line to tell the other UART to hold off transmitting. When it can take more data, the handshake line is released. The problem is that there are several options associated with this and, unless the lines are correctly connected, the handshaking fails to work and data loss is possible. The second method uses software to send flow control characters XON and XOFF. XOFF will stop a data transfer, while XON will restart it. By default, UNIX uses ^S for XON and ^Q for XOFF.

Throughout the link, *stty* gives the user complete control over *all* these operations and there are a lot of options that can be changed. The settings of the most important ones can be displayed by using *stty* with no options. The *-a* option gives a complete list as shown later in the following listing.

```
$stty
speed 9600 baud; evenp hupcl
erase = ^h; kill = ^x; swtch = ^`;
brkint -inpck icrnl onlcr tab3
echo echoe echok
$stty -a
speed 9600 baud; line = 0; intr = DEL; quit = ^|; erase = ^h; kill = ^x;
eof = ^d; eol = ^`; swtch = ^`
parenb -parodd cs7 -cstopb hupcl cread -clocal
-loblk
-ignbrk brkint ignpar -parmrk -inpck istrip
```

```
-inlcr -igncr icrnl -iuclc
ixon ixany -ixoff
isig icanon -xcase echo -echoe -echok -echonl
-noflsh
opost -olcuc onlcr -ocrnl -onocr -onlret -ofill
-ofdel tab3
$
```

Before getting involved with all the various options, it is worth checking that the variable TERM is correct for the terminal in use and that the entry in */etc/ inittab* has the right serial port description. Use the *set* or *env* command to check TERM and change it if necessary. Only the system administrator can change */etc/inittab* if it is wrong.

Control modes

parenb	Enable parity generation and detection.
-parenb	Disable parity generation and detection.
parodd	Select odd parity.
-parodd	Select even parity.
cs5	Select character size of 5 bits (32 characters).
cs6	Select character size of 6 bits (64 characters).
cs7	Select character size of 7 bits (128 characters).
cs8	Select character size of 8 bits (256 characters).
O	Hang up phone line immediately.
50, 75, 110	Set baud rate, e.g, stty 9600.
134, 150	Not all hardware supports all these speed options.
200, 300	
600, 1200	
1800, 2400	
4800, 9600	
hupcl	Hang up a telephone connection on last close.
-hupcl	Do not hang up a telephone connection on last close.
hup	Same as *hupcl*.
-hup	Same as *-hupcl*.
cstopb	Use two stop bits per character.
-cstopb	Use one stop bits per character.
cread	Enable the receiver.
-cread	Disable the receiver.
clocal	Assume a line without modem control.
-clocal	Assume a line with modem control.
loblk	Block output from a noncurrent layer.

Input modes

ignbrk	Ignore break on input.
-ignbrk	Do not ignore break on input.
brkint	Signal INTR on break.
-brkint	Do not signal INTR on break.
ignpar	Ignore parity errors.
-ignpar	Do not ignore parity errors.
inpck	Enable input parity checking.
-inpck	Disable input parity checking.
istrip	Strip input characters to 7 bits.
-istrip)	Do not strip input characters to 7 bits.
inlcr	Map *NL* to *CR* on input.
-inlcr	Do not map *NL* to *CR* on input.
igncr	Ignore *CR* on input.
-igncr	Do not ignore *CR* on input.
icrnl	Map *CR* to *NL* on input.
-icrnl	Do not map *CR* to *NL* on input.
iuclc	Map uppercase alphabetic characters to lowercase on input.
-iuclc	Do not map uppercase alphabetic characters to lowercase on input.
ixon	Enable *START/STOP* output control. Output is stopped by sending an ASCII *DC3* and started by sending an ASCII *DC1*.
-ixon	Disable *START/STOP* output control.
ixany	Allow any character to restart output.
-ixany	Only *DC1* to restart output.
ixoff	Request that the system send *START/STOP* characters when the input queue is nearly empty / full.
-ixoff	Request that the system does not send *START/STOP* characters when the input queue is nearly empty / full.

Output modes

opost	Post-process output.
-opost	Do not post-process output; ignore all other output modes.
olcuc	Map lowercase alphabetic characters to uppercase on output.
-olcuc	Do not map lowercase alphabetic characters to uppercase on output.
onlcr	Map *NL* to *CR-NL* on output.
-onlcr	Do not map *NL* to *CR-NL* on output.
ocrnl	Map *CR* to *NL* on output.

-ocrnl	Do not map *CR* to *NL* on output.
onocr	Do not output *CRs* at column zero.
-onocr	Do output *CRs* at column zero.
onlret	On the terminal *NL* performs the *CR*.
-onlret	*NL* does not perform the *CR* on the terminal.
ofill	Use fill characters for delays.
-ofill	Use timing for delays.
ofdel	Fill characters are *DELs*.
-ofdel	Fill characters are *NULs*.
cr0 crl...	Select style of delay for carriage Returns.
nl0 nll...	Select style of delay for line feeds.
tab0 tabl...	Select style of delay for horizontal tabs.
bs0 bsl...	Select style of delay for backspaces.
ff0 ff1...	Select style of delay for form feeds.
vt0 vtl...	Select style of delay for vertical tabs.

Local modes

isig	Enable the checking of characters against the special control characters *INTR* and *QUIT*.
-isig	Disable the checking of characters against the special control characters *INTR* and *QUIT*.
icanon	Enable canonical input (*ERASE* and *KILL* processing).
-icanon	Disable canonical input (*ERASE* and *KILL* processing).
xcase	Canonical upper/lower case presentation.
-xcase	Unprocessed upper/lower case presentation.
echo	Echo back every character typed.
-echo	Do not echo back every character typed.
echoe	Echo *ERASE* character as a backspace-space-backspace string. Note this mode will erase the *ERASEed* character on many CRT terminals; however, it does not keep track of column position and, as a result, may be confusing on escaped characters, tabs and backspaces.
-echoe	Do not echo *ERASE* character as a backspace-space-backspace string.
echok	Echo *NL* after *KILL* character.
-echok	Do not echo *NL* after *KILL* character.
Ifkc	The same as *echok* ; obsolete.
-lfkc	The same as *-echok*; obsolete.
echonl	Echo *NL*.
-echonl	Do not echo *NL*.

noflsh	Disable flush after *INTR* or *QUIT*.
-noflsh	Enable flush after *INTR* or *QUIT*.
stwrap	Disable truncation of lines longer than 79 characters on a synchronous line.
-stwrap	Enable truncation of lines longer than 79 characters on a synchronous line.
stflush	Enable flush on a synchronous line after every write.
-stflush	Disable flush on a synchronous line after every write.
stappl	Use application mode on a synchronous line.
-stappl	Use line mode on a synchronous line.

Control assignments

erase *char*	Set *char* as *ERASE* character.
kill *char*	Set *char* as *KILL* character.
intr *char*	Set *char* as *INTR* character.
quit *char*	Set *char* as *QUIT* character.
eof *char*	Set *char* as *EOF* character.
eol *char*	Set *char* as *EOL* character.
min *char*	Set *char* as MIN character.
time *char*	Set *char* as TIME character.
line *i*	Set *line* discipline to *i* where $0 < i < 127$.

Combination modes

evenp	Enable *parenb* and *cs7*.
parity	Enable *parenb* and *cs7*.
oddp	Enable *parenb*, *cs7*, and *parodd*.
-oddp	Disable *parenb*, and set *cs8*.
-evenp	Same as *-oddp*.
-parity	Same as *-oddp*.
raw	Enable raw input and output — no ERASE, KILL, INTR, QUIT, EOT, or output post processing.
-raw	Disable raw input and output.
cooked	Same as *-raw*.
nl	Unset *icrnl*, *onlcr*.
-nl	Set *icrnl*, *onlcr* and unsets *inlcr*, *igncr*, *ocrnl*, and *onlret*.
lcase	Set *xcase*, *iuclc*, and *olcuc*.
-lcase	Unset *xcase*, *iuclc*, and *olcuc*.
LCASE	Same as *lcase*.
-LCASE	Same as *-lcase*.
tabs	Preserve tabs when printing.
-tabs	Expand to spaces, any tabs when printing.

tab3   Same as *-tabs*.

ek   Reset *ERASE* and *KILL* characters back to normal # and @ respectively.

sane   Resets all modes to some reasonable values.

term   Set all modes suitable for the terminal type *term*, where *term* is one of tty33, tty37, vtOS, tn300, ti700, or tek.

The use of # as an erase character can cause some problems if transferring C program sources from a another computer as a straight text file. Every # is interpreted as an ERASE character, which corrupts the source. This interpretation must be changed to prevent this problem.

who

who[-aAbdHlnpqrstTu] [am i] [utmp_like_file]

who is used to identify the current system users and can give additional data, such as elapsed time, process ID and so on. The utility gets its information from the file */etc/utmp* but an alternative */etc/wtmp* can be specified instead. This contains a history of all the logins since the file was created. Entering *who am i* identifies the invoking user.

-a   All (Abdlprtu) options.

-A   Accounting information.

-b   Boot time.

-d   Dead processes.

-H   Print header.

-l   Login processes.

-n $ Specify number of users/line for *-q*.

-p   Processes other than getty or users.

-q   Quick who.

-r   Run level.

-s   Short form of who (no time since last output or PID).

-t   Time changes.

-T   Status of tty (+ writable, - not writable, ? hung).

-u   Useful information.

Except for the default *-s* option, the general format for output entries is: *name [state] line time activity pid [comment] [exit].*

```
$who -u
root        console     Aug 17 19:07  3:13      70
root        tty1        Aug 17 22:10    .        209
$who -l
LOGIN       con1        Aug 17 19:01  old       71
LOGIN       con2        Aug 17 19:01  old       72
```

```
LOGIN       con3        Aug 17 19:01  old      73
$who -b
     .      system boot Aug 17 19:01
$who -r
     .      run-level 2 Aug 17 19:01   2   0   S
$who -a
     .      system boot Aug 17 19:01
     .      run-level 2 Aug 17 19:01   2   0   S
brc . Aug 17 19:01   old 12  id=  mt term=0 exit=0
rc2 . Aug 17 19:01   old 16  id=  s2 term=0 exit=0
root        console     Aug 17 19:07  3:14     70
LOGIN       con1        Aug 17 19:01  old      71
LOGIN       con2        Aug 17 19:01  old      72
LOGIN       con3        Aug 17 19:01  old      73
root        tty1        Aug 17 22:10    .     209
$who -d
brc                .    Aug 17 19:01
rc2                .    Aug 17 19:01
$who -p
$who -T
root      + console     Aug 17 19:07
root      + tty1        Aug 17 22:10
$who -t
$
```

tty

tty [-l] [-s]

tty appears to be a useless command. It simply displays the path name of the user's terminal. The *-l* option checks to see if it is a synchronous one and will says so if it is not. The *-s* option does not print or display anything. The main use of *tty* is within shell scripts, where it is used to check if the standard input is assigned to a terminal. It Returns three different exit codes:

2   If invalid options were specified.

0   If the standard input is a terminal.

1   In all other cases.

If the standard input has been redirected to a file, for example, *tty* would Return a message "not a tty" (providing the -s option had not been specified) and an error code of 1.

File compression

pack

pack - -f name

pack is a file compression utility that compresses the file or directory *name* and, if successful, removes the originals. The compressed file is given the suffix .z and is usually about 60 to 70% smaller than the original, although this does depend on the file type and the nature of the data. Object files may only show a compression of about 10%. There are two options available:

-     Prints out compression data on the standard output as the command progresses.

-f   Forces all files specified by name to be compressed. This is often used when compressing directories as it forces *pack* to compress all files, irrespective of their size and compression potential.

    No packing occurs if:

- The file appears to be already packed.
- The file name has more than 12 characters.
- The file has links.
- The file is a directory.
- The file cannot be opened (obvious!).
- No disk blocks will be saved by packing.
- A file called *name.z* already exists.
- The .z file cannot be created.
- An I/O error occurred during processing.

To recover compressed files, use *unpack*. To display their contents use *pcat*.

```
$ pack bigfile
pack: bigfile: no saving - file unchanged
$ pack -f bigfile
pack: bigfile: 41.2% Compression
$ ls big*
bigfile.z
$ pcat bigfile
     1    This is line 1
     2    This is line 2
     3    This is line 3
```

-
-     and so on
-

```
$ unpack bigfile
unpack: bigfile: unpacked
$ ls big*
bigfile
$
```

gzip

gzip [-cdfhlLnNrtvV19] [-S suffix] [file ...]

This utility is is used to compress and decompress files using the GNU zip format and utilities. Compressed files usually have the suffix .gz and this format is probably the most popular Linux compression utility used. The LINUX version of the *tar* utility is also enhanced so that it can use this compression method directly by using the -z option. This saves having to *gzip* the file to decompress it and then use *tar* to extract the data.

-c	Write on standard output, keep original files unchanged.
-d	Decompress file.
-f	Force overwrite of output file and compress links.
-h	Displays help information.
-l	List compressed file contents.
-L	Display software license.
-n	Do not save or restore the original name and time stamp.
-N	Save or restore the original name and time stamp.
-q	Suppress all warnings.
-r	Operate recursively on directories.
-S .suf	Use suffix .suf on compressed files.
-t	Test compressed file integrity.
-v	Verbose mode.
-V	Display version number.
-1	Compress faster.
-9	Compress better.

unpack

unpack *name*

unpack is the decompression utility that complements *pack*. If the decompression is successful, the packed version is replaced by the expanded one with the .z suffix dropped. It will not proceed if the expanded file name already exists or cannot be created.

file

file [-c] [-f ffile] [-m mfile] file...

If a file appears to give no clue as to its type, function or source, this command will try to discover this information. It works through a combination of examining the first few bytes of data and looking at a reference file called /etc/ *magic*. There are three options:

-c	Checks the magic file — usually /etc/magic for format errors. This is not normally done for performance reasons.
-f *ffile*	The *ffile* argument is the name of a file containing a list of files to be investigated.
-m *mfile*	Allows *mfile* to be used instead of /etc/magic.

Communicating with other users

write

write user [line]

write copies lines of data from the keyboard, sends them to the specified user's terminal and displays them. If the receiving user is logged on via two or more terminal lines, the actual line can be specified by adding the line to the command line. The data is taken from the keyboard until end of file is indicated with ^D. If the first character on the line is !, the rest of the command is interpreted as a shell command. Communication with *write* is one-way and therefore it is useful to use a prearranged protocol so each user can take turns sending data. For example, the sender could add "over" to the last line of each transmission to signal the other that it was his or her turn.

```
$write root
How about a beer ? over
$
        Message from root on root@ess2 on ttyp0 at 12:59 ...
Fine.
See you at 12.00 at the bar.
Over and out
<EOT>

$
```

wall

wall *file*

wall sends the contents of file to all users and is used during the shutdown process to send a message to users to log off immediately. To overcome any protections set up by a user via *mesg*, the sender must be the superuser. To send text from a keyboard, enter the command *wall* on its own. Enter the text afterward followed by a ^D. This will then send the text.

mesg

mesg [options]

By itself and without any options, *mesg* reports the current state of a user's terminal, with respect to its acceptance of messages sent via the *write* or *wall* commands. To enable or disable acceptance, the following options are used:

-n   Do not accept messages.

-y   Accept messages.

4 bash shell scripts

The bash (Bourne again shell) program is the standard Linux shell and is based on the standard Bourne shell that most UNIX releases use. It has a lot of very sophisticated features thatallow users to change the environment and use shortcuts when moving around the file system. Probably the most powerful feature is the ability to create applications and utilities using a shell script. This is similar to the batch file concept within MS-DOS, where commands are read from a file rather than from a keyboard and are executed in sequence. Such batch files are used to automatically install software.

While the Linux command structure and the command options in particular are not very intuitive, the system administrator can ease this barrier by providing simpler commands for users using shell scripts. I have a whole set of scripts that I use for disk operations. It is easier to type in *backup /user/steve* than the equivalent Linux commands. Many applications have been written using shell scripts, including replacement interfaces. It is quite possible to write a shell script that simulates another user interface so the user is not aware that Linux is running.

The key to writing and using shell scripts is to recognize that they are fully fledged programs in their own right and that the scripting language provided is a programming language, much the same as BASIC or C. It features variables, arithmetic operations, condition testing, and control structures such as FOR-NEXT, IF-THEN_ELSE and WHILE-DO-DONE loops. One difference is that the shell language is a little strange and occasionally pernickety. Some expressions do not need spaces between them while others do! One big advantage of shell scripts is that the commands can be entered directly from the keyboard to test them or ensure that the syntax is correct. This is extremely useful. However, standard manuals always seem to concentrate on academic definitions of the shell commands that tell you everything except what you want to know! The approach taken in this chapter is to illustrate the many facets of scripting with example routines, some of which can be combined to create useful utilities.

Getting started

All that is needed to create a shell script is the ability to use an editor such as *vi* or *ex*. To create a shell script, use the editor to create a file with the commands in the required sequence and then invoke the script. For very simple, one-line commands, *echo* can be used and the output directed to the shell script file.

There are three ways of executing shell scripts, shown in the following examples. The first two run a second copy of the shell and direct it to use the shell script instead of the keyboard. The third method changes the script access permissions to allow its execution. This is the more normal method of executing a shell script because the script effectively becomes a command for the user. As the example shows, all three methods have the same results.

```
$echo ls -l >DIR
$sh < DIR
total 8
-rw-r-r-1   root other 6   Aug  3 16:39 DIR
-rwxrwxrwx1 root other 67  Jul 31 14:19 backup
-rwxrwxrwx1 root other 403 Jul 31 09:48 cflop
$sh DIR
total 8
-rw-r-r-1   root other 6   Aug  3 16:39 DIR
-rwxrwxrwx1 root other 67  Jul 31 14:19 backup
-rwxrwxrwx1 root other 403 Jul 31 09:48 cflop
$chmod +x DIR
$DIR
total 8
-rw-r-r-1   root other 6   Aug  3 16:39 DIR
-rwxrwxrwx1 root other 67  Jul 31 14:19 backup
-rwxrwxrwx1 root other 403 Jul 31 09:48 cflop
$
```

When any shell command is executed, including a shell script, a copy of the shell program is created that is used to execute the commands. As a result, any changes to home directories and to the shell affect only the copy and not the original version. This is a very good idea because any problem or error will affect only the copy — and allow the original shell to take back control. However, it does cause problems if the shell script needs to modify the original environment. This can be forced by preceding the script file name with a full stop followed by a space on the command line. The next example shows the difference using a shell script that changes the directory. When *pwd* is run to display the current directory after the script has finished, the result depends on how it was executed. With no full stop, the changes it made are not remembered and *pwd* shows the directory */sh*. With the full stop and space prefix, the change is passed back and *pwd* shows */opus/bin*.

```
$cat fullstop
pwd
cd /opus/bin
pwd
$
$pwd
/sh
$fullstop
/sh
/opus/bin
$pwd
```

```
/sh
$. fullstop
/sh
/opus/bin
$pwd
/opus/bin
$
```

An alternative method of executing shell scripts or commands is to place them in background mode. This is done by adding an & immediately after the command name or the last option. The script continues to execute in the background and allows the user to carry on working. If the background command uses *stdout* to display data, this happens, irrespective of what the current screen is. This can be confusing, to say the least. If necessary, redirect the output to a file to prevent this confusion.

```
$cat background
echo This is a message from the background
echo This is another
sleep 10
echo so is this...
$background&
This is a message from the background
This is another
218
$ps
    PID TTY        TIME COMMAND
     78 tty1       0:02 sh
    218 tty1       0:00 sh
    219 tty1       0:00 sleep
    221 tty1       0:00 ps
$so is this...
```

The example *background* displays two messages, sleeps for 10 seconds and then prints a final message. When it is executed, the first two messages appear followed by the Process ID number (PID). This number, 218, refers to the copy of the shell and not to the *sleep* command that is running. *ps* displays all the processes running and shows the shell *sh* with its PID of 218, followed by the *sleep* command. The PID numbers are important, as they are used by the *kill* command to terminate the command or script.

```
$background&
This is a message from the background
This is another
239
$ps
    PID TTY        TIME COMMAND
     78 tty1       0:02 sh
    239 tty1       0:00 sh
    240 tty1       0:00 sleep
    241 tty1       0:00 ps
$kill 240
```

```
background: 240 Terminated
so is this...
$background&
This is a message from the background
This is another
243
$kill 243
$ps
    PID TTY       TIME COMMAND
     78 tty1      0:02 sh
    243 tty1      0:00 sh
    244 tty1      0:00 sleep
    246 tty1      0:00 ps
$ps
    PID TTY       TIME COMMAND
     78 tty1      0:02 sh
    247 tty1      0:00 ps
$
```

In this example, the first *kill* command is given the PID of the *sleep* command. This effectively terminates the *sleep* command but does not affect the remaining *echo*, which proceeds and displays its message. The second *kill* is given the PID returned when the script was started. In this case, the whole script is effectively terminated and all remaining unexecuted commands within it (the *sleep* and *echo* commands) do not complete. To stop a currently executing command or script, press the Control and backspace keys together. This should stop the execution but it is possible to disable this within a script so the key sequence is ignored.

On my system, I have a special directory called /*sh*, where I store all my shell scripts. I have added /*sh* to the PATH variable to tell the Linux system to automatically look in this directory. This keeps scripts separate from standard Linux commands and, by placing /*sh* at the beginning of the PATH list, shell scripts with the same names as standard commands take precedence. This is extremely useful for system administrators, as the more dangerous commands can be replaced with safer shell scripts — without the users knowing.

Shell variables

The shell environment supports three types of variables: those that are built in and are provided automatically by the system, those that are user defined and those used within shell scripts.

Built-in variables

These are normally set up when users log in to the system, and are defined partially by the system and by the users' .*profile* files located in their home directories. These variables have special meanings and uses within the shell environment and can be seen by typing *set*.

```
$ set
EXINIT=set redraw nows sm
HOME=/
IFS=
LOGNAME=root
MAIL=/usr/mail/root
MAILCHECK=600
PATH=:/opus/bin:/bin:/usr/bin:/etc:/usr/ucb
PS1=#
PS2=>
TERM=opus-pc
TZ=GMT0
$
```

The common variables seen on most systems have the following meanings:

EXINIT   Defines options for both the *ex* and *vi* editors.

HOME   Defines the home directory. In this case, the directory is root, shown by the backslash.

IFS   A string of delimiters that can be used to separate words in command lines, such as space, tab and new line.

LOGNAME   The name of the logged-on user.

MAIL   The name of the file for any mail messages to be sent.

MAILCHECK The number of seconds between checks by the shell for any mail. The default is 600 seconds (ten minutes). A value of 0 causes the shell to check before every prompt.

PATH   Specifies the directories that the shell will search to find a command or file. They are searched in order, for example */opus/bin* would be the first.

PS1   Defines the shell prompt. In this case, it is # to denote the superuser. For other users, the default is $.

PS2   Defines the second-level prompt that appears when incomplete lines or more data is needed by the shell.

TERM   Defines the terminal type. The correct selection is vital to use the *vi* editor correctly.

TZ   Defines which time zone the system clock is using. In this example, GMT refers to Greenwich mean time.

Other variables that may be seen are:

MAILPATH   Defines a file list similar to that used by *PATH*, which lists all the files that must be checked for mail.

SHELL   Can be used to invoke another shell. It is normally set to *rsh* to force the use of the restricted shell.

FPU   Defines which floating point unit is used. Linux automatically detects hardware floating point units and therefore this variable is not used.

SHACCT   Defines the file used by the shell to write an account of each
                  shell procedure used.

User-defined variables

The user can change or add extra variables to this list in two ways. The first is
to type the variable name followed by an equals sign and its value. This adds
the new variable to the list produced by *set* as shown. Multiple variables can be
defined on the same command line by separating them with a semicolon.
However, the variables will not be passed to subsequently executed commands
unless the shell is told to do so.

```
$ test1=hello;test2=goodbye
$ set
EXINIT=set redraw nows sm
HOME=/
IFS=

LOGNAME=root
MAIL=/usr/mail/root
MAILCHECK=600
PATH=:/opus/bin:/bin:/usr/bin:/etc:/usr/ucb:/sh
PS1=#
PS2=>
TERM=opus-pc
TZ=GMT0
test1=hello
test2=goodbye
$ export test1
$ export test2
$
```

As a result, although the variables *test1* and *test2* are displayed, any commands
that use them will not recognize them and this can cause several problems, if
not much confusion. To make them visible, they must be exported. This
involves typing the command *export* followed by the names of the variables to
be exported as shown in the preceeding example.

The second method is a variation on the first and involves adding the commands to create the variables and export them to the contents of the *.profile* file
found in every home directory. This file is executed every time a user logs in
and can add variables automatically. The commands are added to the file in
exactly the same way that they are typed from the keyboard.

```
$ cat .profile.old

#ident   "@(#)sadmin:etc/stdprofile     1.2"
#        This is the default standard profile provided to a user.
#        They are expected to edit it to meet
their own needs.
$ cat .profile
```

```
#ident   "@(#)sadmin:etc/stdprofile      1.2"
#        This is the default standard profile provided to a user.
#        They are expected to edit it to meet
their own needs.
test1= hello
test2 = goodbye
export test1
export test2
$
```

Shell script variables

The third type of variable is used within shell scripts in much the same ways that variables are used in other programs — to store or pass data. They normally exist only while the shell script that created them is being executed. As a result, they are local. They are created in the same way as user-defined variables.

The shell automatically creates a special set of variables each time a shell script is executed. These are called parameters and are particularly useful because they contain information about the command line such as its name, the number of arguments on it, and so on.

#	Gives the number of arguments on the command line.
*	A list of all the arguments.
@	Also a list of all the arguments — but each argument is a separate word.
$	The command process number.
!	The process number of the last background task. *kill $!* will terminate the last background task.
0	Contains the name of the command.
?	The exit status of the last executed command. A value of zero is considered true and usually indicates a successful completion. Any other value should be interpreted as false and an indication of an error.

1 ... 9 Contains arguments 1 through 9. Known as positional parameters.

The $ variable is frequently used to name unique temporary files by inclusion in a file name such as *abc$$* or *$$abc*. The shell script *vars* displays the contents of some of these variables.

```
$cat vars
echo No. of arguments = $#
echo The name of the shell script is $0
echo The arguments are $@
echo The process number is $$
echo The second argument is $2
echo The command name is $0
$vars steve -f sue john
No. of arguments = 4
The name of the shell script is vars
```

```
The arguments are steve -f sue john
The process number is 195
The second argument is -f
The command name is vars
$
```

Using variables

Within a programming language such as BASIC, variables are changed☐either by using special string functions if the variable contains text or by using arithmetic functions if the data is numeric. Shell variables can also perform such calculations, but the syntax involved is more complex.

Defining variables

Variables are defined or assigned using an equals sign. The variable name is on the left and its data is on the right. There should be no spaces on either side of the equals sign. If the data contains special characters or spaces, either use quotes to define it or delimit the special characters. The last example in the following is correctly formatted.

```
$ DEMO = Hello World
DEMO: not found
$DEMO= Hello World
Hello: not found
$ DEMO=Hello World
World: not found
$ DEMO="Hello World"
```

If a variable is used that has not been defined, and therefore has no value, a null string is used instead. However, there is no need to define or declare any variables — they can be created and used as needed. Valid names must begin with a letter but can contain letters, numbers and the underscore character.

Displaying variables

To print the contents of a variable, the *echo* command is used but, as can be seen, simply typing *echo* followed by the variable name does unexpected things. The problem is that *echo* sees the variable name as simple text and does not know that it is meant to use the data stored in the variable. To tell *echo* to do this, the variable name is prefixed with a dollar sign. Note that *Hello World* in the example is surrounded by quotes to prevent the shell from simply assigning *Hello* to the variable *DEMO* and interpreting *World* as a file name.

```
$ DEMO="Hello World"
$ echo DEMO
DEMO
$ echo $DEMO
Hello World
$
```

Passing variables to commands

The previous technique is also used to pass variables to commands. It is often referred to as parameter or file name substitution. If the $ is missing, the variable name is interpreted as text or as a file name.

```
$ DEMO=/opus/bin
$ echo $DEMO
/opus/bin
$ cd DEMO
DEMO: does not exist
$ cd $DEMO
$ pwd
/opus/bin
```

When using this technique, note that to pass the variable as part of a command, where the next letter is not a space, the variable name must be enclosed in curly brackets. This tells the shell which part of the text is the variable name. If this is not done, the $ tells the shell to use all of the text as a variable name. If this variable exists, it will be used instead; if not, a null string is used.

```
$echo $name
steve
$echo $name a
steve a
$echo $namea

$echo ${name}a
stevea
$
```

Passing command output to variables

Variables can also be defined by redirecting the output from a command. This is done using the standard equals sign notation but replacing the right-hand side with the command and any options. It is important to remember that the command must be enclosed by grave quotes (`). This is needed to stop the command from being interpreted as text. The grave quote is different from the more normal single (') or double quote. Many errors in shell scripts are due to the improper use of quote marks.

```
$date
Sat Aug  3 15:22:45 GMT 1991
$TODAY=`date`
$echo $TODAY
Sat Aug 3 15:22:57 GMT 1991
$DIR=`ls -x`
$echo $DIR
a.out benchmark book loop m68k_sim m68k_xasm
$
```

Defining variables from the keyboard

Variables can be read in directly from the keyboard. This provides an interactive interface that can be used to request more data or act as a confirmation to go ahead. This is achieved using the *read* command as shown. To make the variables read only and inhibit any modifications, *readonly* is used instead of *read*.

```
$cat interactive
echo What is your name ?
read name
echo Hello $name
$interactive
What is your name ?
Steve Heath
Hello Steve Heath
$
```

Performing arithmetic

To perform arithmetic calculations on variables, the command *expr* is used. It takes two values and performs integer addition, subtraction, multiplication or division and gives remainders, depending on the operator used. The format is critical — there must be spaces between the expressions and the operator and the asterisk used to indicate multiplication must be escaped(enclosed in quotes). In other words, think of the multiplication operator as * and not *. To change a variable, the complete *expr* command is enclosed with grave quotes and used as the right-hand side of a variable assignment.

```
$num=2
$echo $num
2
$expr $num \* 2
4
$expr $num + 2
4
$expr $num - 2
0
$expr $result / $num
3
$expr $result % 5
1
$expr `$num * 2`
2: not found
expr: syntax error
$`expr $num + 2`
4: not found
$result=`expr $num \* 3`
$echo $result
6
$
```

expr can evaluate quite complex operations but because parathenses and brackets are not allowed, the syntax is a little misleading. In the first example, the expression is simple because only addition is used, with no multiplication or division. The second example is ambiguous but is calculated by performing the multiplication first — 3 times 4 equals12, and adding 12 to 2 to gives 14. Similarly, the third example is calculated by dividing 10 by 5 to give 2, multiplying 2 by 3 to give 6, and then adding the two results together to give 8. In other words, all multiplication, division and remainder calculations are performed first using the number or variable on other side of the operator. This reduces the expression to a number of additions or subtractions which are then calculated. Any attempt at bracketing results in a syntax error.

```
$expr 3 + 4 + 5
12
$expr 2 + 3 \* 4
14
$expr 10 / 5 + 2 \* 3
8
$expr (2 + 3) \* 5
syntax error: 'expr' unexpected
$
```

Manipulating data

Simple manipulation of text variables is relatively easy to achieve using a combination of the *echo* command and variable substitution. To concatenate text variables with other text, assign the output of an *echo* command to the target variable and pass the variable data to the *echo* command through the $ prefix. Note the backslash after *surname* to escape the full stop.

```
$name=steve
$surname=heath
$fullname=
$fullname=`echo $name $surname`
$echo $fullname
steve heath
$fullname=`echo My name is $name $surname\.`
$echo $fullname
My name is steve heath.
$
```

More sophisticated manipulation of text data stored in variables is not so straightforward! The data must be transferred to a file, manipulated with *grep* or *sed* to edit the text as required, and the file contents assigned back to the variable, as shown in the next example. The advantage of this is in using the immense power of *grep* or *sed* to edit text that is frequently not available in a normal programming language.

```
$name=steve
$surname=heath
$fullname=
```

```
$fullname=`echo My name is $name $surname\.`
$echo $fullname > temp
$cat temp
My name is steve heath.
$fullname=`sed 's/steve/Stephen/' temp`
$echo $fullname
My name is Stephen heath.
$
```

Quoting

One problem frequently experienced with shell scripts and Linux commands is with the use of certain characters that, in themselves, have a special meaning to the shell. To control how these characters should or should not be interpreted, a system of quoting is used. There are several rules that govern these techniques:

- Single characters can be escaped by prefixing them with a backslash.

  ```
  $ echo "\""
  "
  $
  ```

- Words or partial words can be enclosed in either single or double quotes. Use of single quotes disables all interpretation while using double quotes disables interpretation as a file name. In the example shown, the single quotes force $a to be treated as text and not as a request to substitute the value of variable *a*. The double quotes disable the interpretation of $a if it is being used as a file name. In the example, *echo* was not using $a as a file name and so the variable value is substituted instead and *fred* is printed.

  ```
  $ a=fred
  $ echo '$a'
  $a
  $ echo "$a"
  fred
  $
  ```

- The third option uses grave quotes with commands such as *test* and *expr*. If used, the text within them is treated as a command and its output is either assigned to a variable or passed to a command. In the example, the *sed* command is enclosed within grave quotes to assign its output to the variable *fullname*. Within the command line, *s/steve/Stephen/* is enclosed in single quotes to escape the forward slashes it uses.

  ```
  $cat temp
  My name is steve heath.
  $fullname=`sed 's/steve/Stephen/' temp`
  $echo $fullname
  My name is Stephen heath.
  $
  ```

• Grave quotes are also used with conditional substitution to force a command to be executed if a variable is not assigned or is a null string. More about this later in this chapter.

Conditional flow

It is very rare for all the commands to be executed in a straight sequence, except in very simple programs and scripts. There are frequently times when the program flow must change depending on the status of a variable, or when program loops must be used to repeatedly execute the same code. In these cases, conditional statements are used. Shell scripts are no exception to this and support several different types, which work slightly differently than conditional statements in programming languages.

for loop

for variable **in** word1 word2 ... ... wordn
    do command list
done

A *for* loop repeats a command list for each entry in a word list and assigns that entry to a variable. It does not use the more normal form of simply incrementing the variable until it reaches a defined value. The command list is defined as all commands between *do* and *done*. Loops can be nested but it is recommended that different variable names are used in each loop and that the *for* loops are tabbed inside each other for easier reading.

```
$for TRANSPORT in boat plane horse
> do
> echo $TRANSPORT
> done
boat
plane
horse
$
```

The example shown was typed from the keyboard. The second-level prompt > appears because the shell recognizes the *for* and requests the rest of the command. After *done* is entered, the command is complete and is executed. The second example is a script showing how to nest *for* loops.

```
$cat nest_for
for LOOP1 in first second third
        do
        for LOOP2 in prize place
                do
                echo $LOOP1 $LOOP2
                done
        done
$nest_for
```

```
first prize
first place
second prize
second place
third prize
third place
$
```

One very frequent use of this format is to access all the arguments passed to a shell program. It is used so much that some systems allow *for I in "$@"* to be appreviated to *for I*.

```
$cat get_args
for I in "$@"
do echo $I
done
$get_args one two three
one
two
three
$
```

case

case word **in**
       pattern1)   command list;;
       pattern2)   command list;;
esac

The *case* statement takes the word and sequentially compares it with each pattern in the list. If there is a match, the associated command list is executed and the execution resumes with the next command after *esac*. If there are multiple matches, only the command list associated with the first pattern is executed. All other command lists are ignored. Using an asterisk as a pattern always forces a match and is used to force the execution of a default command list. Multiple patterns that use the same command list can be put on the same line by separating them with a | character.

```
$for number in 1 2 3
> do
>        case $number in
>        1) echo one;;
>        2) echo two;;
>        *) echo It is not one or two;;
>        esac
> done
one
two
It is not one or two
$
```

Again, as this example was typed from the keyboard, the shell provides the second-level prompt until the command finishes. Combining *case* statements with the *read* command provides the basic structure for a command interpreter. The command is read in from the keyboard and assigned to a variable. The variable is checked against a list in a *case* statement and the appropriate action taken. If no match occurs, the default message "command not found" is printed. The second *echo* statement encloses the text in double quotes to escape the angle brackets, which would otherwise cause a problem.

```
$cat dos_mode
echo You are now in DOS mode.
echo "Please enter your command followed by <return>"
read command
case $command in
        dir | DIR | Dir ) ls -x ;;
        vers) who;;
        *) echo $command not found;;
        esac
$dos_mode
You are now in DOS mode.
Please enter your command followed by <return>
dir
background    backup       cflop         demo
$dos_mode
You are now in DOS mode.
Please enter your command followed by <return>
DIR
background    backup       cflop         demo
$dos_mode
You are now in DOS mode.
Please enter your command followed by <return>
vers
root         console      Aug  4 17:00
root         tty1         Aug  4 17:01
$dos_mode
You are now in DOS mode.
Please enter your command followed by <return>
remove
remove not found
$
```

if-else-fi and elif

if	*or*	**if**
command list		command list
then		**then**
command list		command list
fi		**else**
		command list
		fi

This is a general conditional branch. If the command list executes correctly without errors, it returns a value of zero, which is interpreted as meaning

TRUE. If errors occurred, the value is non-zero, meaning FALSE. In the left-hand version, the first command list is always executed. If it returns zero, the condition is TRUE and the second command list between *then* and *fi* is executed. The right-hand version has an optional third command list, which is executed if the first command list returned FALSE.

```
$cat smart_ls
if
ls $1
then
echo Directory listed
else
pwd
echo The directory does not exist.
echo Better luck next time \!
fi
$smart_ls /sh
format
fullstop
interactive
Directory listed
$smart_ls /hjgjh
/hjgjh: No such file or directory
/sh
The directory does not exist.
Better luck next time !
$
```

It is possible to nest *if* statements and, to improve the readability, *elif* can be used to replace *else if*. The script *_elif* uses nested *if* statements to test arguments and check that they are valid directories. Two *fi* lines are needed to complete the two *if* statements. The second version, *_elif2*, replaces the *else if* with *elif* and, because there is now only one *if* statement, only one *fi* is needed to complete the command. Leaving the second in place would cause an error. However, both versions work the same.

```
$cat _elif
if
ls -x $1
then
echo First argument is a valid directory
else
        if
        ls -x $2
        then
        echo Second argument is valid
        else
        echo No arguments are valid
        fi
fi
$_elif /jgjh /hgjhg
```

```
/jgjh: No such file or directory
/hgjhg: No such file or directory
No arguments are valid
$_elif /sh /gjh
DIR          _elif          background    backup       cflop        demo
First argument is a valid directory
$_elif /gjgj /sh
/gjgj: No such file or directory
DIR          _elif          background    backup       cflop        demo
Second argument is valid
$$cat _elif2
if
ls -x $1
then
echo First argument is a valid directory
elif
      ls -x $2
      then
      echo Second argument is valid
      else
      echo No arguments are valid
fi
$_elif2 /fgf /fggfgf
/fgf: No such file or directory
/fggfgf: No such file or directory
No arguments are valid
$
```

while

while
command list
do
command list
done

The *while* structure is different from the others because it loops and repeatedly executes commands until its command list returns a FALSE status. The *while* command list is always executed and if it returns TRUE, the second command list is executed. When this has completed, the *while* command list is executed again and the cycle repeated. If the *while* command list returns FALSE, the second command list is not executed and execution continues from after the *done* statement.

```
# cat _while
while
$command
do
      echo That was a valid command.
      echo Please enter another:
      read command
done
# _while
```

```
That was a valid command.
Please enter another:
pwd
/sh
That was a valid command.
Please enter another:
cd /sh
That was a valid command.
Please enter another:
cd /ghjhghj
_while: /ghjhghj: does not exist
#
```

In the example, the variable command is not set to anything and is a null string. If a null string is executed as a shell command, it returns a TRUE status and so the second command list is executed. This obtains a new value for command from the keyboard. If this is a Linux or shell command that executes correctly, the process repeats. If there is an error, the script ends.

This type of structure is very easy to put into a permanent loop — which effectively locks up the terminal. If the command list always executes correctly or always returns TRUE, the second command list will always execute and there is very little that can be done to break the loop. If pressing ^backspace or ^DELETE does not terminate the loop, the system administrator can kill the user's shell.

until

until
command list
do
command list
done

The *until* structure is like the *while* structure in that it will loop and repeatedly execute commands while its command list keeps returning a FALSE status. The *until* command list is always executed and if this returns FALSE, the second command list is executed. When this has completed, the *until* command list is executed again, and the cycle repeated. If the *until* command list returns TRUE, the second command list is not executed and execution continues from after the *done* statement.

```
# cat _until
command=hgjh
until
$command
do
echo That was not a valid Linux command.
echo Please enter another:
read command
```

```
done
# _until
_until: hgjh: not found
That was not a valid command.
Please enter another:
gfd
_until: gfd: not found
That was not a valid command.
Please enter another:
fgd
_until: fgd: not found
That was not a valid command.
Please enter another:
pwd
/sh
#
```

The example shown is similar to that used to demonstrate the *while* statement. However, to ensure that the *until* command list always causes FALSE to be returned, it must be set to an non-existent command before the *until* statement is executed.

break, continue

These two commands can be used to change the action of loops: *break* causes the shell to break out of a loop and is useful if a loop needs several exit points. *continue* causes the execution to jump to the beginning of the loop and not carry on any further.

```
$cat brk
while
true
do
echo Type a single character and press return.
read a
case $a in
     a|e|i|o|u) echo Typed a vowel;;
     quit) echo Leaving this script;break;;
     retry) continue;;
     *) echo You have typed something else;;
esac
echo end of the loop
done
$brk
Type a single character and press return.
a
Typed a vowel
end of the loop
Type a single character and press return.
g
You have typed something else
end of the loop
Type a single character and press return.
```

```
retry
Type a single character and press return.
quit
Leaving this script
$
```

This example uses both *break* and *continue*. The *while* loop is permanent because the *true* variable has not been set and is a null string — it therefore always returns TRUE. As a result, the second command list continues to execute. Each time through the loop, it asks for a character from the keyboard. This value is used in the *case* statement to identify it and print an appropriate message. Once complete, another message is printed saying the end of the loop has been reached. If *retry* is typed, instead of a character, this forces the *continue* command to be executed, and the script starts at the beginning prompting for a new input. No end of loop message is printed. If *quit* is typed, a message is printed, followed by the *break* command, which breaks the permanent *while* loop and terminates the script. Note that *case* command lists can have multiple commands separated by semicolons but the list must end with ;; to prevent errors.

This type of script can be used to check keyboard input for correct syntax.

Conditional substitution

There is another conditional operation within the shell which is frequently used. This is conditional substitution, where a variable's value is conditionally used depending on its value. The example of prefixing a variable name with $ to use its value in a command is unconditional substitution. By changing the syntax slightly, other values can be used.

${var}   the standard unconditional substitution where *var* is a variable. The curly brackets are only needed if the variable name contains characters other than digits, letters or underscore.

${var:-word}   uses *var* if it is set and not a null string, otherwise *word* is used instead.

${var:=word}   sets *var=word* if *var* is not set or is a null string. Either way, *var* is unconditionally substituted.

${var:?word}   substitutes *var* if it is set and not a null string, otherwise *word* is printed and the shell terminated. If *word* is absent, "parameter null or not set" is printed.

${var:+word}   substitutes *word* if *var* is set and is not a null string, otherwise nothing is substituted.

In all these cases, if the colon is omitted, the check defaults to whether the variable is set or not. Like most things in Linux, the best way to understand them is to look at some examples:

```
$var=data
$echo ${var:-test}
data
$var=
$echo ${var:-test}
test
$echo ${var:=test}
test
$echo $var
test
$var=
$echo ${var:?}
var: parameter null or not set
$echo ${var:?help}
var: help
$var=yes
$echo ${var:+test}
test
$var=
$echo ${var:+test}
$
```

There is one very useful technique that can be used with these substitutions. If the word is replaced by a command in grave quotes, the command is executed and its standard output substituted instead. In the example below, if *var* is a null string or not set, the command *pwd* is executed and its output passed to *echo*, which prints it on the screen.

```
$echo ${var:-`pwd`}
/sh
$
```

This is a clever way of executing commands conditionally, depending on the status of a variable.

Testing

If a shell script conditional statement is compared with one from C or BASIC, the major difference would center around the methods used to evaluate the conditions. With the shell script, the looping structures are controlled by the successful execution of a command list, whereas in BASIC and C, they are controlled by testing variables for certain conditions, such as greater than and so on. This appears to be a fundamental drawback with shell scripts but this facility is provided through the use of another command called *test*.

test uses the standard shell script structures but the command list is replaced by *test* and options that describe the expression to be tested. If the conditions are met, *test* returns TRUE, if not it returns FALSE. In this way, the use of a command list to control branches is extended to that normally found in programming languages.

The conditions that *test* tests for are divided into two groups. The first group contains file tests used for checking file names. The second contains *test* variables used to perform both string and integer arithmetic tests.

-r *file*	True if *file* exists and is readable.
-w *file*	True if *file* exists and is writable.
-x *file*	True if *file* exists and is executable.
-f *file*	True if *file* exists and is a regular file.
-d *file*	True if *file* exists and is a directory.
-c *file*	True if *file* exists and is a character special file.
-b *file*	True if *file* exists and is a block special file.
-p *file*	True if *file* exists and is a named pipe (fifo).
-u *file*	True if *file* exists and its set-user-ID bit is set.
-g *file*	True if *file* exists and its set-group-ID bit is set.
-k *file*	True if *file* exists and its sticky bit is set.
-s *file*	True if *file* exists and has a size greater than zero.
-t [*fildes*]	True if the open file whose file descriptor number is *fildes* is associated with a terminal device.
-z *s1*	True if the length of string *s1* is zero.
-n *s1*	True if the length of the string *s1* is non-zero.
s1 = *s2*	True if strings *s1* and *s2* are identical.
s1 != *s2*	True if strings *s1* and *s2* are not identical.
s1	True if *sl* is not the null string.
nl **-eq** *n2*	True if the integers *n1* and *n2* are algebraically equal. Any of the following comparisons can replace *-eq*:

-ne	Not equal
-gt	Greater than
-ge	Greater than or equal to
-lt	Less than
-le	Less than or equal to

Expressions can be logically combined, inverted and grouped through the use of options:

!	Inverts the test.
-a	ANDs the results of the preceding and following tests.
-o	ORs the results of the preceding and following tests.
(*expr*)	Groups expressions and options as needed. The brackets must be escaped to prevent their interpretation by the shell.

Some implementations allow a pair of square brackets to be used as shorthand for *test*. In this instance, the expression to be tested is put between the brackets.

```
$cat test_ex
if test "$#" = 0
then echo There are no arguments
exit 2
fi
if [ -r "$1" ]
then echo $1 " exists and is readable"
fi
if test -d "$1"
then echo "but it is a directory."
else
echo "and it is not a directory."
fi
if test -d "$1" -a -w "$1"
then echo $1 "exists, is a directory AND is writable."
fi
$test_ex
There are no arguments
$test_ex dos
dos   exists and is readable
but it is a directory.
dos exists, is a directory AND is writable.
$test_ex backup
backup  exists and is readable
and it is not a directory.
$
```

This script can be modified to check a list of arguments by including the second and subsequent *if* statements in a *while* loop that performs the tests, shifts the arguments up one and repeats as long as the argument *$1* is not a null string. This type of structure can be used to process and test arguments. Instead of printing a message, the argument can be transferred to a local variable, or a variable can be set for inclusion in a command line.

```
$cat test_ex
if test "$#" = 0
then echo There are no arguments
exit 2
fi
while test "$1"
     do
     if [ -r "$1" ]
     then echo $1 " exists and is readable"
     else
     echo $1 does not exist\.
     fi
     if test -d "$1"
     then echo "but it is a directory."
     else
     echo "and it is not a directory."
     fi
     if test -d "$1" -a -w "$1"
```

```
        then echo $1 "exists, is a directory AND is writable."
        fi
        shift
done
$test_ex dos ghjhg backup /user $HOME
dos  exists and is readable
but it is a directory.
dos exists, is a directory AND is writable.
ghjhg does not exist.
and it is not a directory.
backup  exists and is readable
and it is not a directory.
/user  exists and is readable
but it is a directory.
/user exists, is a directory AND is writable.
/  exists and is readable
but it is a directory.
/ exists, is a directory AND is writable.
$
```

Commands

Other commands used within shell scripts are:

eval

eval [arguments]

eval evaluates the arguments, reads them as input to the shell and executes them. Its main use within scripts is to evaluate complex arguments before passing them to the shell for execution.

exec

exec [arguments]

exec takes the commands specified by the arguments and executes them without creating a new shell. In other words, if *exec script2* was a command line within a shell script, the commands in *script2* would be executed as if they had been included in the original script.

```
$ cat script
echo "This is the calling script"
exec script1
echo This is calling script again
$ cat script1
echo This is script1
$ script
This is the calling script
This is script1
$
```

The example shows how the command works. A shell script called *script* prints a message and then uses the *exec* command to transfer to *script1*, which prints another message. When *script1* finishes, the complete process terminates — the remaining commands in *script* are not executed and are ignored.

exit

exit [n]

This causes the shell script to stop execution and return an error code. If no number is specified as an argument, the code is that of the last executed command. For example, it can be used as part of a routine to end a script.

```
echo 'Do you want to continue ? y/n'
read a
if test "$a" = n; then exit 1 ; fi
```

basename, dirname

basename and its associated command *dirname* take a file path name and remove the upper levels or the lowest level, respectively. They are frequently used in shell scripts to control file and directory copying or movement. With them, directories and file names can be extracted.

```
$ basename /user/steve/bench
bench
$ dirname /user/steve/bench
/user/steve
$
```

getopts

getopts string name [arg]

getopts is used to process command lines and check option lists for correct syntax. An option is defined as starting with a hyphen, for example *-a -ab -abc* and so on. The letters in the *string* are options. A string of *ab* would mean that the command line would accept *-a*, *-b* or *-ab* as valid options. If a colon immediately follows a letter, that option must be separated by white space i.e. treated as a separate option. Therefore, if the *string* contained *ab:*, the valid options would be *-a* or *-b*.

The command works by taking the positional parameters that contain the command line arguments and processing each one in turn, placing it into the variable *name*. This variable can be checked using a *case* statement and set flags as required. All the option letters must be contained in the *string* so *getopts* can detect illegal options, whereupon it places a ? into the *name* variable.

getopts uses a couple of variables to keep track of what it is doing. OPTIND stores the number of the next argument to be processed and OPTARG is used to store an option that needs a further argument. Again, the easiest way to see this in operation is with some examples.

```
$cat get_opt
while getopts abc name
do
        case $name in
        a|b|c)  echo Valid option $name;;
        \?)     echo illegal option
        esac
done
echo $1 $2 $3
shift `expr $OPTIND - 1`
echo after shifting
echo $1 $2 $3
$
```

The above script processes the command line and checks for any options *a*, *b* or *c*. The *shift* command is used to put any specified file name or other argument into $1. The *echo* commands before and after the *shift* command display exactly what it does. The *case* statement has a catch-all, the escaped ? which prints an illegal option message if any option is passed that does not match. This is a little redundant, as *getopts* prints a similar message when it detects the error. A better use of the *case* structure would be to print some helpful instructions for guidance on the correct syntax.

```
$get_opt -a -b -c
Valid option a
Valid option b
Valid option c
-a -b -c
after shifting
$get_opt -a -b -c ls
Valid option a
Valid option b
Valid option c
-a -b -c
after shifting
ls
$get_opt -a -abc -cab -ca ls
Valid option a
Valid option a
Valid option b
Valid option c
Valid option c
Valid option a
Valid option b
Valid option c
Valid option a
-a -abc -cab
after shifting
ls
```

```
$get_opt fgdf
fgdf
after shifting
fgdf
$get_opt -y ls
get_opt: illegal option - y
illegal option
-y ls
after shifting
ls
$
```

If the script is changed and a colon inserted immediately after the letter *c* in the string, *getopts* takes the next variable as an argument for the option *c* and places it in the variable OPTARG. The *case* statement has been modified to treat the *c* option as a separate case and it now prints the value of OPTARG.

```
$cat get_opt2
while getopts abc:  name
do
      case $name in
      a|b)    echo Valid option $name;;
      c)      echo $OPTARG;;
      \?)     echo illegal option
      esac
done
echo $1 $2 $3
shift `expr $OPTIND - 1`
echo after shifting
echo $1 $2 $3
$$get_opt2 -c -a ls
-a
-c -a ls
after shifting
ls
$get_opt2 -ab -c cargs ls
Valid option a
Valid option b
cargs
-ab -c cargs
after shifting
ls
$
```

hash

hash [-r]

hash provides statistical information on which commands the shell has run and the cost, in time, that was taken to access the commands. The data is split into three columns. HITS is the number of times that the command was accessed, COST a measure of the directory searches it took to locate the command and COMMAND is the full file name for the command. To see the hash table and this data, enter the command with no option. Adding the *-r* option clears the hash table. The data can be used to see which commands are frequently used and to determine if certain commands may be faster by placing them in a directory at the beginning of the PATH variable or, alternatively, reordering the directories in the variable.

```
$hash
hits    cost      command
1*      3         /bin/cat
1*      3         /bin/mail
1*      8         /sh/diskcopy
0*      4         /usr/bin/news
4*      3         /bin/ls
$df
/              (/dev/dsk/c1d0s0 ):      16344 blocks      6469 i-nodes
$hash
hits    cost      command
1*      3         /bin/cat
1*      3         /bin/df
1*      3         /bin/mail
1*      8         /sh/diskcopy
0*      4         /usr/bin/news
4*      3         /bin/ls
$
$
$hash -r
$hash
hits    cost      command
$
```

kill

kill [-signal] Process ID

kill is used to send a signal 15 to the process whose ID is given in the argument. This effectively terminates the process and stops any further execution. It is possible to send other signals to the process by preceding it by a hyphen. Of these, *-9* is probably the most common and useful because it guarantees that the process is killed.

Process IDs or PIDs are returned by the shell when commands are executed in the background or can be obtained by executing the *ps* command. A user may only *kill* his own processes. The superuser can *kill* anything.

kill is useful when a binary file is displayed by mistake and the binary data has locked up the terminal, so it fails to respond to any commands. The superuser can *kill* the shell associated with that terminal and forcibly log off the user. If the terminal is then reset, the user can log in again. This technique can also be applied to shell scripts and programs that go into continuous loops and effectively ignore the user. Again, the superuser or user can log on to another terminal, use *ps* to identify the PID and *kill* the offending process.

```
$ sleep 30&
100
$ ps
    PID TTY        TIME COMMAND
     84 tty1       0:01 sh
    100 tty1       0:00 sleep
    101 tty1       0:00 ps
$ kill 100
100 Terminated
$ ps
    PID TTY        TIME COMMAND
     84 tty1       0:01 sh
    103 tty1       0:00 ps
$
```

newgrp

newgrp [-] [group]

newgrp allows a user to change the group identification and effectively join a new group, as defined in the file */etc/group*. The user remains logged in and the current directory remains the same, but the user is given a replacement shell, irrespective of the success of changing groups. With no arguments, the group is changed back to the user's default, that is, the group specified in the user's entry in */etc/passwd*. Exported variables keep their values and are effectively transferred across, but all others are lost or reset to their default values. If a hyphen is added to the command line, the environment is changed as if the user had logged off and then logged back in using the new group. If the group has a password (not to be recommended) and the user is not associated with the group, a password will be requested.

```
$ echo test > testfile
$ newgrp Cprog
$ echo test > testfile2
$ ls -l test*
-rw-r—r—  1 steve    author      5 Aug 24 02:09 testfile
-rw-r—r—  1 steve    Cprog       5 Aug 24 02:09 testfile2
$
```

set

set returns slightly more information than its companion command *env* and is effectively built into the *sh* shell. It bases much of its data on the environment that is changed by the contents of the *.profile* file. When a user logs on to the system, a *.profile* file is executed that sets up the environment accordingly. This is similar to *autoexec.bat* from the MS-DOS world. As well as allowing changes to the environment, it also changes how the shell responds to commands and error conditions, depending on associated options. The command has several options:

-a   Mark variables that are modified or created for export.

-e   Exit immediately if a command exits with a non-zero exit status. If the command encounters an error or problem and returns a FALSE termination code, the current shell script terminates.

-f   Disable file name generation. Again this is useful for debugging scripts.

-h   Locate and remember function commands when functions are defined (function commands are normally located when the function is executed).

-k   All keyword arguments are placed in the environment for a command, not just those that precede the command name.

-n   Read commands but do not execute them. This is a very dangerous or frustrating command, depending on your viewpoint. If executed from a terminal, all future commands typed from the keyboard are accepted but are not executed, rendering the terminal virtually useless. Typing ^D or ^Z may regain control.

-t   Exit after reading and executing one command.

-u   Treat unset variables as an error when substituting. This forces all variables to be assigned before use and is extremely useful while debugging shell scripts.

-v   Print shell input lines as they are read.

-x   Print commands and their arguments as they are executed. This is similar to the BASIC trace facility. Each command is displayed and the flow through a shell script can be followed.

- -   Do not change any of the flags; useful in setting $1 to a hyphen. Note that this a double hyphen with no space between them.

Using + rather than - causes these flags to be turned off. These flags can also be used when starting the shell. The current set of flags may be found in $-. The remaining arguments are positional parameters and are assigned, in order, to $1, $2, and so on. If no arguments are entered with the command, *set* shows the current variables and their values. The standard environment is shown. The small program *dir()*, which starts after the variables, is a shell script that provides a *dir* command displaying file names and directories, in a similar way to the MS-DOS *dir* command.

```
EXINIT=set redraw nows sm
HOME=/
IFS=

LOGNAME=root
MAIL=/usr/mail/root
MAILCHECK=600
OPTIND=1
PATH=:/opus/bin:/bin:/usr/bin:/etc:/usr/ucb
```

```
PS1=#
PS2=>
TERM=opus-pc
TZ=GMT0
dir(){
if [ "$1" = "" -o "$1" = . ]
then
echo "`pwd`:"
else
if [ $# -eq 1 -a -d "$1" ]
then
echo "${1}:"
fi
fi
/bin/ls -CF $*
}
```

shift

shift [n]

shift shifts all the positional variables, ($1 to $9), up one place. When executed, $1 is discarded and is replaced by $2. $2 is replaced by $3, and so on. It is often used to process arguments from a command line. If a numerical value is given for n, the command starts with variable *$n+1*. If it is not specified, a default of 1 is assumed.

```
$cat shift3
echo $1 $2 $3
shift
echo $1 $2 $3
shift
echo $1 $2 $3
$ shift3 a b c
a b c
b c
c
$
```

times

times prints the accumulated user and system times for both commands and processes.

```
$ times ls -Rl
0m0s 0m1s
$ times diskcopy
0m0s 0m1s
$
```

trap

trap [arguments]

trap allows the user to take control of any interrupts or other messages that the shell would normally process or receive. It is usually used to disable ^DEL from terminating a command. The argument is a command that is executed when the signal specified by *n* is received or trapped — hence the command name. If the command is a null string, the signals are effectively ignored. If there is no argument, the signals are set to their default and interrupts and so on are effectively enabled. Common signals and their causes that are trapped are:

0	exit from a shell script
1	hangup — line disconnect
2	interrupt
3	quit
15	kill or terminate process

To remove any temporary files, either at the end of of a shell script or if a hangup, interrupt, *quit* or *kill* message is generated, include a *trap* statement like this:

trap 'rm /tmp/junk$$; exit' 0 1 2 3 15

tty

tty [-l] [-s]

tty appears to be a useless command. It displays the path name of the user's terminal. The *-l* option checks to see if it is a synchronous terminal and will say so if it is not. The *-s* option does not print or display anything. The main use of *tty* is within shell scripts, where it is used to check if the standard input is assigned to a terminal. It will return three different exit codes:

2	if invalid options were specified
0	if the standard input is a terminal
1	in all other cases

If the standard input has been redirected to a file, *tty* would return a message "not a tty" if the *-s* option had not been specified and an exit code of 1.

type

type [arguments]

type displays what the arguments evaluate to, and is a good way of checking a file name before execution.

```
$ type $HOME/$TERM
/user/steve/opus-pc not found
$ type $HOME/*
/user/steve/script is /user/steve/script
/user/steve/script1 is /user/steve/script1
$
```

ulimit

ulimit [no of blocks]

Linux limits the maximum size of a file. A user can lower this limit and the superuser can raise it. Typing *ulimit* without a limit number displays the current limit. In the example, the user has attempted to raise the limit unsuccessfully:

```
$ ulimit
32768
$ ulimit 100000
Bad ulimit
$ su
Password:
# ulimit 100000
# ulimit
100000
#
```

umask

umask changes the standard octal value used to assign read, write and execute permissions. *umask* on its own displays the standard setting of octal 0022, which gives read and write permission to the owner and read only permission to group and others. To change this, the new octal value is added. Any files subsequently created automatically have the new permissions.

```
$umask
0022
$echo this is a test > newfile
$ls -l newfile
-rw-r—r—  1 root other 15 Aug  8 00:58 newfile
$umask 0055
$echo this is another test > newfile2
$ls -l newfile?
-rw—w—w-  1 root other 21 Aug  8 00:59 newfile2
$
```

unset

unset is followed by a list of variable names. It removes or deletes that variable from the shell environment. The standard variables, such as *PATH, PS1,PS2, MAILCHECK* and *IFS* cannot be unset.

```
$var1=a;var2=b;var3=c
$set
HOME=/
IFS=

LOGNAME=root
MAIL=/usr/mail/root
MAILCHECK=600
PATH=:/opus/bin:/bin:/usr/bin:/etc
```

5   tcsh shell scripts

The tcsh is an equivalent to the C shell developed at Berkeley and is gaining favor within the UNIX world. Although it provides the same functionality as the bash (Bourne) shell, it has several unique facilities and a different shell script language. Apart from very simple bash shell scripts, the tcsh shell is largely incompatible with Bourne derived scripts, and vice versa. The reason for this is simple. The C shell, as its name implies, uses control structures similar to those used in the C programming language and are therefore not compatible with the Bourne shell. As most users use either one shell or the other, this chapter is a duplicate of the preceding chapter, except that it is totally based on *tcsh* (the Linux equivalent of the C shell), and all the example scripts have been converted. To compare the two shells, compare the relevant sections in these two chapters.

While the Linux command structure and the command options, in particular, are not very intuitive, the system administrator can ease this barrier by providing simpler commands for users using shell scripts. I have a whole set of such scripts that I use for disk operations. It is easier to type in *backup /user/ steve* than the equivalent Linux commands. Many applications have been written using shell scripts, including replacement interfaces. It is quite possible to write a shell script that simulates another user interface so the user is not aware that Linux is running.

The key to writing and using shell scripts is to recognize the fact that they are fully fledged programs in their own right and that the scripting language provided is a programming language in much the same way as BASIC or C. It features variables, arithmetic operations, condition testing and control structures. One big advantage of shell scripts is that the commands can be entered directly from the keyboard to test them or ensure that the syntax is correct. This is extremely useful. However, standard Linux manuals always seem to concentrate on an academic definition of the shell commands, which tell users everything except what they want to know! The approach taken in this chapter is to go through the many facets of scripting and illustrate them with some example routines, some of which can be combined to create useful utilities.

Getting started

All that is needed to create a shell script is the ability to use an editor such as *vi* or *ex*. To create a shell script, use the editor to create a file with the commands in sequence and invoke the script. For very simple, one-line commands, *echo* can be used and the output directed to the shell script file. There are three ways of doing this, shown in the following example. The first two run another copy of the shell and direct it to use the shell script instead of the keyboard. The third method changes the script's access permissions to allow execution. This is the more normal method of executing a shell script as the script effectively becomes a command for the user. As the example shows, all three methods have the same result. Note that the prompt in the examples is a number in brackets. The number increases by one every time a command is executed. This is fully explained later in this chapter.

```
(1)echo ls -l >DIR
(2)csh < DIR
total 8
-rw-r-r-  1 root other   6 Aug  3 16:39 DIR
-rwxrwxrwx 1 root other  67 Jul 31 14:19 backup
-rwxrwxrwx 1 root other 403 Jul 31 09:48 cflop
(3)csh DIR
total 8
-rw-r-r-  1 root other   6 Aug  3 16:39 DIR
-rwxrwxrwx 1 root other  67 Jul 31 14:19 backup
-rwxrwxrwx 1 root other 403 Jul 31 09:48 cflop
(5)DIR
total 8
-rw-r-r-  1 root other   6 Aug  3 16:39 DIR
-rwxrwxrwx 1 root other  67 Jul 31 14:19 backup
-rwxrwxrwx 1 root other 403 Jul 31 09:48 cflop
(6)
```

One important point to remember is that the first character of the shell script must be a #. Without it, there is a danger that the system will treat it as a Bourne shell script and fail to understand the different syntax. A suggested way of doing this is to start the script with a comment line beginning with a # to stop the rest of the line from being interpreted as a command line.

When any shell command is executed, including a shell script, a copy of the shell program is created and this copy is used to execute the commands. As a result, any changes to home directories and to the shell affect only the copy and not the original version. This is a very good idea because any problem or error affects only the copy and allows the original to take control. However, it does cause problems if the shell script needs to modify the original environment.

An alternative method of executing shell scripts or commands is to place them in background mode. This is done by adding an & immediately after the command name or the last option. The script continues to execute in the background and allows the user to carry on working. If the background command uses *stdout* to display data, this happens irrespective of what the current screen is and this can be confusing. If necessary, redirect the output to a file to prevent this.

```
(10) cat background
echo This is a message from the background
echo This is another
sleep 10
echo so is this...
(11) background&
[1] 103
(12) This is a message from the background
This is another
ps
     PID TTY        TIME COMMAND
      83 tty1      0:01 csh
     103 tty1      0:00 sh
     104 tty1      0:00 sleep
     105 tty1      0:00 ps
(13) so is this...

[1]     background
          10.7r 0.0u 0.1s
```

The example *background* displays two messages, sleeps for 10 seconds and prints a final message. When it is executed, the first two messages appear, followed by the Process ID number (PID). This number, 218, refers to the copy of the shell and not to the *sleep* command that is running. *ps* displays all the processes that are running and shows the shell *sh* with its PID of 218, followed by the *sleep* command. The PID numbers are important because they are used by the *kill* command to terminate the command or script. In these examples, the Bourne shell is called because there is no # at the start of the first line. This is why the *ps* command displays *sh* instead of *csh* as the shell process.

```
(10) cat background
echo This is a message from the background
echo This is another
sleep 10
echo so is this...
(11) background&
[1] 103
(12) This is a message from the background
This is another
ps
     PID TTY        TIME COMMAND
      83 tty1      0:01 csh
     103 tty1      0:00 sh
     104 tty1      0:00 sleep
     105 tty1      0:00 ps
(13) so is this...

[1]     background
          10.7r 0.0u 0.1s

(13) background&
[1] 106
```

```
(14) This is a message from the background
This is another
ps
    PID TTY        TIME COMMAND
     83 tty1      0:01 csh
    106 tty1      0:00 sh
    107 tty1      0:00 sleep
    108 tty1      0:00 ps
(15) kill 107
background: 107 Terminated
so is this...

[1]    background
(16) background&
[1] 112
(17) This is a message from the background
This is another
ps
    PID TTY        TIME COMMAND
     83 tty1      0:01 csh
    112 tty1      0:00 sh
    113 tty1      0:00 sleep
    114 tty1      0:00 ps
(18) kill 112
(19)
[1]    Exit -48                background
        10.1r 0.0u 0.0s
```

In this example, the first *kill* command is given the PID of the *sleep* command. This effectively terminates the *sleep* command but does not affect the remaining *echo*, which proceeds and displays its message. The second *kill* is given the PID returned when the script was started. In this case, the whole script is effectively terminated and all remaining unexecuted commands within it (e.g. the *sleep* and *echo*) do not complete.

The C shell also supports other job control functions that are not available with the Bourne shell.

jobs

jobs displays all the executing commands or jobs and their status. The format is usually the job ID followed its status and name. There are several shorthand methods for the job ID which can be used with other commands.

%*number*	Job with id *number*.
%*name*	Job with the name *name*. The name need not be a complete match For example, %m would find *mail*, *mv* and so on.
%+	The most recently suspended job.
%1	The next most recently suspended job.

fg

fg jobid

fg restarts a suspended job that is identified by its *jobid*. If no ID is given, the current job (the last one suspended) resumes. In many ways this command is unnecessary because simply typing the *jobid* on its own is enough to bring it to the foreground.

^Z

^Z

This suspends the currently executing command or job. It can be used to regain control of a terminal if a script or command has locked up the keyboard. Once the offending job is suspended, it can be terminated using the *kill* command.

To terminate a currently executing command or script, press both the Control and the backspace keys. This should stop the execution, but it is possible to disable this facility within a script, so the key sequence is ignored. Some systems also support ^C or ^\.

Aliases

The C shell provides an alias mechanism that allows the user to give existing commands and shell scripts new names which are easier to remember. The new names can be longer or shorter than the originals. The main use of aliases is in defining simple names for commands with complex options.

The *alias* command takes two arguments. The first is the new name and the second is the renamed command with whatever options, and so on, that are needed. The second argument frequently requires quoting. The command on its own displays all the current aliases and the *unalias* command is used to remove them. Many aliases are set up by the *.login* file, which is executed when users log in and start a session using the system.

```
(63) alias
dir      ls -CF
h        history
ls       ls -CF
(64) alias pg more
(65) alias
dir      ls -CF
h        history
ls       ls -CF
pg       more
(66) pg vars
echo No. of arguments = $#
```

```
echo The name of the shell script is $0
echo The process number is $$
echo The second argument is $2
echo The command name is $0
echo The third argument is $3
(67) alias append 'cat >> '
(68) echo Hello steve | append temp
(69) pg temp
My name is steve heath
Hello steve
(70) unalias append
(71) append
Append: Command not found
(72) alias pg
more
(76)
```

The facility does not support situations where the new name is referred to in the command it represents. Command lines like *alias ls 'ls -adi'* are not accepted.

History mechanism

The history mechanism records all the command lines entered during a session and makes them available for further use in command lines and shell scripts. The main advantage of this is the reduction in keystrokes it allows. If a mistake is made in a complex command, the whole command line need not be entered from scratch — the original copy can be used, with the mistake corrected. Commands can also be repeated. This is such a useful utility that the *bash* shell was extended to support it. The key to its operation is the *history list* and the history substitution character, *!* . The history list is a list of events where each event is numbered and is the command line that was executed. The prompt in the examples within this chapter displays the current event number. After each command is entered, it is added to the history list and the current event number increased by one. To display the history list, the *history* command is executed. Events can be extracted from the list through the use of special substitutions as shown:

!n	The *n*th event.
!-n	The *n*th previous event.
!!	The last event.
!prefix	The most recent event with the specified *prefix*.
^xx^zz	The last event with the string *xx* replaced by *zz*.
!*	All the arguments of the last event.
!$	The last argument of the last event.
*!^*	The first argument of the last event.

!:n   The *n*th argument of the last event.

!12:s/*xx*/*zz*/ The 12th event with the string *xx* replaced by *zz*.

These substitutions are used instead of retyping command lines and/or arguments. To execute the last command again, enter !! from the keyboard. To execute the command in event number 23, enter !23, and so on. Here are some further examples of their use:

```
(1) wc temp2
        1          1          6 temp2
(2) !!
wc temp2
        1          1          6 temp2
(3) ^temp2^temp3
wc temp3
        2          2         12 temp3
(4) h
        1   wc temp2
        2   wc temp2
        3   wc temp3
        4   h
(5) echo hello world
hello world
(6) banner !$
banner world

    #     #   ####   #####    #      #####
    #     #   #   #  #    #    #      #   #
    #     #   #   #  #    #    #      #   #
    # ## #   #   #  #####    #      #   #
    ## ##  #   #  #    #    #      #   #
    #     #   ####   #    #   ######  #####
(7) !5:s/hello/HELLO/
echo HELLO world
HELLO world
(8) echo !*
echo HELLO world
HELLO world
(9) echo !^
echo HELLO
HELLO
(10) !-4
banner world

    #     #   ####   #####    #      #####
    #     #   #   #  #    #    #      #   #
    #     #   #   #  #    #    #      #   #
    # ## #   #   #  #####    #      #   #
    ## ##  #   #  #    #    #      #   #
    #     #   ####   #    #   ######  #####

(11) !b
```

```
banner world

   #     #   ####   #####    #      #####
   #     #  #    #  #    #    #      #    #
   #     #  #    #  #    #    #      #    #
   #  ## #  #    #  #####     #      #    #
   ## ## #  #    #  #    #    #      #    #
   #     #   ####   #    #    ######  #####

(12) !bant
bant: Event not found.
(12) !b:s/world/hello/
banner hello

   #     #  ######  #          #      ####
   #     #  #       #          #     #    #
   ######  #####   #          #     #    #
   #     #  #       #          #     #    #
   #     #  #       #          #     #    #
   #     #  ######  ######  ######   ####

(13)  h
      1   wc temp2
      2   wc temp2
      3   wc temp3
      4   h
      5   echo hello world
      6   banner world
      7   echo HELLO world
      8   echo HELLO world
      9   echo HELLO
     10   banner world
     11   banner world
     12   banner hello
     13   h
(14)
```

There are a couple of points to remember. If there are multiple events that match a prefix, the first one that matches when working back from the current event will be executed. The prefix need not be a complete match. In the previous example, the prefix l was matched with event 5, the *ls* command. Be careful with argument lists as they may change — they always refer to the last event and are updated after any command execution. In the example shown, the two *cat* commands, events 17 and 18, display the same file because the last argument is the same in both cases. This is not always the case and as soon as another command is executed, the same command receives a different argument — with different results.

```
(16) cat temp2 temp3
Hello
Hello
World
```

```
(17) cat !$
cat temp3
Hello
World
(18) cat !$
cat temp3
Hello
World
(19) wc temp2
         1       1       6 temp2
(20) cat !$
cat temp2
Hello
(21)
```

Shell variables

The shell environment supports three types of variables: those that are built in and are provided automatically by the system, those that are user defined and those used within shell scripts.

Built-in variables

These are normally set up when the user logs in to the system, and are defined partially by the system and partially by the users' *.login* file located in their home directories. They have special meanings and uses within the shell environment and can be seen by typing the command *set*.

```
(26) set
argv    ()
cwd     /usr/stevebsd
history 50
home    /usr/stevebsd
ignoreeof
mail    /usr/mail/stevebsd
notify
path    (. /opus/bin /bin /usr/bin /etc )
prompt  (!)
shell   /usr/ucb/csh
status  0
time    10
(27)
```

The common variables can be divided into two types — toggle and value. Toggle variables are either set or unset while value variables can take values. The common variables seen on most systems are:

ignoreeof   If set, prevents ^D from logging out from tcsh and forces the use of the *logout* command. If unset, it terminates the shell.

noclobber   Restricts redirection so files are not destroyed accidentally if redirected files actually exist.

noglob   If set, stops file name expansion.

nonomatch If set, prevents a file pattern that has no matches from generating an error.

notify If set, notifies background job completions as necessary without waiting for a convenient break such as a prompt.

home Defines the home directory. In this case, the directory is root, shown by the backslash.

mail The name of the file for any mail messages to be sent.

cwd The home directory of the user.

path Specifies the directories the shell searches to find a command or file. They are searched in order; for example */opus/bin* would be the first.

prompt Defines the shell prompt. The default is % although (*!*) is frequently used — the exclamation mark is interpreted as the current history event number. This is the prompt that has been used within this chapter.

time Controls the timing of commands. If a command takes more than *time* CPU seconds, timing information is displayed when it completes.

status Contains the exit status for the last executed command. It is used to test for a successful command completion.

history Specifies the number of history events that will be kept. If this is too big, the memory allocated to the shell may be exceeded.

savehist Specifies the number of history events that are saved in the file *~/.history* when the user logs out.

histchars Allows the history substitution characters to be changed. The first character replaces the default ! and the second replaces ^ in substitution.

User-defined variables

Users can define new variables either by using the *set* or *setenv* commands. *set* is similar to its namesake in the bash shell and uses a similar format, comprising the command name followed by the variable name, an equals sign and the string the variable will contain. This creates a variable the user can use from the shell — but cannot use from within a shell script. The reason for this is simple — the newly created variable is limited to working in the current shell. When a shell script is executed, a new shell is created and the variable is not passed over — and is not recognized.

To make variables recognizable by shell scripts, they must be created using the *setenv* command. Its format is a little different from *set* in that the equals sign is not needed. With both commands, the string may need to be in quotes to prevent the shell from interpreting special characters.

```
(13) setenv demo2 Hello
(14) set demo = hello
(15)  set_test
demo was created using set.
demo =
demo2 was created using setenv
demo2 = Hello
(16)
```

To remove a variable created using *set*, use the *unset* command followed by the variable's name. This does not work with variables that were created using *setenv*. To remove these, the command *unsetenv* is used.

```
(19) unset demo
(20) unset demo2
(21) set_test2
demo2 was created using setenv
demo2 = Hello
(22) echo $demo
demo: Undefined variable.
(23)
```

Shell script variables

The third type of variable in use within shell scripts is used in much the same ways that variables are used in other programs — to store or pass data. They normally exist only while the shell script that created them is being executed. As a result, they are local. They are created in the same way for user-defined variables.

The shell automatically creates a special set of variables each time a shell script is executed. These are called parameters and are particularly useful because they contain information about the command line, such as its name, the number of arguments, and so on.

# argv	Gives the number of arguments on the command line.
#	Can also be the number of arguments on the command list — used by some systems for compatibility with the Bourne shell.
argv[*]	A list of all the arguments.
argv[n]	The *n*th argument. Note that n=0 is an undefined variable. This is an alternative to the $*n* variables.
$	The command process number.
status	The exit status of the last command executed. A value of zero is considered true and usually indicates a successful completion. Any other value should be interpreted as false and an indication of an error.
0	Contains the name of the command.
1 ... 9	Contains arguments 1 through 9. Known as positional parameters.

The $ variable is frequently used to name unique temporary files by inclusion in a file name such as *abc$$* or *$$abc*. The shell script *vars* displays the contents of some of these variables. Please note that all the variable names are preceded by $ to allow *echo* to recognize them.

```
(22) cat vars
echo No. of arguments = $#
echo The name of the shell script is $0
echo The process number is $$
echo The second argument is $2
echo The command name is $0
echo The third argument is $3
(23) vars abc def ghj klm
No. of arguments = 4
The name of the shell script is vars
The process number is 98
The second argument is def
The command name is vars
The third argument is ghj
(24)
```

Using variables

Within a programming language such as BASIC, variables are changed either by using special string functions if the variable contains text, or by using arithmetic functions if the data is numeric. Shell variables can also perform such calculations but the syntax involved is more complex.

Defining variables

Variables are defined or assigned using the *set* command as shown. The variable name is on the left and its data is on the right. If the data contains special characters or spaces, either use quotes to define it or delimit the special characters. Lists of words, letters, and numbers can be assigned by inserting the list between two brackets.

```
(1) set DEMO = Hello World
(2) DEMO
DEMO: Command not found.
(3) echo $DEMO
Hello
(4) set DEMO = "Hello World"
(5) echo $DEMO
Hello World
(6) set LIST = ( a b c d )
(7) echo $LIST
a b c d
(8)
```

If a variable is used in a shell script that has not been defined and therefore has no value, a null string is used. However, there is no need to define or declare any variables — they can be created and used as needed. Valid names must begin with a letter but can contain letters, numbers and the underscore character.

Displaying variables

The *echo* command is used to print the contents of a variable but, as can be seen, typing *echo* followed by the variable name does unexpected things. The problem is that *echo* sees the variable name as simple text and does not know that it is meant to use the data stored in the variable instead. To tell *echo* to do this, the variable name is prefixed by a dollar sign. Note that *Hello World* was surrounded by quotes to prevent the shell from simply assigning *Hello* to the variable *DEMO* and interpreting *World* as a file name.

```
(20) set DEMO="Hello World"
(21) echo DEMO
DEMO
(22) echo $DEMO
Hello World
(23)
```

Modifying variables

The C shell has two clever ways of modifying — or, more correctly, extracting the information stored in a variable. Neither technique modifies the actual data stored in the variable — they both extract part of it which is used in the expression or command instead.

The first technique allows individual parts of a list that has been stored in a variable to be extracted. This is done by adding a pair of square brackets to the variable name, together with a number or range of numbers specifying which part of the list is to be used. This is similar to the string construction used within C. Adding # to the beginning of its name will return the number of elements in a variable. This can be used inside the square brackets to get the last variable.

```
(30) set LIST = ( a b c d )
(31) echo $LIST[*] $LIST[3]
a b c d c
(32) echo $LIST[2-3]
b c
(33) echo $#LIST
4
(34) echo $LIST[$#LIST]
d
(35)
```

The second technique uses modifier codes, which are added to the the variable name after a colon to extract part of its contents. The main modifier codes are:

h   Removes a trailing path name.

t   Removes all leading path names.

r Removes a file extension, leaving the main file name.

e Removes the main file name, leaving the extension.

Note that these modifiers only work on the first element of a list. To modify all parts, the prefix *g* is added to the modifier.

gh Removes a trailing path name for all parts of a list.

gt Removes all leading path names for all parts of a list.

gr Removes a file extension, leaving the main file name for all parts of a list.

ge Removes the main file name, leaving the extension for all of a list.

q Places the extracted data in quotes.

Usually, only one modifier can be used at a time. These modifiers are extremely powerful and are frequently used to manipulate file and path names as shown below.

```
(41) set file=(/user/steve/temp.cff /user/sue/doc)
(42) echo $file[2]:h
/user/sue
(43) echo $file[2]:t
doc
(44) echo $file:gh
/user/steve /user/sue
(45) echo $file:gt
temp.cff doc
(46) echo $file:r
/user/steve/temp /user/sue/doc
(47) echo $file:e
cff /user/sue/doc
(48) echo $file:ge
cff
(49) echo $file:q
/user/steve/temp.cff /user/sue/doc
(50)
```

Passing variables to commands

The display technique can also be used to pass variables to commands. It is often referred to as parameter or file name substitution. If the $ is missing, the variable name is interpreted as text or as a file name.

```
(23)  set DEMO=/opus/bin
(24) echo $DEMO
/opus/bin
(25) cd DEMO
DEMO: does not exist
(26) cd $DEMO
(27) pwd
/opus/bin
(28)
```

To pass the variable as part of a command when the next letter in the command is not a space, the variable name must be enclosed in curly brackets. This tells the shell which part of the text is the variable name and which is not. If this is not done, the $ sign tells the shell to use all of the text as a variable name. If a variable of this name actually exists, it will be used instead. If not, a null string is used.

```
(23)echo $name
steve
(24)echo $name a
steve a
(25)echo $namea

(26)echo ${name}a
stevea
(27)
```

Passing command output to variables

Variables can also be defined by redirecting the output from a command. This is done using the standard equals sign notation but replacing the right-hand side with the command and any options. It is important to remember that the command must be enclosed by grave quotes(`). This prevents the command from being interpreted as text. Many errors in shell scripts are due to the improper use of quote marks.

```
(1) set TODAY = `date`
(2) echo $TODAY
Tue Oct 29 04:03:16 GMT 1991
(3) set DIR = `ls -x`
(4) echo $DIR
DIR _elif _until _while background
(5)
```

Defining variables from the keyboard

Variables can be read directly from the keyboard. This provides an interactive interface, which can be used to request more data or to act as a confirmation to go ahead. This is done using a special variable $<, which can be assigned to another variable, if needed.

```
(57) cat interactive
#Interactive demo
echo " Hello. What is your name ?"
set nam = $<
echo Hello $nam

(58) interactive
 Hello. What is your name ?
Steve
Hello Steve
(59)
```

Testing variables

To test a variable to see if it is exists, precede the variable with *$?*. This returns a 1 if the variable is set and 0 if not and can be used as a control expression in *if, while* statements, and so on.

```
(37) echo $?new_var
0
(38) set new_var = 1000
(39) echo $?new_var
1
(40)
```

Performing arithmetic

The command @ is used to perform arithmetic operations on variables. It is a subset of the *set* command, which allows the right hand side of an expression to be an arithmetic expression. The supported syntax is taken from the C language and uses the standard +, -, * and / division operators as well as the ++ and --increment and decrement syntax.

```
(50)@ j = 3 * 4
(51) echo $j
12
(52) @ j ++
(53) echo $j
13
(54) @ j —
(55) echo $j
12
(56)
```

Complex calculations can be bracketed as shown below instead of separating into several smaller calculations.

```
(60) @ k = (3 * 4) / 2
(61) echo $k
6
(62)
```

Manipulating data

Simple manipulation of text variables is relatively easy using a combination of the *echo* command and variable substitution. To concatenate text variables with other text, the output of an *echo* command is assigned to the target variable which is then passed to the *echo* command using the $ prefix.

```
(62) set name=steve
(63) set surname=heath
(64) set fullname=`echo $name $surname`
(65) echo $fullname
steve heath
(66)
```

More sophisticated manipulation of text data stored in variables is not so straightforward! The data must be transferred to a file, manipulated with *grep* or *sed* to edit the text as required and the file contents assigned back to the variable, as shown. The advantage this offers is in using the immense power of *grep* or *sed* to edit text, which is frequently not available in a normal programming language.

```
(62) set name=steve
(63) set surname=heath
(64) set fullname=`echo $name $surname`
(65) echo $fullname
steve heath
(66) echo My name is $fullname > temp
(67) set fullname=`sed 's/steve/STEPHEN/' temp`
(68) echo $fullname
My name is STEPHEN heath
(69)
```

Quoting

One problem frequently experienced with shell scripts and commands concerns the use of certain characters with certain Linux commands which, in themselves, have a special meaning to the shell. To control how these characters should or not be interpreted, a system of quoting is used. There are several rules that govern these techniques:

- Single characters can be escaped by preceding them with a backslash.

  ```
  (1)echo \"
  "
  (2)
  ```

- Words or partial words can be enclosed in either single or double quotes. Using single quotes disables all interpretation while double quotes disables interpretation as a file name. In the example shown, the single quotes force $a to be treated as text and not as a request to substitute value of the variable *a*. The double quotes disable the interpretation if *echo* was using $a as part of a file name. It doesn't and so the variable value is substituted and *fred* is printed.

  ```
  (3)set a=fred
  (4)echo '$a'
  $a
  (5)echo "$a"
  fred
  (6)
  ```

- If grave quotes are used, the text within them is treated as a command and its output is either assigned to a variable or passed to a command. In the example, the *sed* command is enclosed within grave quotes to assign its output to the variable *fullname*. Within the command line, the *s/steve/Stephen/* option is enclosed in single quotes to escape the forward slashes it uses.

```
(66) echo My name is $fullname > temp
(67) set fullname=`sed 's/steve/STEPHEN/' temp`
(68) echo $fullname
My name is STEPHEN heath
(69)
```

- If a variable is used as part of a command line and the next letter after the variable name is not a space, the variable must be quoted in curly brackets.

```
(23)echo $name
steve
(24)echo $name a
steve a
(25)echo $namea
(26)echo ${name}a
stevea
(27)
```

Conditional flow

Except for very simple programs and scripts, it is very rare for all the commands to be executed in a straight sequence. There are frequently times when the program flow must change depending on the status of a variable, or when program loops must be used to repeatedly execute the same code. In these cases, conditional statements are used. Shell scripts are no exception to this and support several different types, which work slightly differently than conditional statements in programming languages.

foreach

foreach variable (wordlist)
command list
end

A *foreach* loop repeats a command list for each entry in a word list and assigns that entry to a variable. It does not use the more normal form of incrementing the variable until it reaches a certain value. The command list is defined as all commands between the *foreach* and *end*. Loops can be nested but it is recommended that different variable names are used in each loop and that the for loops are tabbed inside each other for easier reading.

```
(7) foreach TRANSPORT (horse boat plane)
? echo $TRANSPORT
? end
horse
boat
plane
(8)
```

The example shown was typed from the keyboard. The second-level prompt ? appears because the shell recognizes the *foreach* and requests the rest of the command. After *end* has been entered, the command is complete and is executed. The second example is a script that shows how to nest *foreach* loops.

```
(26) foreach LOOPA (first second third)
? foreach LOOPB (prize place)
? echo $LOOPA $LOOPB
? end
? end
first prize
first place
second prize
second place
third prize
third place
(27)
```

One very frequent use of this format is to access all the arguments passed to a shell program. The word list is replaced with *($argv[*])* as shown.

```
(36) cat get_args
#Get_args script
foreach x ($argv[*])
echo $x
end
(37) get_args one two three
one
two
three
(38)
```

switch

switch (string)

case pattern1 :
    command list
    breaksw
case pattern2 :
    command list
    breaksw
default:
    command list
endsw

The *switch* statement takes the word and sequentially compares it with each pattern preceded by the word *case*. If there is a match, the associated command list is executed and the execution resumes with the next command after *endsw*.

The default part of the structure is used to trap any string that has no pattern match.

```
(27) cat switcher
#Switcher
foreach NUM (1 2 3 )
        switch ($NUM)
        case 1:
        echo ONE
        breaksw
        case 2:
        echo TWO
        breaksw
        default:
        echo not 1 or 2
        endsw
end
(28) switcher
ONE
TWO
not 1 or 2
(29)
```

Combining *switch* statements with the $< command provides the basic structure for a command interpreter. The command is read in from the keyboard and assigned to a variable. The variable is checked against in a *switch* statement and the appropriate action taken. If no match occurs, the default message of "command not found" is printed. The second *echo* statement encloses the text in double quotes to escape the angle brackets that would otherwise cause a problem. This example also shows how to have two or more *case* patterns execute the same command list — add the extra *case* statement after the first one and before the associated command list.

```
(36) cat dos_mode
#dos_mode
while (1)
echo You are now in DOS mode.
echo "Please enter your command followed by <return>"
set command = $<
switch ($command)
        case dir:
        case DIR:
        ls -x
        breaksw
        case vers:
        who
        breaksw
        case unix:
        break
        default:
        echo $command not yet implimented.
endsw
```

```
end
(37) dos_mode
You are now in DOS mode.
Please enter your command followed by <return>
dir
DIR          _elif          _until
You are now in DOS mode.
Please enter your command followed by <return>
DIR
DIR          _elif          _until
You are now in DOS mode.
Please enter your command followed by <return>
Dir
Dir not yet implimented.
You are now in DOS mode.
Please enter your command followed by <return>
vers
stevebsd   tty1          Nov  3 18:12
You are now in DOS mode.
Please enter your command followed by <return>
unix
19.6r 0.1u 0.2s
(38)
```

if-else-endif

if	*or*	**if**	
expression		expression	
then		**then**	
command list		command list	
endif		**else**	
		command list	
		endif	

This is a general conditional branch. If the expression executes correctly without errors, it returns a value of non-zero, which is interpreted as meaning TRUE. If errors occurred, the value is zero, meaning FALSE. The right-hand version has an optional third command list that is executed if the first command list returns FALSE. Unlike the Bourne shell, the expression cannot be a command and the *then* must be on the same line as the *if*. It is possible to nest *if* statements — but remember to have enough *endif* statements to match the number of *if* statements.

```
(45) cat iftest
#if test
set input = $<
if $input =~ "unix" then
        who
else
if $input =~ "dir"   then
```

```
        ls -x
else
        echo "I don't understand."
endif
endif

(46) iftest
unix
stevebsd   tty1          Nov  3 18:12
(47) iftest
ghgh
I don't understand.
(48)
```

It is possible to use the success of a command as the expression to be tested. A special variable *$status* contains the exit status of the last completed command and can be used as the tested expression as shown.

```
(64) cat test_command
#command tester
echo Hello
if ( ! $status ) then
echo OK
else
echo NOT OK
endif
ghgh
if ( ! $status ) then
echo OK
else
echo Command failed
endif

(65) test_command
Hello
OK
ghgh: Command not found.
Command failed
(66)
```

while

> **while** expression
> command list
> **end**

The *while* structure is different from the others because it loops and repeatedly executes commands while its command list keeps returning a TRUE (non-zero) status. The *while* expression is always evaluated and if this returns TRUE, the second command list is executed. When this has completed, the *while* expression is again executed and the cycle repeated. If it returns FALSE, the command list is not executed and execution continues after the *end* statement.

```
(78) cat _while
#While example
set stat = 0
while ( ! $stat )
echo Please enter a command
set command = $<
$command
set stat = $status
end
(79) _while
Please enter a command
who
stevebsd    tty1          Nov  3 18:12
Please enter a command
hjh
hjh: Command not found.
(80)
```

In the previous example, a *while* statement is used to create a loop where commands can be entered from the keyboard and executed until the command fails. The expression uses an exclamation mark to test for the NOT conditions stored in the variable *stat*. If the exclamation mark is missing, the *while* command list is not executed at all. *stat* contains the exit status of the command. The *$status* variable can only be used directly if the last line in the *while* command list is the command to be tested. While this is the case in this example, it stores the status to allow other command lines to be added without affecting the execution. This type of loop is used to repeatedly execute a command either until it succeeds or fails, depending on how the testing is constructed.

Break, continue

These two commands can be used to change the action of *foreach* and *while* loops. *break* causes the shell to break out of the loop and is useful if a loop needs several exit points. *continue* causes execution to jump to the beginning of the loop and not carry on any further.

```
(86) cat brk
#Break and continue
while (1)
echo Type a single character and press return.
set a = $<
switch ($a)
        case a:
        case b:
        case c:
        echo Your letter is either a b or c
        breaksw
        case x:
        break
        default:
```

```
            continue
            endsw
echo Thank you
end
echo Leaving script
(87) brk
Type a single character and press return.
a
Your letter is either a b or c
Thank you
Type a single character and press return.
f
Type a single character and press return.
x
Leaving script
(88)
```

The previous example uses both *break* and *continue*. The *while* loop is permanent because the expression is always set to 1 and thus always returns TRUE. As a result, the command list continues to execute. Each time through the loop, it asks for a character from the keyboard. This value is used in the *switch* statement to identify it and print an appropriate message. Once complete, "Thank you" is printed, indicating the end of the loop has been reached. If a character other than *a*, *b* or *c* is entered, this executes the *continue*, the script starts at the beginning of the *while* loop and prompts for a new input. No "Thank you" message is printed. If *x* is typed, the *break* command is executed which breaks the permanent *while* loop and the script terminates. Again, no "Thank you" message is printed, execution continues after the *end* statement and the last *echo* command prints its message. This type of script can be used to check input from the keyboard for correct syntax.

goto

goto destination

This is an unconditional jump instruction that forces the shell script to go to the line marked with the *destination* and continue executing from there. This command is usually ignored by purists who claim that a well-structured program should not need to use it. However, it can be invaluable during debugging to change a script flow quickly. The destination is defined within the shell script by a line with the label followed by a colon.

onintr

onintr label

onintr -

onintr

If terminated through some error or a signal passed to it, most scripts stop execution and return the user to the normal shell script. An example of such an interrupt is a ^C or ^DELETE typed from the keyboard. It is possible to take control of this within the shell script through the use of the *onintr* command. This can take one of three formats. If a label follows it, the script transfers to the label and continues execution from there. If a hyphen follows it, all interrupts are ignored and if the command is on its own, default interrupt handling is restored.

Expressions

The standard control structures use the result of an expression to determine program flow. The C shell supports many different types of expression as shown below.

Logical operations

||	OR
&&	AND
!	NOT
0	FALSE
1	TRUE

File operators

-r *file* True if *file* exists and is readable.

-w *file*True if *file* exists and is writable.

-x *file* True if *file* exists and is executable.

-e *file* True if *file* exists.

-f *file* True if *file* exists and is an ordinary file.

-o *file* True if *file* is owned by the user.

-d *file* True if *file* exists and is a directory.

-z *file* True if *file* has a size of zero.

Arithmetic operators

*	times
/	quotient
%	remainder
+	plus
-	minus

Logical bit operators

&	bitwise AND
|	bitwise OR
^	bitwise exclusive OR
<<	left shift
>>	right shift
~	one's complement

Relational operators

!=	not equal
==	equal to
>	greater than
>=	greater than or equal to
<	less than
<=	less than or equal to

String operators

s1 =~ s2	string match
s1 !~ s2	not a string match

With the bash shell, the *test* command is used to test expressions. This is not needed with tcsh — the expression is included in the control statement as needed. This construction is very similar to that used in C programming.

eval

eval [arguments]

eval evaluates the arguments, reads them as input to the shell and executes them. Its main use within scripts is to evaluate complex arguments before passing them to the shell for execution.

exec

exec [arguments]

This command takes the commands specified by the arguments and executes them without creating a new shell. In other words, if *exec script2* was a command line within a shell script, the commands in *script2* would be executed as if they had been included in the original script.

```
(23) cat script
echo "This is the calling script"
exec script1
echo This is calling script again
(24) cat script1
echo This is script1
(25) script
This is the calling script
This is script1
(26)
```

The example shows how *exec* works. A shell script called script prints a message and uses the *exec* command to transfer to *script1*, which prints another message. When script1 finishes, the complete process terminates. The remaining commands in script are ignored and not executed.

exit

exit [n]

exit causes the shell script to stop execution and return an error code. If no number is specified as an argument, the code is that of the last executed command. It can be used as part of a routine to end a script.

```
echo 'Do you want to continue ? y/n'
set a = $<
if ($a =~ n) then exit 1
endif
```

shift

shift [n]

shift shifts all the positional variables ($1 to $9) up one place. When executed, $1 is discarded and is replaced by $2. $2 is replaced by $3, and so on. It is often used to process arguments from a command line. If a numerical value is given for *n*, the command starts with variable *$n+1*. If it is not specified, a default of 1 is assumed.

```
(1)cat shift3
echo $1 $2 $3
shift
echo $1 $2 $3
shift
echo $1 $2 $3
(2) shift3 a b c
a b c
b c
c
(3)
```

wait

wait [process ID]

wait forces the script to wait for either all associated background processes or, if a process ID is given as an argument, to wait for that specific process to complete. When waiting for all processes, a return code of zero is given; while waiting for a specific process it returns the code from that process. In the example, *waitdemo* displays the current data and time and starts another script called *snore* in the background which sleeps for 20 seconds. The *wait* command forces it to wait until *snore* has completed. This causes the 20 second difference in the times.

```
(49) cat snore
sleep 20
(50) cat waitdemo
date
```

```
echo Now starting snore in the background
exec snore&
wait
date
(51) waitdemo
Thu Oct 24 02:58:43 GMT 1991
Now starting snore in the background
Thu Oct 24 02:59:03 GMT 1991
20.2r 0.0u 0.1s
(52)
```

6   Editors

UNIX and thus Linux is infamous for its editors. They have, at various times, been considered difficult to use and understand — and yet extremely flexible and powerful in their capabilities. Compared with current word processors and text editors, which use graphical interfaces and mice, they do seem cumbersome and out of date. However, it should not be forgotten that they provided cut and paste functions and complex search and replace facilities years before the current word processor favorites were conceived.

Despite reservations about their interfaces and command structures, a basic knowledge and understanding of these editors is essential because they have to be used during system administration and program development. Some traditionalists would say that coming to grips with *vi*'s unintuitive command interface is part of the indoctrination into the world of Linux — I disagree and, whenever possible, perform any text editing off-line on a PC and then upload the files. However, if you are sitting in front of a dumb terminal, you do not have this option and the only way out is to use a Linux editor. Four editors are normally supplied with Linux: *ed* and *ex* are line based editors and *vi* is a full screen editor that incorporates the functions of *ed* and *ex*. There is a fourth editor called *emacs* that is extremely powerful but has a steep learning curve. As a result, this chapter concentrates on the first three editors.

The line editors *ed* and *ex*

ed was the standard line editor for many of the earlier UNIX systems and, although it has been effectively superseded by *ex* and *vi*, its basic ideas have been included in these later editors. It is a line editor in which the text is displayed line by line and not using a complete screen. This is due to historical circumstances, such as the use of teletypes instead of display terminals, and an effort to keep communication traffic and costs to a minimum. In both cases, the aim was to minimize the amount of data that was printed or to keep telephone costs down.

ex and *vi*

ex and its relative *vi*, which is described later, are two versions of the same editor, except that *vi* is a full-screen editor that uses the whole of the screen to display the current lines and their contents and *ex* is line based. *ex* commands can be executed in *vi* by prefixing them with a colon, such as, *:wq* to write and quit the file that is being edited.

Invoking ex

There are two ways of invoking the editor *ex*. Both have similar options but the *edit* editor is a restricted version of *ex* .

ex - **-v -t** *tag* **-r** file **-R -x** *+command file*
edit -r file **-x** *file*
where:

-	Stops all interactive user messages.
-v	Invokes *vi* mode and uses *ex* as a full screen editor.
-t *tag*	Positions the editor in the file where the *tag* is located.
-r *file*	Recovers *file* from the crash save area. If no file is specified, a list is printed.
-R	Read only mode.
-x	An encryption option. The encryption algorithms used within Linux are subject to U.S. export restrictions and many systems outside of the U.S. do not support encryption.
file	The name of the file to be edited. If not specified, *ex* creates a new file.
+command	Begins executing with the editor command. For example:
	+5 move to line 5.
	+/*error*/ move to the first line containing *error*.

ex commands

The *ex* command format is fairly simple and consists of either two or three components. With the two-component version, a line address or range is specified, followed by a command that will act on the specified lines. The three component version precedes the line address with another command, which modifies the behavior of the last command.

One advantage the three-component version has is that the line address, which is normally a number or some similar reference, can be replaced with a regular expression identifying lines by their contents. Using regular expressions, it is very easy to delete all lines containing the word "error", or replace "mike" with "MIKE", and so on. Regular expressions are explained later in this chapter.

The editor keeps track of its place within the file through the use of line numbers. Each line in the file is consecutively numbered by the editor and operations on the file are performed on specified lines. This is done by supplying a line address as follows:

.   (period) This is the current line and is automatically updated. If no line address is given, the command operates on the current line.

5	References a single line — line 5 in this case.
1,5	References a range of lines — lines 1 to 5 in this case.
1,$	References the whole file. Line 1 is always the first line and $ is a marker for the end of the file. In this example, the address range is from line 1 to the end of the file.
.+5	Go forward 5 lines from the current line.
.-5	Go back 5 lines from the current line.
^	Go back one line (early versions only).
-	Go back one line.
+	Go forward one line.

To see data, the user must tell the editor to print out the required lines because, unlike full screen editors, *ex* does not automatically update the screen or have any cursor commands that scroll data or allow the user to roam through the data file. The command interface is relatively simple. Except for inserting and appending text, all keyboard input is interpreted as command sequences. These have several different formats.

Text insertion takes the format of a line address, followed by a command, such as *append* or *insert*, followed by the text that is required and terminated by a line with a full stop. This is the only way to insert text because all other keyboard input is interpreted as commands.

```
address command
text
.
```

The second format takes a line address followed by a command and, if needed, a destination address. The *move*, *print* and *delete* commands take this type of format.

```
address command destination
```

The third format is used for text search and replace commands, which use an address followed by a command, and regular expressions that are used to identify text and replace it. In some cases, other options can be added at the end.

```
address command regular expression options
```

The fourth format is used for utility commands or line addresses on their own.

```
command
```

Displaying lines

n p	Where *n* is the line number.
n,m p	Where *n* is the first line of a range and *m* the last number.
set number	Displays a line number whenever a line is printed using *p*. To remove line numbers, use *nonumber* instead.

n	Prints the line *n*. If no command (such as *p*) is given with a line number, *ex* uses *print* as the default command and displays the line.
1,$ p	Prints all the lines in the file starting at line 1 and ending with the line containing the last character. The dollar symbol is shorthand for the last line.

Deleting and restoring lines

n d	Where *n* is the line number.
n,m d	Where *n* is the first line of a range and *m* the last number.
1,$ d	Deletes all the lines in the file starting at line 1 and ending with the line containing the last character. The dollar symbol is shorthand for the last line.
d	Deletes the current line. If no line number is given, *ex* uses the current line as default with the command.
ndm	Delete *m* lines starting at line number *n*.
put	Restores the last set of deleted lines and inserts them after the current line.

```
:4d5
This is line 4
:1,$p
This is line 1
This is line 2
This is line 3
This is line 4
This is line 5
:5
This is line 5
:put
This is "inserted line" 5
:1,$p
This is line 1
This is line 2
This is line 3
This is line 4
This is line 5
This is "inserted line" 1
This is "inserted line" 2
This is "inserted line" 3
This is "inserted line" 4
This is "inserted line" 5
```

If a buffer name is specified after the *put* command or *delete* command, the deleted lines are stored in that buffer. A valid buffer name is a lowe case letter of the alphabet. If the name is placed in uppercase, the data is appended to the buffer during delete. The uppercase is ignored by *put*.

Manipulating lines

a   *append* inserts a new line after the current line. New lines will be added until a new line only containing a full stop is entered. This stops the *append* operation. To *append* lines after a certain line number, precede the command with the line number.

```
: 1 a
       2   This is an appended line
       3   .
:1,$ p
       1   This is line 1
       2   This is an appended line
       3   This is  line 2
       4   This is line 3
:
```

co   *copy* duplicates selected lines and inserts them. The number of the line to be copied precedes *co* and the destination line number follows it. The new line is inserted after the destination line.

```
:1 co 4
       5   This is line 1
:
```

i   *insert* works in a similar way to *append*, except that the new line or lines are inserted before the destination line.

```
:1,$ p
       1   This is line 1
       2   This is line 2
       3   This is line 3
:2
       2   This is line 2
:i
       2   This is an extra line
       3   .
:1,$ p
       1   This is line 1
       2   This is an extra line
       3   This is line 2
       4   This is line 3
:
```

j   *join* splices the specified line with that below. If no line number is specified, the current line is joined with the one below.

```
:2 j
       2   This is an extra line This is line 2
```

m   *move* performs a similar job to *co* but moves the line to a destination, instead of copying it.

```
:p
       5   This is line 1
:5 m 3
       4   This is line 1
:1,$ p
```

```
1  This is line 1
2  This is an appended line
3  This is line 2
4  This is line 1
5  This is line 3
:
```

put [*buffer*] *put* takes the lines from the buffer and inserts them immediately after the current line. The buffer takes as its name any lowercase letter from the alphabet. To load a buffer, use *yank*. If no buffer is specified, the data goes into a special default buffer which is also used for deleted lines.

yank[*buffer*] *yank* copies lines into either the default buffer or a specified buffer, for further use by *put*. If the buffer name is in uppercase, it is appended to the buffer.

```
:1,$ yank
5 lines yanked
:1,$list
This is line 1$
This is line 2$
This is line 3$
This is line 4$
This is line 5$
:1 yank a
:2 yank A
:5
This is line 5$
:put a
This is line 2
:1,$p
This is line 1
This is line 2
This is line 3
This is line 4
This is line 5
This is line 1
This is line 2
:
```

Indenting lines

<   Shifts the current line to the left.

>   Shifts the current line to the right.

```
:2
    2  This is an appended line
:>
    2          This is an appended line
:>
    2                  This is an appended line
:<
    2          This is an appended line
```

Search and replace

ex has a powerful search and replace facility, based on that provided by *ed*. It can search for a text string and replace it, or simply find the lines that contain the string. The search strings can be replaced with regular expressions that allow the use of wildcard characters. As with the *ed* description, this section concentrates on how the commands work and uses simple text strings. The next section covers their use with regular expressions.

/s1/   This searches for the text *s1* and moves to the first line where it occurs. The search is carried out going forward. Replacing the slashes with question marks makes the search go backwards.

```
:1,$p
This is line 1
This is line 2
This is line 3
:2
This is line 2
:/line/
This is line 3
:2
This is line 2
:?line?
This is line 1
:
```

Several search commands can be combined by separating them with semi-colons or commas. A semicolon forces the search to be consecutive — the second item is searched for after the first one has been located. With a comma, the searches are carried out in parallel.

```
:1,$p
This is line 1
This is line 2
This is line 3
This is the last line
:/3/;/This/
This is the last line
:/3/,/This/
This is line 1
:
```

/s1/comm   Adding a command to the */s1/* construction forces it to act like a line address for the command.

```
:1,$p
This is line 1
This is line 2
This is line 3
This is the last line
:/3/d
:/2/d
:1,$p
```

```
This is line 1
This is the last line
:
```

s/*s1*/*s2*/ Substitute text *s1* with text *s2* in the current line. If a range of lines precedes the command, the substitution is performed on each line. The second text string can be removed, in which case the first text string is deleted from the line.

```
:p
THIS is lineLINE 1
:s/LINE//
:p
THIS is line 1
:s/THIS/This/
:p
This is line 1
:
```

1,5s/*s1*/*s2*/ Line addresses can be added to the command to tell *ex* to perform the substitution on all the specified lines. The action is taken on each individual line in turn but only on the first match of each line.

```
:1,$p
This is line 1
This is line 2
This is line 3
This is the last line
:1,3s/line/LINE/
:1,$p
This is LINE 1
This is LINE 2
This is LINE 3
This is the last line
:4s/last/LAST/
:4
This is the LAST line
```

1,5s/*s1*/*s2*/n The substitution can be made to operate on the *n*th match within the line by adding *n* to the command, where *n* is an integer from 1 to 512. This operates on each line separately. If n=2, the second match on each line is modified — and not the second match within the range of lines that has been specified.

```
:1
This is line 1
:1s/i/QQ/2
:1
This QQs line 1
:1,2s/i/qq/
:1,3p
Thqqs QQs line 1
Thqqs is line 2
This is line 3
:
```

1,5s/*s1*/*s2*/g If a *g* is added, the substitution works on all matches.

```
:1,3p
Thqqs QQs line 1
Thqqs is line 2
This is line 3
:1,3s/i/qq/g
:1,3p
Thqqs QQs lqqne 1
Thqqs qqs lqqne 2
Thqqs qqs lqqne 3
:
```

1,5s/*s1*/*s2*/c If a *c* is added, confirmation of each change is requested.

```
:1,$s/line/LINE/c
This is line 1
        ^^^^y
This is line 2
        ^^^^n
This is line 3
        ^^^^y
This is LINE 3
:1,$p
This is LINE 1
This is line 2
This is LINE 3
:
```

&   If used in the second text within a substitute command, the ampersand is interpreted as a special character and the first text string is used as a replacement for it, as shown in the example. If used as a command, it repeats the last substitution.

```
:1
This is line 1
:s/line/&LINE/
:p
THIS is lineLINE 1
:
```

1,$g/*s1*/*list*

This is a variation of the substitute command where the *g* replaces *s* and a command list replaces the second text string. It works by looking at each line for a match with text *s1*. If there is a match, the list of commands is executed. The list is made up of standard *ed* commands, separated by an escaped semicolon (\;) but not including *g* and *v*. If the list is empty, the command *p* is assumed and the matching lines printed out.

1,$v/*s1*/*list*

By replacing *g* with *v*, the command list is executed on every line that does not match with text *s1*. In all other respects, it behaves like *g*.

regular expressions

All the commands in the search and replace section use a text string to locate a particular line and then manipulate it. Instead of a simple text string, a regular expression can be employed, which uses special characters to identify specific characteristics. To identify all words beginning with the letter "a" would be virtually impossible using simple text. However, with a regular expression, it is very easy. The special characters used in regular expressions are:

^	Beginning of line.
$	End of line.
.	Any character.
\<	Beginning of word.
\>	End of word.
[*string*]	Any character in *string*.
[≠*string*]	Any character NOT in *string*.
[^*string*]	Any character NOT in *string*.
[x-y]	Any characters between *x* and *y*.
.*	Any number of any characters.
x*	Any number of character *x*.

If any of these characters are needed as simple text, they must be escaped (for example, * "*" and so on). Here are some examples of their use.

/\<.../	Find three-letter words.
/\<[0-9]/	Find any words beginning with a number from 0 to 9.
/^$/	Find any blank lines.
/a.c/	Find any string of three characters where the first character is "a" and the third is "c".
/\<a.c\>/	Find any three-letter word whose first character is "a" and third is "c".
/\<[aeiou]/	Find any word beginning with a vowel.
/\<[^aeiou]/	
	Find any word beginning with a consonant (not a vowel).
/[^1-5]/	Find any number that is not 1, 2 , 3, 4 or 5.
/.*/	Find any line (matches any number of any character).

These regular expressions can be used with substitution commands to increase their power. In the example shown, the first regular expression finds any occurrence of lowercase or uppercase "qq" and replaces it with the letter "i" — and thus corrects the spelling. The second example finds the line with the numbers 1 and 2, irrespective of any characters between them, and replaces the text with "1". This effectively deletes all the text after the number 1.

```
:1,$p
Thqqs QQs line 1   This is line 2
Thqqs is line 3
This is the last line
This is line 1
:1,$s/[qQ][qQ]/i/g
:1,$p
This is line 1   This is line 2
This is line 3
This is the last line
This is line 1
:1,$s/1.*2/1/
:1,$p
This is line 1
This is line 3
This is the last line
This is line 1
:
```

File commands

e *file*   *edit* fetches *file* and goes into the edit mode without leaving the editor.

f [*file*]   *file* changes the name of the current file to *file* or, if typed on its own, displays the current file name. A good use for this command is to ensure that an original file is not overwritten by accident.

```
:edit unique
:f unique.two
:w
```

In the example, the file called *unique* is loaded but the default file name is changed to *unique.two* so any write operation creates a file called *unique.two* rather than overwriting the original.

re   *fileread* inserts the contents of *file* immediately after the current line.

```
$ ex list
"list" 5 lines, 75 characters
:3
This is line 3
:read insert
"insert" 5 lines, 75 characters
:1,$p
This is line 1
This is line 2
This is line 3
This is line 4
This is line 5
```

rew   *rewind* fetches the last stored version of the file and discards any changes that have been made since the original version was loaded. The command can force a return to the stored version by adding an exclamation mark to the end (such as rew!).

w [*file*]   *write* writes back any changes to *file*. If a file name is specified, this is used instead.

leaving ex

sh   *shell*n returns temporarily to the shell until *exit* is typed. This is useful to check file names before writing a file back to disk.

```
:sh
$ dir
/user/book/test:
dd1    ddresult2   file1      filea      target3
dd2    ddtest      file2      target1    test
$ exit
!
:
```

xit   *exit* and return to shell.

q   *quit* and return to the shell only if any changes have been written back.

quit! *quit ex* even if changes have not been written back to the file.

q!   same as *quit!*

line numbering

nu   *number* adds line numbers to the output produced by *print*.

ma   *mark* notes a line number or range and assigns it to a marker, which can be any lowercase letter of the alphabet. The markers can be used instead of line numbers, provided they are preceded with ' (single quote) and not used on their own.

```
:1,$p
This is line 1
This is line 2
This is line 3
This is "inserted line" 1
This is "inserted line" 2
This is "inserted line" 3
This is "inserted line" 4
This is "inserted line" 5
This is line 4
This is line 5
:4
This is "inserted line" 1
:ma a
:8
This is "inserted line" 5
:ma b
:'a,'bp
This is "inserted line" 1
This is "inserted line" 2
This is "inserted line" 3
This is "inserted line" 4
```

```
This is "inserted line" 5
:3ma d
:1,3ma f
:'fp
This is line 1
:1,'fp
This is line 1
This is line 1
This is line 1
:
```

Scrolling the screen

visual   *vi* switches the editor into the visual editor mode.

z   *window* clears the screen and puts the cursor at the top.

^D   *scroll* scrolls the screen display.

Utilities

map   This displays how cursor keys are mapped.

```
:map
inschar ^_R     i
up      ^_H     k
down    ^_P     j
left    ^_K     h
right   ^_M     l
```

unm   *unmap* changes the cursor key map.

ve   *version* prints out the Linux version that *ex* is running under.

u   *undo* undoes the last operation and is extremely useful in cases where the wrong command has been executed or has not performed as expected.

ab   *abbrev* allows command abbreviations.

una   *unabbrev* does not allow command abbreviations.

ar   *args* displays the arguments passed with the *ex* command line. The argument within square brackets is the current argument.

```
$ex abc def ghj
3 files to edit
"abc" [New file]
:ar
[abc] def ghj
```

next   *next* forces *ex* to move on to the next argument and evaluate it. In the example, the file *def* does not exist and the result is an error message, as well as changing any further output from *ar*.

```
$ex abc def ghj
3 files to edit
"abc" [New file]
:ar
[abc] def ghj
:next
```

```
"def"  No such file or directory
:ar
abc [def] ghj
:
```

! command *escape* executes the shell command that follows it and is useful for looking at directories, and so on. If the command is *sh*, another shell is run in a similar way to the *sh* command and control returns to *ex* when *exit* is typed.

```
:!ls -x
insert  list
!
:!sh
# exit
!
:sh
# exit
!
:
```

l   *list* prints out lines in a similar way to the *print* command, except that ^I is used instead of tab and $ is printed at the end of each line.

```
:1,$p
This is line 1
This is line 2
This is line 3
This is line 4
This is line 5
:1,$list
This is line 1$
This is line 2$
This is line 3$
This is line 4$
This is line 5$
:
```

pre   *preserve* is the *save my data at all costs* command and should only be used if a *write* does not work. The command effectively dumps the file into a crash save area. This is normally used to store diagnostic or other data if the Linux system crashes. If *pre* is used, seek help from the system administrator immediately to find out why the *write* command would not work. To recover the data, use the *recover* command or invoke *ex* with the -r option.

rec   *recover* restores a file from the system crash save area and is normally used after the *preserve* command.

Initializing options

To change the *ex* environment, the *set* command is used with a list of options:

set *x*	Enable option *x*.
set no*x*	Disable option *x*.
set x=*val*	Give value *val*.
set	Show changed options.
set all	Show all options.
set *x***?**	Show value of option *x*.

Some useful options for *set*:

ai	*autoindent* — supply indent.
ap	*autoprint* — print current line after buffer changed.
aw	*autowrite* — write before changing files.
bf	*beautify* — discard all control characters other than new-line and form-feed.
dir	*directory* — specify the directory.
ed	ed compatible.
ic	*ignorecase* — ignore case in pattern searches.
list	Tabs will print as ^l.
nu	*number* — lines are displayed with their line numbers.
para	*paragraphs* — the names of *nroff* macros that start paragraphs for the { and } commands. Initially, these are set to IPLPPPQPbpP LI.
sect	*sections* — the name of macros that start sections for the [[and]] commands. The initial values are NHSHH HU.
term	The name of the terminal type being used.
EXINIT	This environment variable is inspected to see if there are any special options. The *set* options that are required should be listed in this variable.
./.exrc	This is an editor initialization file.

vi

vi, the visual editor, is a full-screen editor that displays the file and any modifications on screen. It uses the terminal definition defined by the *TERM* environment variable. If this definition does not match the actual terminal used, the displayed data is garbled and does not respond correctly to cursor keys and other commands. In this situation, it is all too easy to corrupt the file by incorrectly modifying data. The reason for this is simple — the editor uses the terminal control characters to move the cursor around the screen and insert/delete data and so on. While most terminals respond in the same way for the common commands, like carriage return and line feed, the cursor control commands are often different. Similar problems exist with cursor and other special functions on the keyboard. While cursor keys may look the same, they do not send the same characters! The result is a mess on the screen.

If the screen does not appear correctly, type *<esc>:quit!<cr>* and ignore any beeps or bells that may be sounded. The *<esc>* ensures that any character insertion mode is stopped — but causes the terminal to sound its bell or beep, if this is not so. The *:quit!<cr>* sequence immediately leaves *vi*. Once out of the editor, the *TERM* variable can be displayed using the *set* or *env* commands, changed by *TERM=vt100*, where *vt100* is the name of the terminal type, and exported to inform the system of the change. This sequence is shown below:

```
# env
EXINIT=set redraw nows sm
HOME=/
LOGNAME=root
MAIL=/usr/mail/root
PATH=:/opus/bin:/bin:/usr/bin:/etc:/usr/ucb
TERM=opus-pc
TZ=GMT0
# TERM=vt100;export TERM
# env
EXINIT=set redraw nows sm
HOME=/
LOGNAME=root
MAIL=/usr/mail/root
PATH=:/opus/bin:/bin:/usr/bin:/etc:/usr/ucb
TERM=vt100
TZ=GMT0
#
```

For those with the tcsh shell, *TERM* can be set by using the *setenv* command: *setenv TERM vt100*. Some implementations specify the *TERM* variable in lowercase as *term*.

This problem can also be caused by the terminal, especially when using terminal emulation packages on PCs or terminals that are capable of emulating other terminal types. Again, it is important to have a match between the terminal type being emulated and that expected by the Linux system. The method of configuring the terminal emulation depends on the software being used, but most support the DEC vt100 terminal type, and this is frequently the default that is emulated and expected by the system.

It is prudent to check the *TERM* variable before invoking *vi* on any strange system, or when logging on remotely. The *TERM* variable can be changed by a *.profile* shell script, manually, as previously explained, or by the system administrator in the setup files for that user. If the terminal cannot be matched to the system, it is safer for the data, at the expense of speed and comfort for the user, to not use *vi*. Use the line editors, *ed* or *ex* instead, as these are not so critical in needing a terminal match.

Invoking vi

There are three ways of invoking *vi*. All have the same set of options but the *view* editor is a read-only version of *vi* while *vedit* is a restricted version of *vi* for novices.

vi   -v -t *tag* -rfile -R -x +*command* **file**
view -v -t *tag* -rfile -R -x +*command* **file**
vedit -v -t *tag* -rfile -R -x +*command* **file**

where:

-w*n*	Sets the window size, where *n* is the number of lines.
-v	Invokes *vi* mode and uses *ex* as a full-screen editor.
-t *tag*	Positions the editor in the file where the *tag* is located.
-r*file*	Recovers a file from the crash save area. If no file is specified, a list is printed.
-R	Read only mode.
file	The name of the file to be edited. If not specified, *vi* creates a new file.
-x	An encryption option. The encryption algorithms used within Linux may be subject to U.S. export restrictions and many systems outside of the U.S. do not support encryption.
+*command*	Begin executing with the editor command for example:
	+5 move to line 5
	+/error/ move to the first line containing the text error

vi **commands**

vi has three input modes — the *vi* command mode, where text is interpreted as a *vi* command to move the cursor, scroll the display and so on; a text input mode, where keyboard input is accepted as text until the escape key is pressed; and an *ex* command mode, which is enabled by typing a colon while in the *vi* command mode.

Leaving the editor

Q	Quits *vi* screen editor for the line editor *ex*. A : prompt is supplied.
ZZ	Exits *vi* after writing any changes to the file and returns to the shell.
:x<CR>	The same as ZZ.
:q!	Forces an exit from *vi* and returns to the shell.
:wq	Updates the file with any changes and returns to the shell.

Moving the page

^d or ^D	Scrolls the window forward.
^u or ^U	Scrolls the window backward.

^f or ^F	Moves forward a page.
^b or ^B	Moves backward a page.

A count can be placed before these commands to specify a repetition. For example, *5^f* moves forward 5 pages, *9^U* scrolls backward 9 times.

Moving the cursor

<cr>	Moves the cursor down.
+	Moves the cursor down.
j	Moves the cursor down.
^N	Moves the cursor down.
-	Moves the cursor up.
k	Moves the cursor up.
^P	Moves the cursor up.
space	Moves the cursor right.
l	Moves the cursor right.
<backspace>	
	Moves the cursor left.
h	Moves the cursor left.
B	Moves the cursor back a word.
E	Moves the cursor forward to the end of a word.
W	Moves forward to the beginning of a word.
b	Moves the cursor backward to the beginning of a word in the current line.
e	Moves the cursor forward to the end of a word in the current line.
w	Moves the cursor forward to the beginning of a word in the current line.
t	Moves the cursor up to the character before the next character typed.

A count can be placed before these commands to specify a repetition. For example, *5j* moves the cursor down 5 lines, *9l* moves the cursor right 9 spaces. In addition, some terminal cursor keys are also supported.

†	Moves to the first non-white position on the current line and is also used to match a pattern at the beginning of a line.

Moving to a specific line

z <cr>	Redraws the screen with the current line at the top.
z.	Redraws the screen with the current line in the center.
z-	Redraws the screen with the current line at the bottom.

A count can be placed before these commands to specify a repetition. For example, *nz<cr>* redraws the screen with line number *n* at the top, *nz-* redraws the screen with line number *n* at the bottom, and so on.

G	Goes to the line number that has been typed before the command. If no number is given, *vi* goes to the end of the file. The screen is redrawn if necessary (e.g. *5G* goes to line 5, *345G* goes to line 345, and so on). If the line does not exist, the terminal beeps and the cursor stays at its current position.
H	Moves the cursor to the top line of the screen and the first non-white character on the line (such as a letter, number or punctuation mark). If a count is given before it, the cursor is moved to that line.
L	Moves the cursor to the bottom line of the screen and the first non-white character on the line (a letter, number or punctuation mark). If a count is given before it, the cursor is moved to that line.
M	Moves the cursor to the middle line of the screen and the first non-white character on it.
[[	Moves the cursor back to the previous section boundary. A section boundary can be defined either by a form-feed character ^L or by a .NH or .SH macro. Lines beginning with a {, which declare a function in C programs, also act as a section boundaries. This makes skipping through functions very easy indeed.
]]	The reverse of *[[*. It moves forward to a section boundary. It alsos stop at C functions defined by {.

Adding and deleting lines and characters

dd	Deletes the current line.
*n***dd**	Deletes *n* lines starting with the current line and moving downward.
dw	Delete text up to the next word. This command is actually two: *d* is a delete operator that deletes all text passed over by the cursor, while *w* tells the cursor to move to the next word and so deletes the text up to the next word. The operator can be combined with other cursor movement commands.
D	Deletes the current line.
x	Deletes the current character.
X	Deletes the character before the cursor.
r*x*	Replace the current character with the character *x*.
R *...<esc>*	Replaces characters starting with the current character until <esc> is pressed:

```
The quick brown fox jumps.
```
type *Rgreen cat<esc>*
```
The quick green cat jumps.
```

A ...*<esc>*   Appends characters to the end of the current line until *<esc>* is pressed.

C ...*<esc>*   Changes the rest of the line until *<esc>* is pressed. This is very similar to the *R* command

cw   Changes text up to the next word. This command is actually two: *c* is a change operator that deletes all text passed over by the cursor, while *w* tells the cursor to move to the next word, and so changes the text up to the next word. The operator can be combined with other cursor movement commands.

A count can be placed before these commands to specify a repetition. This includes commands such as *R*, *C* and *A*, where the command can be repeated *n* times, where *n* is the count. With each repetition, the editor inserts characters entered from the keyboard until *<esc>* is pressed.

J   Joins the current line with the one below it. It is fairly intelligent in that it inserts a space between words, two spaces after a full stop, and so on. If a count is given before the *J* command, such as *nJ*, then *n* lines of text are joined together.

U   Restores the current line to its original state before the changes started. Remember *U* for undo!

u   Undoes the last change.

.   Repeats the last change.

^E   Exposes an extra line at the bottom of the display in some versions of *vi*. The data that appears has not been inserted or added: all that has happened is that an additional line has been added to the display.

^Y   Exposes an extra line at the top of the display in some versions of *vi*. The data that appears has not been inserted or added: all that has happened is that an additional line has been added to the display.

Inserting text

a ...*<esc>*   Inserts characters, starting to the right of the current cursor location until *<esc>* is pressed.

I ...*<esc>*   Inserts characters at the beginning of the current line until *<esc>* is pressed.

i ...*<esc>*   Inserts characters, starting to the left of the current cursor location until *<esc>* is pressed:

                The quick brown fox jumps
                type *iyoung <esc>*
                The quick young brown fox jumps.

o ...*<esc>*   Inserts a new line below the current cursor, moves the cursor to the beginning and inserts characters until *<esc>* is pressed.

O ...*<esc>*   Inserts a new line above the current cursor, moves the cursor to the beginning of the new line and inserts characters until *<esc>* is pressed.

^H   Erases last character.

^W   Erases last word during text insertion.

Finding characters or phrases

/   Searches forward for the character string that follows it:

```
The quick brown fox jumped.
```
type */mped<cr>* or */mp<cr>*
```
The quick brown fox jumped.
```

?   Searches backward for the character string that follows it:

```
The brown fox jumped over the dog.
```
type *?br<cr>* or */brow<cr>* and so on
```
The brown fox jumped over the dog.
```

F   Finds a single following character, working backward from the cursor. A preceding count, *n*, looks for the *n*th occurrence.

```
The quick brown fox jumped.
```
type *Fb*
```
The quick brown fox jumped.
The quick brown fox jumped.
```
type *2Fo*
```
The quick brown fox jumped.
```

N   Scans for the next occurrence of the last pattern used in an /.../ or ?...? search. The scan direction is in reverse.

n   Scans for the next occurrence of the last pattern used in an /.../ or ?...? search. The scan direction is the reverse of that invoked by *N*.

f   Finds the first instance of the following character after the cursor. A count repeats the operation. This is similar to the *F* command:

```
The fox jumped over the lazy dog.
```
type *fz*
```
The fox jumped over the lazy dog.
The fox jumped over the lazy dog.
```
type *2Fo*
```
The fox jumped over the lazy dog.
```

T   Takes the following single character, locates the character before the cursor and places the cursor just after that character. It is frequently used with the *d* operator to delete characters as the cursor is moved:

```
The brown fox jumped over the dog.
```
type *tu*
```
The brown fox jumped over the dog.
The brown dog jumped over the dog.
```
type *dTw*
```
The quick browover the lazy dog
```

t   Moves the cursor forward to just before the next character that follows the *t* command. It is frequently used with the *d* operator to delete character as the cursor is moved:

```
The brown fox jumped over the dog.
```
type *tp*
```
The brown fox jumped over the dog.
The brown dog jumped over the dog.
```
type *dtu*
```
The brown dumped over the dog
```

,   Reverses the last *f, F, t* or *T* command and looks the other way in the current line. A preceding count repeats the search.

```
The fox jumped over the lazy dog.
```
type *fo*
```
The fox jumped over the lazy dog.
```
type *,*
```
The fox jumped over the lazy dog.
```

;   Repeats the last character find that was used in the last *f, F, t* or *T* command. A preceding count repeats the search.

```
The fox jumped over the lazy dog.
```
type *fo*
```
The fox jumped over the lazy dog.
```
type *,*
```
The fox jumped over the lazy dog.
```

Writing and retrieving files

These are essentially *ex* commands and must be preceded by a colon. The response from *vi* is to move to the bottom of the screen, print the colon and await the rest of the command.

:e *file*   *edit* fetches *file* and goes into edit mode without leaving *vi*.

:f [*file*]   *file* changes thename of the current file to *file* or, if typed on its own, displays the current file name.

A good use for this command is to ensure that an original file is not overwritten by accident.

```
:edit unique
:f unique.two
:w
```

In the example, the file called *unique* is loaded but the default filename is changed to *unique.two* so that any write operation creates a file called *unique.two*, rather than overwrite the original.

:re *file*   *read* inserts the contents of file immediately after the current line.

```
$ ex list
"list" 5 lines, 75 characters
:3
```

```
This is line 3
:read insert
"insert" 5 lines, 75 characters
:1,$p
This is line 1
This is line 2
This is line 3
This is line 4
This is line 5
```

:rew   *rewind* fetches the last stored version from the file and effectively discards any changes that have been made since that version was saved. The command can force a return to the stored version if no changes have been made by adding an exclamation mark to the end, for example *rew!*

:w [*file*]   *write* any changes to *file*. If a new name is given, this is used instead.

:wq   Write back any changes and quit *vi*.

Using text markers

'   Returns to a previous context or a marker, depending on the subsequent character.

m   Marks the current cursor position in one of 26 mark registers that is specified by a character from *a* to *z*.

Using text buffers

P   Puts (inserts) the last deleted text block using the current cursor position as a reference. If the deleted text comprises whole lines deleted, for example, with the *d* or *dd* command, the lines are inserted above the cursor position. If the text contains characters, they are inserted before the cursor. This command can be extended to use a specific buffer by preceding it with "*n*, where *n* is either 1-9 or a-z and specifies which buffer is used.

```
"ap    "1p
```

p   The same as *P*.

Y   Takes a copy of the current line or number of lines, if preceded by a count, and places it into a buffer for later use by either the *p* or *P* commands.

```
"ay    "1y
```

yy   Does the same as *Y*.

y   Does the same as *Y* but can be used with cursor commands. *yw* puts the next word into a buffer.

^G   Displays the file number, current line number and other statistical information, including the number of lines in the current buffer at the bottom of the screen. The percentage is the amount of buffer storage space that is taken from line 1 to the current line and gives some indication of the size of the buffer and the amount of data that is in front of the cursor.

```
~

~
"prose" [Modified] line 3 of 11 —27%—
```

Special operations

!	Used to process lines from the buffer through another program or utility.
^?	Interrupts *vi* and returns it to a state where further commands will be accepted.
#	Normally the erase character and, while inputting data, it acts as a backspace. When followed by a number, it can act as a function key and invoke a macro. If it is the erase character, the command must be preceded with a \ to prevent it from being interpreted as a backspace.
%	Moves to the parenthesis or brace that corresponds to the parenthesis or brace at the current cursor position. This is extremely useful when editing C programs and other similar text.
$	Moves the cursor to the end of the current line.
(	Moves the cursor to the beginning of a sentence and can be preceded by a count. For example,

      2 (moves the cursor backwards two sentences.

)	Moves the cursor forwards to the beginning of a sentence and can be preceded by a count. For example,

      3)   moves the cursor forwardsthree sentences.

Both the (and) commands define the end of a sentence as either a . or ! or ? followed by at least two spaces or a line end. If the spaces are not present, the sentence end will not be recognized and the behavior of these commands may appear to be erratic!

Setting options

vi supports several options that control the behavior of the screen, and so on. These options are set using the :*set* command in the following forms:

To set an option

:set option<cr>

:set option=value<cr>

To clear an option

:set no option<cr>

These are the common supported options. The names on the right are recognized abbreviations. As can be seen from the command *set all*, there are a lot more !

ai   *autoindent* automatically indents program loops.

aw   *autowrite* automatically writes before *:n* and *!.* commands are executed.

ic   *ignorecase* ignores upper or lower case when searching.

list   Tabs print as ^L.

nu   *number* lines are displayed with their line numbers.

para   *paragraphs* the names of nroff macros that start paragraphs for the *{* and *}* commands. Initially, these are set to IPLPPPQPbpP LI.

re   *redraw* simulates a smart terminal and redraws the screen after any changes.

sect   *sections* the name of macros that start sections for the *[[* and *]]* commands. The initial values are NHSHHHU.

term   The name of the terminal type being used. Useful if *vi* is invoked and the terminal specification is incorrect. *term* allows it to be changed without leaving *vi*.

```
:set all
noautoindent      number              noslowopen
autoprint         nonovice     tabstop=8
noautowrite nooptimize  taglength=0
nobeautify        paragraphs=IPLPPPQPbpPLI
tags=tags /usr/lib/tags
directory=/tmp    prompt              term=vt100
noedcompatible    noreadonly  noterse
noerrorbells      redraw              timeout
flash remap ttytype=vt100
hardtabs=8  report=5    warn
noignorecase      scroll=11    window=23
nolisp            sections=NHSHHHUuhsh+c
nowrapscan  nolist          shell=/bin/sh
wrapmargin=0      magic        shiftwidth=8
nowriteany        mesg  showmatch
```

ex commands

vi supports *ex* commands from a command line at the bottom of the screen. Indeed, many of the commands described so far are in fact *ex* commands. The command line is invoked by typing a colon while in the *vi* command mode. To be absolutely certain of which mode you are in, press Escape before typing — and ignore any beep. The response is to move the cursor to the bottom of the screen and display : as a prompt. Any *ex* command can now be executed.

7 System administration

As discussed in Chapter 1, Linux is quite capable of supporting large numbers of users. To bring some degree of control to the system, one user is nominated as a superuser and given the task of system administration. This task can vary in complexity, depending on the number of users, their level of knowledge, the type of system and other factors. Obviously, the administration of a single-user Linux workstation will be different from a system supporting several hundred users although the techniques are similar.

There are three basic jobs that the administrator carries out. The first is to organize the users into groups and provide working directories for them. Individual user, group and others access permissions control access to files. If several users need to share data, they can become members of the same group and the appropriate group permission for the files is set to allow access to them. The second function is to control access to removable media, such as floppy disks and tapes, so that a user's data is not accidently removed from the file system by another who wants to mount a different floppy disk and access different files. Included in this function is the need to maintain adequate file system backups.

The final administrative role is one of accounting and system setup. This may range from a simple, one-off session to configure the system or a full-time job, calculating individual access costs for each user. The system administrator needs superuser status and frequently logs in as the user *root* to gain the appropriate powers. Some systems have other user names, such as *adm* and *mountfsys*, which can be used to perform some administrative tasks that need superuser status — but with some restrictions.

Adding users

Before a new user can use the system, several files must be modified to enable Linux to recognize the new login name. This process is relatively simple to perform. The user's name must be entered in the file */etc/passwd* together with the associated group and other details. If the group is new, this must be added to */etc/group*. Finally, a home directory must be created, if needed.

Creating a new group

To create a new group, a new entry must be made in the file */etc/group*. Each entry consists of four fields separated by colons. The fields specify:

group name	The group name.
password	This should be empty. Group passwords are not recommended because of the high security risk and the facility may be removed in later versions of Linux.
group ID	A number from 0 to 65535, although numbers 0 to 99 are reserved.
membership	A list of user names that can join or are members of this group. It is possible for a user to be a member of several different groups, but only one is selected when the user logs in. To change to another group, the command *newgrp* is used.

An easy way to add a new entry is to use the *echo* command and redirection. To remove a user or group, edit the appropriate entry as needed. In the example shown, a new group called *author* is created, with an ID of 100 and two users as members, *steve* and *sue*.

```
#cat /etc/group
root::0:root
other::1:
bin::2:root,bin,daemon
sys::3:root,bin,sys,adm
adm::4:root,adm,daemon
mail::6:root
daemon::12:root,daemon
#echo "author::100:steve,sue" >> /etc/group
#cat /etc/group
root::0:root
other::1:
bin::2:root,bin,daemon
sys::3:root,bin,sys,adm
adm::4:root,adm,daemon
mail::6:root
daemon::12:root,daemon
author::100:steve,sue
#
```

Creating a new user

To create a new user, a new entry must be made in the file */etc/passwd*. Each entry consists of seven fields, separated by colons. The fields specify:

user name	The user name that will be entered at login.
password	Contains an encrypted password and should be left empty. The command *passwd* fills it if a password is assigned to this user.
user ID	A number from 0 to 65535, although numbers 0 to 99 are reserved with 0 for superuser.
group ID	A number from 0 to 65535, although numbers 0 to 99 are reserved and should match the group ID for the entry in */etc/group*.

account   Used to identify the user by some accounting programs and should contain the user name, department and account number.

login-directory

The directory that the user will be put into after logging into the system.

program   The program that will be invoked after a successful login. If blank, */bin/bash* is executed to provide a shell for the user. A common alternative is */bin/tcsh*.

In the example that follows, a new user *steve* has been added with a user ID of 200 and a group ID of 100. His accounting information is *Heath*1234* and login directory is */user/author/steve*. When *steve* logs in, the standard bash shell will be run.

```
#cat /etc/passwd
root:cH14bAuH/8aCU:0:1:0000-Admin(0000):/:
daemon::1:1:0000-Admin(0000):/:
bin::2:2:0000-Admin(0000):/bin:
sys::3:3:0000-Admin(0000):/usr/src:
adm::4:4:0000-Admin(0000):/usr/adm:
uucp::5:5:0000-uucp(0000):/usr/lib/uucp:
nuucp::10:10:0000-uucp(0000):/usr/spool/uucppublic:/usr/lib/uucp/uucico
lp::71:2:0000-lp(0000):/usr/spool/lp:
setup::0:0:general system administration:/usr/admin:/bin/rsh
powerdown::0:0:general system administration:/usr/admin:/bin/rsh
sysadm::0:0:general system administration:/usr/admin:/bin/rsh
checkfsys::0:0:check diskette file system:/usr/admin:/bin/rsh
makefsys::0:0:make diskette file system:/usr/admin:/bin/rsh
mountfsys::0:0:mount diskette file system:/usr/admin:/bin/rsh
umountfsys::0:0:unmount diskette file system:/usr/admin:/bin/rsh
#echo "steve::200:100:Heath*1234:/user/author/steve:/bin/bash" >>/etc
/passwd
#cat /etc/passwd
root:cH14bAuH/8aCU:0:1:0000-Admin(0000):/:
daemon::1:1:0000-Admin(0000):/:
bin::2:2:0000-Admin(0000):/bin:
sys::3:3:0000-Admin(0000):/usr/src:
adm::4:4:0000-Admin(0000):/usr/adm:
uucp::5:5:0000-uucp(0000):/usr/lib/uucp:
nuucp::10:10:0000-uucp(0000):/usr/spool/uucppublic:/usr/lib/uucp/uucico
lp::71:2:0000-lp(0000):/usr/spool/lp:
setup::0:0:general system administration:/usr/admin:/bin/rsh
powerdown::0:0:general system administration:/usr/admin:/bin/rsh
sysadm::0:0:general system administration:/usr/admin:/bin/rsh
checkfsys::0:0:check diskette file system:/usr/admin:/bin/rsh
makefsys::0:0:make diskette file system:/usr/admin:/bin/rsh
mountfsys::0:0:mount diskette file system:/usr/admin:/bin/rsh
umountfsys::0:0:unmount diskette file system:/usr/admin:/bin/rsh
steve::200:100:Heath*1234:/user/author/steve:/bin/bash
#
```

Before the user can log in correctly, the user's login directory must be created (if it does not already exist) and a *.profile* copied across. The *.profile* is a shell script that is executed automatically when the user logs in to the system and sets up the environment for the user. In the next example, a standard version is copied across. Finally, a password is assigned to *steve* by the system administrator. The password is shown as six asterisks, but in practice, it is invisible.

```
# mkdir -p /user/author/steve
# cp /etc/stdprofile /user/author/steve/.profile
# passwd steve
New password: ******
Re-enter password:  ******
#
opus
login: steve
password: ******
UNIX System V Release 3.1 88000
opus
Copyright (c) 1984 AT&T
All Rights Reserved
$ pwd
/user/author/steve
$
```

Adding terminals

For Linux systems not connected to a network, the number of users that can simultaneously log in to the system is determined by the number of serial ports and thus terminals that the system can support. However, even if ports are available to physically plug into, they will not allow a user to log in unless they have been activated in the eyes of Linux.

The first action is to ensure that the system is in multiuser mode. Linux runs in one of eleven different operating levels, levels 0 to 6, levels a, b, and c, and a special single-user level, s. In most systems, level 1 and 0 are used for single-user mode, level 2 is for multiuser mode and level 3 is often used for networking. The operating level that is invoked when the system is started is usually defined in a file called */etc/rc*. However, System V derivatives moved away from this method and have a specific "*/etc/rc*" for each level, that is *rc2* for level 2, and so on. Such systems boot automatically into multiuser mode. Earlier systems required *root* to start multiuser operation, by issuing an *init 2* command from the system console. Needless to say, a multiuser system requires users and groups to be defined before anyone can log in. When a Linux system is first installed, this is one of the normal tasks needed to commission the system.

The first operation is to modify a file */etc/inittab*, which is a database of commands for the command *init*. It contains part of the startup sequences and, more important, controls the checking of terminal ports for users wanting to log in. Each terminal port requires an individual entry. Each entry has four fields, separated by colons, which specify the following:

id   An identifier name of 1 to 4 letters which is used to identify the process in the kernel's process table. It is also used as an entry in */etc/utmp* and */etc/wtmp,* which can be interrogated by the *who* command.

level   The level here is compared with the operating level that *init* is trying to establish. If it matches, the entry is active. This field can be any number from 0 to 6 or the letters a, b or c. If it is empty, the entry is valid with any numeric level.

type   This further determines the entry's validity and how the entry will be executed.

Valid types are:

off   The entry will not run.

once   The entry only runs when *init* is moving Linux to another operating level.

wait   Similar to *once* but forces *init* to wait until the process has finished processing before getting the next entry.

respawn Causes the entry to run as long as *init* remains at its current operating level. This is the *type* used for enabling terminal ports.

boot   Similar to *once* but is only started when the operating level becomes numeric, that is, when the system is started.

bootwait Similar to *wait* but is only started when the operating system becomes numeric, that is, when the system is started.

power   Similar to *once* but is only started if *init* receives a SIGPWR signal indicating a power failure.

powerwait Similar to *wait* but is only started if *init* receives a SIGPWR signal indicating a power failure.

initdefault A special case where its level determines the operating level that *init* will establish when the system is booted up. If there is no entry, *init* asks for the level. It accepts any numeric state .

process The action that *init* asks the shell to execute. The *process* can use shell syntax but must take care to redirect *stdin*, *stdout* and *stderr* as necessary. To enable a terminal, the *process* invokes */etc/getty*, which polls the terminal port for any activity.

The *inittab* file shown below has examples of the various *types* and *processes* described above. The last four entries enable four terminal ports using the *type respawn* and */etc/getty* as the *process*. Two arguments are passed to */etc/getty*: The first is the terminal port name, which is found in the directory */dev*, and the second is a reference stored in */etc/gettydefs*. The port name depends on the system and the Linux implementation — look at the system information for the name. The *gettydefs* reference tends to be fairly consistent — the most important ones are named after baud rates — 19,200, 9,600, 2,400, and so on. Each reference is to a set of parameters that control how the terminal port works. Needless to say, the right reference must be used to ensure correct functioning.

```
#cat inittab
zu::sysinit:/etc/bzapunix </dev/console >/dev/console 2>&1
tu::sysinit:touch -c /unix </dev/console >/dev/console 2>&1
fs::sysinit:/etc/bcheckrc </dev/console >/dev/console 2>&1
mt:23:bootwait:/etc/brc </dev/console >/dev/console 2>&1
is:2:initdefault:
p3:s1234:power:/etc/shutdown -y -i0 -g0 >/dev/console 2>&1
s0:056:wait:/etc/rc0 >/dev/console 2>&1 </dev/console
s1:1:wait:/etc/shutdown -y -iS -g0 >/dev/console 2>&1 </dev/console
s2:23:wait:/etc/rc2 >/dev/console 2>&1 </dev/console
s3:3:wait:/etc/rc3 >/dev/console 2>&1 </dev/console
of:0:wait:/etc/uadmin 2 0 >/dev/console 2>&1 </dev/console
fw:5:wait:/etc/uadmin 2 2 >/dev/console 2>&1 </dev/console
RB:6:wait:echo "\nThe system is being restarted."
>/dev/console 2>&1
rb:6:wait:/etc/uadmin 2 1 >/dev/console 2>&1 </dev/console
co:234:respawn:/etc/getty console console
c1:234:respawn:/etc/getty con1 console
c2:234:respawn:/etc/getty con2 console
c3:234:respawn:/etc/getty con3 console
#
```

To find out which references are available, print out */etc/gettydefs* — but be warned, it's a big file! The parameters are similar to those used in *stty*. The entry format is:

label # initial flags # final flags # login msg # next label

where:

label   is the reference name.

initial flags are the settings used by *getty* to print out the login message and get the user name and password.

final flags   are the settings used after the login has been completed.

login msg   is the login message that is printed (*login:*).

next label   is the name of the next reference.

The easiest method of making a new entry is to copy an existing one and modify it, not forgetting to change the *label* and *next label* fields. In the addition made to */etc/inittab* shown, the *gettydefs* reference 19200 sets the terminal port to 19,200 baud rate.

```
# echo "sh:234:respawn:/etc/getty tty1 19200" >> /etc/inittab
#cat inittab
zu::sysinit:/etc/bzapunix </dev/console >/dev/console 2>&1
tu::sysinit:touch -c /unix </dev/console >/dev/console 2>&1
fs::sysinit:/etc/bcheckrc </dev/console >/dev/console 2>&1
mt:23:bootwait:/etc/brc </dev/console >/dev/console 2>&1
is:2:initdefault:
p3:s1234:power:/etc/shutdown -y -i0 -g0 >/dev/console 2>&1
s0:056:wait:/etc/rc0 >/dev/console 2>&1 </dev/console
s1:1:wait:/etc/shutdown -y -iS -g0 >/dev/console 2>&1 </dev/console
s2:23:wait:/etc/rc2 >/dev/console 2>&1 </dev/console
s3:3:wait:/etc/rc3 >/dev/console 2>&1 </dev/console
of:0:wait:/etc/uadmin 2 0 >/dev/console 2>&1 </dev/console
fw:5:wait:/etc/uadmin 2 2 >/dev/console 2>&1 </dev/console
RB:6:wait:echo "\nThe system is being restarted." >/dev/console 2>&1
rb:6:wait:/etc/uadmin 2 1 >/dev/console 2>&1 </dev/console
co:234:respawn:/etc/getty console console
c1:234:respawn:/etc/getty con1 console
c2:234:respawn:/etc/getty con2 console
c3:234:respawn:/etc/getty con3 console
sh:234:respawn:/etc/getty tty1 19200
$
```

With the modifications made, the final operation is to tell *init* to scan the modified *inittab* list. This is done using the command *init n*, where *n* is the appropriate operating level (usually 2, 3 or 4). *init* scans the file and finds the new entry at the end. The level is set at 2, 3, 4 — and therefore matches. The type *respawn* causes the process to run while *init* is still executing and so the process */etc/getty tty1 19200* is executed. This goes to the terminal port and prints out the login message if a terminal is connected. If there is no terminal, the system continues to try to establish contact with a user. If the terminal port does not exist, frequent messages are sent to *root* complaining that the hardware does not exist. These messages are infuriating, to say the least, and the only remedy is to change the entry in */etc/inittab* from *respawn* to *off* and execute *init* again. The moral is to only enable the terminal ports that are physically connected to the system and set any other terminal entries to off. Many systems are supplied with */dev* files for all the possible hardware devices the system could use. However, just because the */dev* file is present, it does not follow that the hardware is present.

Passwords

Many Linux systems have large numbers of users whose data needs to be shared or restricted, and access to the superuser is restricted. This inevitably requires password protection to be set up — and strictly adhered to. When delivered, most systems do not have any password protection enabled. It is the responsibility of the system administrator to enable passwords for all users. Here are some suggestions:

- *All* users that appear in */etc/passwd* must be allocated passwords — not just *root*, *adm*, and so on.
- Change the passwords regularly and, for the best security, do not make them obvious.
- If necessary, create some "guest" users with a restricted shell. This allows infrequent users to access the system in a controlled manner.

Checking the file system

Linux systems perform a file system check as part of their startup routines. The *fsck* command is normally used. If new disks or partitions are added they are not automatically checked unless the startup script — usually one of the *rc* scripts stored in the */etc/rc.d* directory — is modified to include them.

fsck

fsck [-AVRTNV] [-s] [-t fstype] [fs-options] filesys [...]

The *fsck* command examines the file system specified and will repair as necessary. It operates interactively, although this can be overruled by setting some of the options. The file system is not the normal / or other file name, but is the special */dev* name for the disk that contains it. If the file system is not mounted, the raw device can be checked — and this is considerably faster. The command *df* displays the file system names of all disks that are mounted. The following options are interpreted by *fsck*:

-A   Walk through the */etc/fstab* file and try to check all file systems in one run. This option is typically used from the */etc/rc* system initalization file, instead of multiple commands for checking a single file system.

-R   When checking all file systems with the *-A* flag, skip the root file system (in case it's already mounted read-write).

-T   Don't show the title on startup.

-N   Don't execute, just show what would be done.

-s   Serialize *fsck* operations. This is a good idea if you are checking multiple file systems.

-V   Produce verbose output, including all file-system-specific commands that are executed.

-t fstype   Specifies the type of file system to be checked. When the -A flag is specified, only file systems that match *fstype* are checked. If *fstype* is prefixed with *no* only file systems whose file system does not match *fstype* are checked.

fs-options	Any options that are not understood by *fsck*, or that follow the -- option are treated as file-system-specific options to be passed to the file-system-specific checker. Currently, standardized file system-specific options are somewhat in flux. Although not guaranteed, the following options are supported by most file system checkers.
-a	Automatically repair the file system without any questions (use this option with caution).
-r	Interactively repair the file system (ask for confirmations).

If there are files that exist without owners, these are put into a directory called */lost+found*. To create space for these files, the directory must have some files copied into it to allocate storage space. These files are subsequently removed to free the directory for the orphan files.

```
$df
/ (/dev/dsk/c1d0s0 ): 15736 blocks 6330 i-nodes
$fsck -f /dev/dsk/c1d0s0\

  /dev/dsk/c1d0s0
  File System: root Volume: Rev:G4
  ** Phase 1 - Check Blocks and Sizes
  ** Phase 5 - Check Free List
  2998 files 57778 blocks 15736 free
$fsck -n /dev/dsk/c1d0s0

  /dev/dsk/c1d0s0 (NO WRITE)
  File System: root Volume: Rev:G4

  ** Phase 1 - Check Blocks and Sizes
  ** Phase 2 - Check Pathnames
  ** Phase 3 - Check Connectivity
  ** Phase 4 - Check Reference Counts
  ** Phase 5 - Check Free List
  2998 files 57778 blocks 15736 free

$
```

Using floppy disks

In Linux, unlike many operating systems, floppy disks and other removable media cannot be interchanged at will. Linux only recognizes a floppy disk as part of the file system if it is mounted, and it presumes that it is present until it is unmounted. If the medium is removed or replaced without following a strict protocol, data can be lost or corrupted. This protocol is simple — before using media, they are mounted using the *mount* command. Before they are removed, *umount* is used to ensure it is updated and removed from the file system. Once this command has successfully completed, the medium can be removed.

mount

mount device target [-r]

mount tells the system that a removal file system is present on *device* and that it can be accessed via the directory *target*. The *-r* option makes the directory target read only. *device* is normally the special device file for a floppy disk or other removable media contained in the directory */dev*. Consult your system documentation for the correct name — it will probably be */dev/fd0* for drive A and */dev/fd1* for drive B. The directory target must exist and the convention in most systems is to use */mnt*, although this is not mandatory — I use */flopA* and */flopB*. If other files exist in the target directory, they will become inaccessible after the mounting procedure and are effectively replaced by the medium's file system. The files are not deleted or changed, although it may appear that they have gone. When the file system is unmounted, the original files in the target directory appear again.

It is good practice to use the *-r* (read only) option with strange media to prevent any corruption. It was possible, on some older systems, to corrupt a floppy disk by mounting it using the wrong format. The read only option prevents such problems.

If there is an entry in */etc/fstab* then the directory name can be used with *mount* and *umount* without having to type in all the details.

```
ess2:/etc# cat /etc/fstab
/dev/hda3   swap      swap        defaults   1   1
/dev/hda2   /         ext2        defaults   1   1
/dev/hda1   /MSDOS    msdos       defaults   1   1
none        /proc     proc        defaults   1   1
/dev/fd0    /flopA    msdos       defaults   1   1
ess2:/etc# mount /flopA
mount: block device /dev/fd0 is write-protected, mounting read-only
ess2:/etc# ls -alsi /flopA
total 1396
      1    7 drwxr-xr-x    2 root     root        7168 Jan  1  1970 ./
      2    1 drwxr-xr-x   19 root     root        1024 Nov 20 05:53 ../
    441    1 -rwxr-xr-x    1 root     root         537 Dec 28  1995 302.db_*
    442    1 -rwxr-xr-x    1 root     root         768 Dec 28  1995 332.db_*
    443    1 -rwxr-xr-x    1 root     root         783 Dec 28  1995 340.db_*
```

umount

umount device

Umount is the opposite of *mount* and removes the file system associated with the device. It should be executed prior to removal of any media. It sends a message if any file within the file system is being used (still being accessed) or if a user's current directory is within the file system.

Both *mount* and *umount* are normally privileged and require superuser status to execute. The reason is simple — the whole file system can be at risk if there is uncontrolled exchange of media without obeying the protocol. The main danger arises when media are replaced without using *umount* and *mount*. The system assumes that the current media have not been changed and may update it and thus, destroy both the new system data and the data originally on the media. To control this potential problem, some systems only allow removable media to be used for archive and backup and force all access to be made via *cpio* or *tar*. Other implementations have more trust in their users and change the permissions so any user can use *mount* and *umount* as necessary.

Formatting media

Before any disk can be mounted, it must be formatted and a file system created on it. Disks are usually formatted using the *dinit* command, although many PC-based systems rely on the MS-DOS *format* command to do the job instead. Linux is no exception to this! Once the media have been formatted, the file system is created using the *mkfs* command. This creates the file and directory structures and is an essential prerequisite for a mountable disk.

Backing up hard disks

Every Linux administrator should have to go through that terrible moment when the system fails to recognize a hard disk and the nightmare of "when did I last back it up?", leading to the thought of the hundreds of hours of work that have been lost! It is at such times, or when a file has been mistakenly deleted, that the importance of backing up the files stored on fixed disks to floppy disks or some other media, is realized, and backing up is no longer seen as another chore thatcan be put off. After all, until this happens, the "it will never happen to me" syndrome exists!

To put the records straight, I have experienced eight hard disk failures — five due to software corruption and three to head crashes. The average amount of data stored on each disk was about 600 Mbytes. Fortunately, all the data was backed up and after either reformatting or repairing the disk, the data was re-installed. Hard disks can fail, and unless a game of Russian Roulette with your data and the time taken to create it appeals, make sure data is regularly backed up. While this is good practice with all computer systems, it is especially so with a Linux system because of the ease with which it is possible to corrupt the file system. The biggest danger concerns the use of memory buffers and caches, which mean that the mass storage is not immediately updated following a write — and therefore the only copy of the data is in memory. If the system loses power, this data is lost and the data on the hard disk will be incomplete. Worse still, if the lost data contained *inode* or *superblock* information, there is a good chance that the entire file system may be corrupted. While good discipline can prevent the system from being accidentally switched off, the only protection the administrator can offer is a regular backup procedure and/or the provision of an uninterruptable power supply.

Backup suggestions

- Regularly save current files as you work — a power outage can happen at any time!
- Execute the *sync* command frequently to force the disk to be updated.
- Work on copies of important files — this is important when performing "major surgery" on system files and so on. Never make changes to a master copy.
- Back up using at least two sets of backups. This may seem extravagant — but relying on a single set can be extremely dangerous. I have had three separate incidents of floppy-based backups destroyed because of a floppy disk failing. Two of them were due to a faulty disk drive that scratched the disk when they were inserted. Although the drive was easy to replace, there was not a second backup copy — and a lot of data was lost. If there is only a single backup and this is corrupted during restoration, the data is irretrievably lost. I use three sets of backups — two copies of the current data and a third stored off site in case of fire, flood or other catastrophe.
- Treat backup disks or tapes with great care; they are your insurance policy.
- Clearly label backup tapes and disks.
  Include the command that was used to create the backup.
  Use different-colored disks, labels or marking.
  Mark the backup sets so they can easily be identified: odd, even, set 1, set 2 etc.
- Call the disks or tapes by a unique set name e.g. Duplicate and Copy.
- Mark the set with the date of the last backup. I include the current date within the file name e.g. Data Duplicate 12-10-96.
- Back up regularly! Never put it off! If there is not time to backup completely, copy the changed files onto a floppy disk or tape.
- Always label the backup media! If a label is not available, use a pencil to write a name on the disk or tape and write-protect it, to prevent it from being mistaken as blank media.

There are several methods of backing up disks, depending on the media and backup program used.

Media

The traditional medium is the humble floppy disk, which is cheap and reliable — but an awful lot can be required to back up up several hundred megabytes. Most systems have a floppy disk drive and this method is available on most smaller systems. Larger systems tend to use magnetic tape, either as a 9-track reel or in a cassette or cartridge. Tape streamers are getting faster and their popularity is definitely increasing. They offer large amounts of data storage on a small tape at a low cost. For systems with very large file systems, tape is really the only viable option when compared with using several hundred floppies. Data transfer rates of 10-20 Mbytes per second can be achieved and there is usually no need to constantly monitor the operation.

Removable hard disks are a faster alternative. Data transfer is fast — but the amount of storage is not as great as that of tape — digital tapes can hold several gigabytes today. One big advantage of removable disks is that it is easy and quick to retrieve a single file. With the low cost of hard disks, it is economic to add a second drive and use this to back up the main disk.

Backup commands

The commands *cpio*, *tar* and *dd* are all capable of backing up data, although the first two are probably the most commonly used. Whichever technique is used, it is highly recommended that the complete command line that was used to create the backup is written on the disk or tape label. Although these commands perform similar functions, they are not cross-compatible. For further information on these commands, refer to Chapter 2.

The boot disk

One often forgotten aspect of backup is the boot disk or tape, which is needed to start the system after a failure. This should include the utilities used to create the backup in the first place. Without such a disk or tape, the work saved in the backups is effectively lost. With MS-DOS, this involves creating a system disk and installing the system files, together with any specific device drivers and software. This process is relatively simple. With Linux systems, this process is extremely varied — some systems supply a master copy of a boot disk or tape and recommend its duplication. Others supply documentation describing how such media can be created; some implementations do neither and rely on the whole system being reinstalled before any backups can be used. Consult the system documentation to find out which method should be used. Duplicate the relevant media and treat them just like backups — make three copies and store one off-site.

Shutting the system down

This section is dedicated to all those who have switched off a Linux machine by simply pulling out the main plug or switching off the electricity supply. **THIS IS AN EXTREMELY FOOLHARDY THING TO DO**. Linux does not update all the files and directories immediately after they are changed and this must be done *before* switching the computer off. In addition, users on the system may have programs running — and switching the computer off in the middle of these activities can also damage the system. If the system is not shutdown in a controlled manner, it is possible for the whole file system to be corrupted and lost. It is very much like playing Russian Roulette. In the majority of cases, nothing will happen — but there is always that risk. For the record, I have had to restore more Linux systems due to the supervisor typing the wrong commands than through file corruption from interrupting the power supply. However, I have lost a complete file system twice. The first time was due to a power failure and the second was when a cleaner unplugged the computer to use the electric socket!

There are several ways of shutting the system down. The standard method uses a *shutdown* utility that brings the system down and ensures that all data is written safely to disk. It also sends a message to all users, telling them that the system is about to close down and that they should log off immediately to make sure that their files and data are not corrupted. There are times when these utilities do not work, in which case, an alternative method is to use the *sync* command — although this is slightly more risky.

The general method for a controlled system shutdown is straightforward. The superuser moves to the root directory using the system console, executes the *shutdown* command and waits for a message from the system to indicate that the system is in single-user mode. At this point, the command *sync* is executed three times by the supervisor and the system checked to ensure that no disks are being accessed — no access lights are lit and there are no access sounds from the disk drives. At this point, the system can be powered off. This general technique varies from implementation to implementation.

If the system needs to be brought down in a hurry, if the supervisor is not available or the *shutdown* commands are missing (yes, I have deleted the *shutdown* commands by mistake!), any user can execute the *sync* command three times and wait until any disk access has completed before switching off. The risk with this approach is that no warning is automatically given to other users and their files may still be open when the system is switched off. As a result, these files may be corrupted. However, it is still a far better method than just powering off the computer!

shutdown

shutdown [-krhfnc] [-t secs] time [warning message]

-k	Don't really shutdown, only warn.
-r	Reboot after shutdown.
-h	Halt after shutdown.
-f	Do a "fast" reboot.
-n	Do not go through "init" but go down real fast.
-c	Cancel a running shutdown.
-t secs	Delay between warning and kill signal.

For example,

shutdown -r   will shut down the system immediately and reboot the system.

shutdown 60 will shut down the system in 60 seconds time.

Shutdown performs the following tasks:

- It broadcasts a warning message to all logged on users, informing them that the system will close down in 60 (usually) seconds and that they should log off now.
- It then executes the *init 0* command, which returns the system to its single user state.
- *shutdown* then uses *sync* to ensure that all data is written to disk.

Shutdown can only be executed by the superuser from the *root* directory when using the system console. If the system is shut down from another terminal other than the console, the system will appear to hang when it is next booted. To get around this, the terminal that was used to shutdown the system must be re-instated. The only way I have found to get around this problem is to re-install the software!

sync

Some Linux implementations allow the system to be shut down from any terminal, while others insist on the system console(the terminal that was used to bring the system up). If a terminal other than the system console is used to shut down the system, this can cause problems the next time the system is started up. The reason for this is simple: Linux usually starts up using the terminal that was last used to shut it down. If another terminal is used, the system console sees the beginning of the startup messages, but all further messages are transferred to the other terminal. To the system console, the system appears to have crashed, when all that is needed is to use the other terminal. On a large system, this may be physically impossible or impractical, in which case, the system may need to be rebuilt or restored from backups.

8 Linux Networking

Telnet and FTP

Using terminal emulation programs, it is possible to access the Linux host as a terminal. It is also possible to exchange files using transfer protocols such as Kermit, which is installed on both the Linux system and the PC.

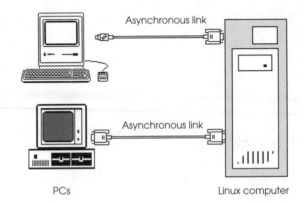

PCs   Linux computer

Although very simple, this approach does have some disadvantages. Each user needs a separate cable to the Linux system which, in turn, needs a dedicated serial port for each user. With a large number of PCs connected, the cabling can rapidly become unwieldy. Anyone who has seen 20 or more serial lines going into the back of a machine will immediately understand the problem. In addition, the serial line will only work over distances greater than 10 meters if special line drivers are used to boost the signal. This adds to the cost. Data transfer rates of about 9,600 to 38,000 baud are fine for updating a screen – but very slow for transferring data.

This solution is acceptable for small numbers of users who only need terminal access and the occasional ability to transfer files.

Terminal emulation via Ethernet

It is possible to use Ethernet to replace serial communication and improve data transfer rates, without having to implement a full traditional network, complete with networking software, and so on.

This is often done using TCP/IP and a set of associated utilities commonly referred to as Telnet. Telnet started out as a utility that ran on UNIX machine and allowed users to log into other UNIX machines or hosts that were linked to the Ethernet network using the TCP/IP protocol. This software is now so commonly used that it has become part of the standard software supplied with most UNIX machines. In addition, there are many Telnet-compatible utilities available for other PCs and workstations that allow them to act as terminals across the Ethernet network. There are many utilities available either as commercial products or in the public domain. NCSA Telnet and Cabletron's TCP/IP Connect are good examples.

Using TCP/IP in this way, the PCs are effectively acting as clients and the Linux machine acts as a server. There is one important difference between this configuration and a PC-only network. In this configuration, the PCs are only acting as terminals logging into and using the processing power in the Linux machine. There are two Linux utilities that are then used to link the PC as a terminal to the Linux computers and provide file transfer. Telnet provides the communication link and its associated ftp utility provides the ability to file transfer.

Setting up the link

The first prerequisite is to install the TCP/IP networking software that provides the communication protocols that allow Telnet to link into the system. There are two ways of doing this with Linux: either recompile a kernel and include the appropriate network support or use a prebuilt kernel with the networking support already included. Such kernels often have the descriptions or keywords *net* or *network* in their documentation. The next step is to link the PCs onto the Ethernet network using the appropriate connectors. After this, certain Linux files must be updated with information defining the various Linux computer names, any aliases and most importantly, their IP addresses.

The main details of how to rebuild the kernel are covered in Chapter 2. The next sections describe the main options that have to be set within the kernel configuration file to ensure that the common networking facilities described in this chapter can be used. The underlined option is the one that is recommended for a simple functional installation.

Selecting the file system support

File systems can be shared over the network using a protocol called NFS that assigns a special file system to the shared files so that the system knows that the files are located on the network and not locally. As a result, this file system has to be included in the kernel to allow it to recognize requests for access to shared files and directories across the network. This is done by selecting NFS support in the configuration file as shown. There are two parameters: the first simply includes the NFS file system or not and the second allows the kernel to use a root file system that is located on another Linux system connected to the network. As the notes say, most people say no to this option.

NFS filesystem support (CONFIG_NFS_FS) [Y/m/n/?] ?

If you are connected to some other (usually local) Unix computer (using SLIP, PLIP, PPP or ethernet) and want to mount files residing on that computer (the NFS server) using the Network File Sharing protocol, say Y. If you don't know what all this is about, say N. If you might be or think you will be connecting to a Sun workstation, select Y.

Root file system on NFS (CONFIG_ROOT_NFS) [N/y/?] ?

If you want your Linux box to mount its whole root filesystem from some other computer over the net via NFS (presumably because your box doesn't have a harddisk), say Y. Read Documentation/nfsroot.txt for details. Most people say N here.

Selecting the network software

Network facilities require additional driver support and again these must be enabled within the kernel configuration file. Most of the options are not needed. My recommended replies are underlined.

Network device support (CONFIG_NETDEVICES) [Y/n/?] ?

You can say N here in case you don't intend to connect to any other computer at all or all your connections will be either via UUCP. If unsure, say Y.

Dummy net driver support (CONFIG_DUMMY) [M/n/y/?] ?

If you use SLIP or PPP, you might want to enable it.

EQL (serial line load balancing) support (CONFIG_EQUALIZER) [N/y/m/?] ?

For most users, this is not needed so select N. It allows two serial links to be combined to create a faster virtual link.

PLIP (parallel port) support (CONFIG_PLIP) [N/y/m/?] ?

PLIP (Parallel Line Internet Protocol) is used to create a mini network consisting of two (or, rarely, more) local machines. It's safer to say N here.

PPP (point-to-point) support (CONFIG_PPP) [N/y/m/?] ?

PPP (Point to Point Protocol) is a newer and better SLIP. It serves the same purpose: sending Internet traffic over telephone (and other serial) lines. If unsure, say N.

SLIP (serial line) support (CONFIG_SLIP) [N/y/m/?] ?

Say Y if you intend to use SLIP or CSLIP (compressed SLIP) to connect to your Internet service provider or to connect to some other local Unix box or if you want to configure your Linux box as a Slip/CSlip server for other people to dial in.If not select N.

Radio network interfaces (CONFIG_NET_RADIO) [N/y/?] ?

Radio based interfaces for Linux. Most users don't want or need this and select N. If unsure, say N.

Ethernet (10 or 100Mbit) (CONFIG_NET_ETHERNET) [Y/n/?] ?

```
Ethernet is the most common protocol used on Local Area Networks and this
option is undoubtedly a Y if you need to connect the target system to any
other computer. You will need to know the Ethernet card type/manufacturer
in order to respond to further questions.  If the system is being used in
isolation, select N.
```

Hardware selection

The final choice is to select the driver for the installed Ethernet card. There are many drivers available and the process involves going through the list and selecting the required one. Some of the questions are generic and try to prevent you from having to scroll through tens of options. One point: the NE1000/ NE2000 drivers are in the Other ISA cards section after the HP cards. Once configured, rebuild and reinstall the kernel.

3COM cards (CONFIG_NET_VENDOR_3COM) [N/y/?] ?

```
If you have one of these cards installed, select Y. If not select N.
```

AMD LANCE and PCnet (AT1500 and NE2100) support (CONFIG_LANCE) [N/y/?] ?

```
If you have one of these cards installed, select Y. If not select N.
```

Western Digital/SMC cards (CONFIG_NET_VENDOR_SMC) [N/y/?] ?

```
If you have one of these cards installed, select Y. If not select N.
```

Other ISA cards (CONFIG_NET_ISA) [Y/n/?] ?

```
If you have a different card to one of the previos mentioned types select
Y. If not select N.
```

One final point: the Ethernet drivers will search through the I/O addresses to find a configured card. This can cause a hangup if it finds a card that it thinks is an Ethernet card but is not. It is a good idea to tell the kernel where the card is by adding a parameter such as *eth0=0x300* to the *lilo* configuration file or typing it in on the command line.

Checking the kernel

To check that the kernel is running, look at the logon messages for confirmation that all is well. Once logged in, the command *dmesg* can also be used to see them.

```
Swansea University Computer Society NET3.030 Snap #1 for Linux 1.3.4
NET3: Unix domain sockets 0.07 BETA for Linux NET3.030.
Swansea University Computer Society TCP/IP for NET3.030 (Snapshot #1)
IP Protocols: ICMP, UDP, TCP
NE*000 ethercard probe at 0x300: 00 20 e4 80 06 9d
eth0: NE2000 found at 0x300, using IRQ 10.
ne.c:v1.10 9/23/94 Donald Becker (becker@cesdis.gsfc.nasa.gov)
```

To check that the network software is running, look at the daemon list in the boot-up messages. This is only displayed on the boot up terminal and cannot be seen by using *dmesg*. If it contains *nfsd*, all well and good.

To check that the NFS file system is installed, look at the file */proc/filesystems*.

```
hosts1:/proc# cat /proc/filesystems
        minix
        ext2
        umsdos
        msdos
nodev   proc
nodev   nfs
        iso9660
        hpfs
hosts1:/proc#
```

With the kernel rebuilt and running, the final operation is to configure the network information that identifies the computer to the network.

Using netconfig

The network utilities such as Telnet, identify which Linux computer or host that it will link to by a name and·a four-part Internet Protocol address (IP) which should be unique. Each host computer on the Ethernet network that wishes to support Telnet logons must have a unique IP address. This should not be confused with the Ethernet address, which is has a six-part value.

The Ethernet address is supplied by the individual Ethernet controller while the IP address is defined in a file called */etc/hosts* which provides the master list of which computers are on the network and accessible. In the examples that follow there are two Linux computers on the same network as an Apple Macintosh. The Apple Mac runs NCSA Telnet to log into either of the two Linux computers.

```
# cat /etc/hosts
# Sample /etc/hosts file
hosts1:~# cat /etc/hosts
#
# hosts         This file describes a number of hostname-to-address
#               mappings for the TCP/IP subsystem.  It is mostly
#               used at boot time, when no name servers are running.
#               On small systems, this file can be used instead of a
#               "named" name server.  Just add the names, addresses
#               and any aliases to this file...
#
# By the way, Arnt Gulbrandsen <agulbra@nvg.unit.no> says that 127.0.0.1
# should NEVER be named with the name of the machine.  It causes problems
# for some (stupid) programs, irc and reputedly talk. :^)
#

# For loopbacking.
127.0.0.1        localhost
200.200.200.30          ess2.tvr.com ess2
89.16.32.01             hosts1
89.16.32.02             hosts2
#
```

As the example shows, there are four addresses allocated to the network for the machines called *hosts1*, *hosts2* and so on. Although there are four addresses allocated, they do not all have to physically connected. This file contains the IP addresses for each machine. By changing the entry for the appropriate name, this address can be changed. When the TCP software is started, this file is used to locate the IP address for the Linux computer. Its node name is used to locate the address. If no match is found, the TCP initialization is stopped and remote users cannot log in. The two Linux computers are called *hosts1* and *hosts2* and have the same */etc/hosts* file.

Please note that the addresses in */etc/hosts* and in the startup message for the computer *hosts1* are in fact the same although they have different numbering. The message has converted the */etc/hosts* address from decimal into hexadecimal. There is a second file called */etc/hosts.equiv* which is used to define Linux computers that share accounts and are thus equivalent. This file is used by two utilities called *rsh* and *rcp* which are remote access programs that provide remote command execution and file copying.

```
# cat /etc/hosts.equiv
ess2
host1
host2

#
```

This file should contain all the names of the Linux computers described in */etc/hosts*. One common mistake is to create the */etc/hosts* file and then forget to change the hostname of the machine to the appropriate name to match the entry in */etc/hosts*. The node name is changed using the *hostname* command. Note that the cursor will not be updated until after the user has logged in again.

```
hosts1:~# hostname
hosts1
hosts1:~# hostname ess2
hosts1:~# hostname
ess2
hosts1:~#
```

A quick way of setting all this information up is to use the *netconfig* script which will ask for the required information. It asks for the names and addresses that the computer will need. If the system is attached to a fully supported network, these details should come from the system administrator. If not, then you will have to provide them yourself. Here is a set of examples.

Hostname   This can be any name without whitespace or punctuation e.g. cerbera, steve but not sally-anne or dave's.

Domain name   This is common to the computers on the network and should be the same as all the other systems. The name can be any alphanumeric name and full stops are allowed. For public networks, there is a name registration process but for private ones this is not the case. Example names are *tvr.com*, *study.com* and so on.

IP number   This is a four-digit number with a full stop between each one. The numbers can be between 0 and 255 e.g. 200.200.200.30, 102.0.34.89.

Gateway   If you don't have one, simply enter the IP address.

Netmask   Unless told otherwise, use 255.255.255.0

Loopback   This is a testing mode that uses a special IP address. If you want to use networking, you will not be using this mode only.

Name server   For most systems except this with specialized networks, the name server is not used.

Configuring the remote terminal

The remote terminal must also be configured with the various host names and the respective IP addresses. With other hosts, this is done by ensuring that their own copy of the file */etc/hosts* contains all the host names and addresses. For other remote terminals such as PCs and Apple Macintoshes, this is usually done by a special configuration file, similar to the */etc/hosts* file but unique to each application. Many applications are now using a simple concept where all that is needed is the IP address and do not need to modify a */etc/hosts* file or equivalent.

```
ftp=yes
termtype="vt100"
arptime=5
block=200
hardware=Ether
commandkeys=yes
name=default
scrollback=200
erase=delete
tektype=1
vtwrap=yes
vtwidth=80
vtlines=24
clearsave=yes
contime=20
retrans=30
mtu=512
maxseg=512
rwin=512
name=hosts1 ; hostip=89.16.32.01 ; nameserver=1
name=hosts2 ;hostip=89.16.32.02; nameserver=2
#
#Here is the corresponding /etc/hosts file from the UNIX system
```

```
#
#        89.16.32.01 hosts1
#        89.16.32.02 hosts2
#        89.16.32.03 hosts3
#        89.16.32.04 hosts4
#        89.16.32.05 hosts5
#
# The system name is host1
#
```

As in the file listing above for the Apple Macintosh NCSA Telnet program configuration file *config.tel*, the file will often contain other information about the link such as terminal characteristics and Ethernet configuration data. The two hosts that this Macintosh links to are *hosts1* and *hosts2* and their IP addresses are located towards the bottom of the file. The corresponding */etc/hosts* file for the UNIX hosts has been appended as a set of *rem* statements – prefixed by # – to act as a reminder of how they are named.

Logging in

To log into another host from your own Linux system, the telnet utility is used as shown. The first login procedure logs the terminal into its main UNIX machine called *hosts1*. Once logged in, the user can execute telnet to access the second host called *hosts2*.

```
Linux 1.3.20 (hosts1) (ttyp0)

hosts1 login: root
Last login: Sat Nov 16 11:02:46 from 200.200.200.200
Linux 1.3.20.
hosts1:~#
#
# telnet hosts2
Trying...
Connected to hosts2.
Escape character is '^]'.

Linux 1.3.20 (hosts2)

hosts2 login: root
Last login: Sat Nov 16 11:02:46 from 200.200.200.200
Linux 1.3.20.
hosts2:~#
#
```

To exit from the other machine, the escape character is used, which normally defaults to ^] (CONTROL-]). Once the link has been made, the login prompt will appear as usual and allow you to log in. The normal procedure of checking the login name against the entries in */etc/passwd* is carried out as normal and as if the login was from the system console or from a serial port.

From an Apple Mac or PC, the process is similar but slightly different. Normally the link is opened by making a connection in which a name will be asked for that will be used to locate the IP address in the configuration file and thus locate the hosts itself. In the example shown, this is called *hosts2*.

Once the connection has been established, the normal login message is displayed in a window and the session continues in a similar manner to that of a login over a serial port. Note that the terminal or *stty* settings may be different – a common problem is the lack of local echo so that the data sent to the host is not seen. This can be changed by using the *stty* command directly or as part of a *.profile* file or by configuring the application to support local echo.

To end the session and log off, CONTROL-D is normally sufficient.

Telnet and ftp commands

There are several commands associated with the telnet utility that allow a user to remotely log in to another UNIX or Linux host, copy files, execute commands on the remote machine and even remote file copying.

telnet

telnet [host [port]]

telnet is used to communicate with another host using the TELNET protocol. If *telnet* is invoked without arguments, it enters command mode, indicated by its prompt (telnet>). In this mode, it accepts and executes the commands listed below. If it is invoked with arguments, it performs an *open* command with those arguments.

Once a connection has been opened, *telnet* enters an input mode. The input mode entered will be either character-at-a-time or line-by-line depending on what the remote system supports.

While connected to a remote host, *telnet* command mode may be entered by typing the *telnet* escape character (usually CONTROL-]). When in command mode, the normal terminal editing conventions are available.

The following commands are available. Only enough of each command to uniquely identify it need be typed (this is also true for arguments to the *mode*, *set*, *toggle*, and *display* commands).

open *host [port]*

Open a connection to the named host. If no port number is specified, *telnet* will attempt to contact a TELNET server at the default port. The host specification may be either a host name or an IP address. If a host name is used it must be contained in the file */etc/ hosts.*

close   Close a *telnet* session and return to command mode.

quit   Close any open *telnet* session and exit *telnet* command mode. Logging off will also close a session and exit.

mode *type*   This changes the transmission mode to either character-by-character (mode character) or line-by-line (mode line).

z   Suspend *telnet*. This command only works when the user is using the C shell.

?   Show the current status of *telnet*. This includes the connection, as well as the current mode.

display *argument*

Displays all, or some, of the *set* and *toggle* values.

? *command* Get help. With no arguments, *telnet* prints a help summary. If a command is specified, *telnet* will print the help information for just that command.

send *arguments*

Sends one or more special character sequences to the remote host. The following are the arguments that may be specified (more than one argument may be specified at a time):

escape   Sends the current *telnet* escape character such as (CONTROL-]).

synch   Sends the *telnet* SYNCH sequence. This sequence causes the remote system to discard all previously typed (but not yet read) input.

brk   Sends the *telnet* BREC (Break) sequence, which may have significance to the remote system.

tp   Sends the *telnet* IP (Interrupt Process) sequence, which should cause the remote system to abort the currently running process.

ao   Sends the *telnet* AO (Abort Output) sequence, which should cause the remote system to flush all output from the remote system to the user's terminal.

ayt   Sends the *telnet* AYT (Are You There) sequence, to which the remote system may or may not choose to respond.

ec   Sends the *telnet* EC (Erase Character) sequence, which should cause the remote system to erase the last character entered.

el   Sends the *telnet* EL (Erase Line) sequence, which will cause the remote system to erase the line currently being entered.

ga   Sends the *telnet* GA (Go Ahead) sequence, which likely has no significance to the remote system.

nop   Sends the *telnet* NOP (No Operation) sequence.

?   Prints out help information for the *send* command.

set *argument value*

Set any one of a number of *telnet variables* to a specific value. The special value *off* disables the function associated with the variable. The values of variables may be interrogated with the **display** command. The variables thatmay be specified are:

echo   This is the value (initially CONTROL-E) which, when in line-by-line mode, toggles between local echoing of entered characters (for normal processing), and suppressing echoing of entered characters (for entering, say, a password).

escape   This is the *telnet* escape character (initially CONTROL-]) which causes entry into *telnet* command mode (when connected to a remote system).

interrupt   This is initially taken to be the terminal interrupt character and is used to interrupt the host activity.

quit   This is used to set the character which quits the telnet session. This is initially assigned to CONTROL-].

flushoutput   If *telnet* is in *localchars* mode and the *flushoutput* character is typed, an AO sequence is sent to the remote host. The initial value for the flush character is taken from the terminal's own flush character.

erase   If *telnet* is in *localchars* mode and if *telnet* is operating in character-at-a-time mode, then when this character is typed, an EC sequence is sent to the remote system. The initial value for the erase character is taken from the terminal's own erase character.

kill   If *telnet is* in *localchars* mode and if *telnet is* operating in character-at-a-time mode, then when this character is typed, an EL sequence is sent to the remote system. The initial value for the kill character is taken from the terminal's own kill character.

eof   If *telnet is* operating in line-by-line mode, entering this character as the first character on a line will cause this character to be sent to the remote system. The initial value of the eof character is taken to be the terminal's eof character.

toggle *arguments...*

Toggle (between TRUE and FALSE) various flags that control how *telnet* responds to events. More than one argument may be specified. The state of these flags may be interrogated with the *display* command. Valid arguments are:

localchar   If this is TRUE, then the *flush, interrupt, quit, erase* and *kill* characters are recognized locally, and transformed into the appropriate TELNET control sequences. The initial value for this toggle is TRUE in line-by-line mode, and FALSE in character mode.

autoflush   If *autoflush* and *localchars* are both TRUE, when the *ao, intr,* or *quit* characters are recognized and transformed into TELNET sequences, *telnet* refuses to display any data on the user's terminal until the remote system acknowledges that it has processed those sequences.

autosynch   If *autosynch* and *localchars* are both TRUE, then when either the *intr* or *quit* characters is typed, the resulting TELNET sequence sent is followed by the TELNET SYNCH sequence. This procedure will cause the remote system to begin throwing away all previously typed input until both TELNET sequences have been read and acted upon. The initial value of this toggle is FALSE.

crmod   Toggle carriage return mode. When this mode is enabled, most carriage return characters received from the remote host will be mapped into a carriage return followed by a line feed. This mode does not affect those characters typed by the user, only those received from the remote host. This mode is not very useful unless the remote host only sends carriage return, but never a line feed. The initial value for this toggle is FALSE.

debug   Toggles socket level debugging (useful only to the superuser). The initial value for this toggle is FALSE.

options   Toggles the display of some internal *telnet* protocol processing. The initial value for this toggle is FALSE.

netdata   Toggles the display of all network data (in hexadecimal format). The initial value for this toggle is FALSE.

?   Displays the legal *toggle* commands.

Here is an example *telnet* session:

```
# telnet
telnet> ?
Commands may be abbreviated. Commands are:

close    close current connection
display    display operating parameters
mode    try to enter line-by-line or character-at-a-time mode
open    connect to a site
quit    exit telnet
send    transmit special characters ('send ?' for more)
set     set operating parameters ('set ?' for more)
status    print status information
toggle    toggle operating parameters ('toggle ?' for more)
?    print help information
telnet> ? display
will flush output when sending interrupt characters.
won't send interrupt characters in urgent mode.
won't map carriage return on output.
won't recognize certain control characters.
won't turn on socket level debugging.
won't print hexadecimal representation of network traffic.
won't show option processing.

[^E] echo.
[^]] escape.
[^H] erase.
[off] flushoutput.
[^?] interrupt.
[^X] kill.
[^\] quit.
[^D] eof.
telnet> open hosts2
Trying...
Connected to hosts2.
Escape character is '^]'.


Linux 1.3.20 (hosts2) (ttyp0)


hosts2 login: root
Last login: Sat Nov 16 11:02:46 from 200.200.200.200
Linux 1.3.20.
hosts2:~#
telnet> quit
Connection closed.
#
```

While *telnet* allows you to login to another UNIX host on the network, it does not allow you to transfer files between the hosts. There is a program called *ftp* that does allow this.

ftp

ftp [-v] [-d ~ [-i l [-n] [-g] [host]

ftp is used to perform remote file transfer and other related services between two machines on a network. It has many commands but the most important are *open* and *user* to create the initial connection and login, and *get* and *put* which transfer files between the machines.

! *[command [args] 1*

> Invoke an interactive shell on the local machine. If there are arguments, the first is taken to be the command to execute directly, with the rest as its arguments.

$ *macro-name [args]*

> Execute the macro *macro-name* that was defined with the *macdef* command. Arguments are passed to the macro unglobbed.

account *[passwd]*

> Supply a supplemental password required by a remote system for access to resources once a login has been successfully completed.

append local-file [remote-file]

> Append a local file to a file on the remote machine. If *remote-file* is left unspecified, the local file name is used in naming the remote file after being altered by any *ntrans* or *nmap* setting. File transfer uses the current settings for type, format, mode, and structure.

ascii   Set the file transfer type to network ASCII. This is the default type.

bell   Arrange that a bell be sounded after each file transfer command is completed.

binary   Set the file transfer type to support binary image transfer.

bye   Terminate the *ftp* session with the remote server and exit ftp. An end of file will also terminate the session and exit.

case   Toggle remote computer file name case mapping during *mget* commands. When case is on (default is off), remote computer file names with all letters in uppercase are written in the local directory with the letters mapped to lowercase.

cd *remote-directory*

> Change the working directory on the remote machine to *remote directory*.

cdup   Change the remote machine working directory to the parent of the current remote directory.

close   Terminate the *ftp* session with the remote server, and return to the command interpreter. Any defined macros are erased.

cr   Toggle carriage return stripping during ASCII type file retrieval. Records are denoted by a carriage return linefeed sequence during ASCII type file transfer. When *cr* is on (the default), carriage returns are stripped from this sequence to conform with the UNIX single linefeed record delimiter. Records on non-UNIX remote systems may contain single linefeeds; when an ASCII type transfer is made, these linefeeds may be distinguished from a record delimiter only when *cr* is off.

delete *filename*
                Delete the file *filename* on the remote machine.

debug [*debug_value*]
                Toggle debugging mode. If an optional value is included, it is used to set the debugging level. When debugging is on, each command is printed.

dir [*remote-directory*] [*local-file*]
                Print a listing of the directory contents in the directory, *remote-directory*, and optionally, placing the output in a local file.

disconnect A synonym for *close*.

form *format* Set the file transfer form to *format*. The default format is file.

get *remote-file* [*local-file*]
                Retrieve the file *remote-file* and store it on the local machine. If the local file name is not specified, it is given the same name it has on the remote machine, providing it is not remapped.

glob   Toggle file name expansion for *mdelete, mget* and *mput*. If globbing is turned off with *glob*, the file name arguments are taken literally and not expanded.

hash   Toggle hash-sign ("#") printing for each data block transferred. The size of a data block is 1,024 bytes.

help [*command*]
                Print an informative message about the meaning of a command. If no argument is given, *ftp* prints a list of the known commands.

lcd [*directory*]
                Change the working directory on the local machine. If no directory is specified, the user's home directory is used.

ls [*remote-directory*] [*local-file*]
                Print an abbreviated listing of the contents of a directory on the remote machine. If *remote-directory* is left unspecified, the current working directory is used. If no local file is specified, the output is sent to the terminal instead.

macdef *macro-name*

>   Define a macro.

mdelete *[remote-files]*

>   Delete the *remote-files* on the remote machine.

mdir *remote-files local-file*

>   Like *dir*, except multiple remote files may be specified. If interactive prompting is on, *ftp* will prompt the user to verify that the last argument is indeed the target local file for receiving *mdir* output.

mget *remote-files*

>   Expand the *remote-files* on the remote machine and do a get for each file name thus produced.

mkdir *directory-name*

>   Make a directory on the remote machine.

mls *remote-files local-file*

>   Like ls, except multiple remote files may be specified. If interactive prompting is on, *ftp* will prompt the user to verify that the last argument is indeed the target local file for receiving *mls* output.

mode *[mode-name]*

>   Set the file transfer mode to *mode-name*. The default mode is stream mode.

mput *local-files*

>   Expand wildcards in the list of local files given as arguments and do a *put* for each file in the resulting list.

nmap *[inpattern outpattern]*

>   Set or unset the file name mapping mechanism.

ntrans *[inchars [outchars]]*

>   Set or unset the file name character translation mechanism.

open *host [port]*

>   Establish a connection to the specified host FTP server. An optional port number may be supplied, in which case, *ftp* will attempt to contact an FTP server at that port. If the *auto-login* option is on (default), *ftp* will also attempt to automatically log the user in to the FTP server.

prompt   Toggle interactive prompting. Interactive prompting occurs during multiple file transfers to allow the user to selectively retrieve or store files. If prompting is turned off (default is on), any *mget* or *mput* will transfer all files, and any *mdelete* will delete all files.

proxy *ftp-command*

Execute an *ftp* command on another secondary control connection. This command allows simultaneous connection to two remote FTP servers for transferring files between the two servers.

put *local-file [remote-file]*

Store a local file on the remote machine. If *remote-file* is left unspecified, the local file name is used after processing according to any *ntrans* or *nmap* settings in naming the remote file.

pwd   Print the name of the current working directory on the remote machine.

quit   A synonym for **bye**.

quote *arg~ arg2 ...*

The arguments specified are sent, verbatim, to the remote FTP server.

recv *remote-file local-file*

A synonym for *get*.

remotehelp *command*

Get help on *command* from the remote server.

rename *file1 newname*

Rename *file1* on the remote machine using the new file name *newname*.

reset   Clear reply queue. This command resynchronizes command/reply sequencing with the remote ftp server.

rmdir *directory*

Delete a directory on the remote machine.

runique   Toggle storing of files on the local system with unique file names. If a file already exists a number starting with 1 is appended to the name to differentiate the file and prevent confusion.

send *local-file remote-file*

A synonym for *put*.

sendport   Toggle the use of PORT commands.

status   Show the current status of *ftp*.

struct *struct-name*

Set the file transfer structure to *struct-name*. By default stream structure is used.

There are sometimes restrictions placed on *ftp* for security reasons that prevent it from working the first time or in a system where passwords are not used. If *ftp* makes the connection but prevents a login then check the following:

- The user name must be in the password data file */etc/passwd* and must have a password. A null password will stop the login.
- The user name must not be in the file */etc/ftpusers*.
- The users must use a standard shell. Special system administration users are not supported and cannot log in. If the user name is *anonymous* or *ftp* – this is the anonymous name which is often used to allow anyone partial access – the user name *ftp* must be in the password file */etc/passwd*.

Here is an example of how it is used:

```
# ftp hosts2
Connected to hosts2.
220 hosts2 FTP server (Version 4.140 Mon Jun 12 12:25:02 PDT 1989) ready.
Name (hosts2:root): root
331 Password required for root.
Password:
230 User root logged in.
ftp> la
ftp> ls
200 PORT command successful.
150 Opening data connection for /bin/ls (89.16.32.1,1047) (0 bytes).
bck
bin
boot
dev
etc
install
lib
lost+found
mnt
opus
save
shlib
tmp
unix
usr
who
226 Transfer complete.
97 bytes received in 0.05 seconds (1.9 Kbytes/s)
ftp> get who who.re
200 PORT command successful.
150 Opening data connection for who (89.16.32.1,1048) (15 bytes).
226 Transfer complete.
local: who.re remote: who
16 bytes received in 0 seconds (0.016 Kbytes/s)
ftp> bye
221 Goodbye.
# cat who.re
This is hosts2
#
```

Using *rcp* and *rlogin*

There are two simpler ways of logging into a remote host and transferring files using the two commands *rlogin* and *rcp*.

rcp

rcp [-p] file1 file2
rcp [-p] [-r] file ... directory

rcp will copy files between two machines. The file names are either a local file name or a remote name where the host name is prefixed to the more normal path name. A semicolon is used to separate the host name and path. The *-p* option will attempt to duplicate the modification times and other similar data when the file is transferred. The *-r* option is used if any of the source files are a directory where the subdirectories will be transferred as well. In this case, the destination file must be a directory as well.

The local user name is used to log in automatically into the other machine prior to the file transfer. The other host must recognize the local user name and support the remote command execution shell. If not, the command will fail. Passwords are not used and if the remote user has password protection, this command can fail with an "access permission denied" message. Such remote access is controlled by restricting the use of the remote shell *rsh*. This is done through the use of group permissions and execution rights.

It is possible to log in using another's name by adding the user name to the host name but separated by an "at" sign (@) as shown in the example.

```
# rcp hosts2:/who who2
# cat who2
This is hosts2
# rcp steveh@hosts2:/whos who3
# cat who3
This is Steve's directory on hosts2
#
```

rlogin

rlogin rhost [-ec] [-8] [-L] [-l username]

rlogin will allow the user of one machine to log in to another host on the network. In some ways it is very similar to the *telnet* command but it is simpler and far less sophisticated. It has several options:

e*c*   This allows a different escape character, *c*, to be used to end the login session. There is no space between the *e* and the new escape character.

8   specifies the use of 8-bit characters all the time.

L   specifies the use of the litout mode. This mode is rarely used in practice.

l *username*   specifies which user name will be used to attempt the login.

Here are some examples of how the *rlogin* command is used. The first one is a normal remote login where the login uses the current user name by default. In the second example, the remote login is done using the user name *sysadm*. This is a special name on the system that immediately invokes the system administration package supplied with the system.

```
# rlogin hosts2
UNIX System V Release 3.2 88000
hosts2
Copyright (c) 1984 AT&T
All Rights Reserved
Login last used: Wed Mar 30 12:55:36 1994
#

# rlogin hosts2 -l sysadm
UNIX System V Release 3.2 88000
hosts2
Copyright (c) 1984 AT&T
All Rights Reserved
Login last used: Wed Mar 30 09:18:12 1994

      SYSTEM ADMINISTRATION

 1 diskmgmt   disk management menu
 2 filemgmt   file management menu
 3 machinemgmt machine management menu
 4 packagemgmt package management menu
 5 softwaremgmt software management menu
 6 syssetup   system setup menu
 7 ttymgmt    tty management menu
 8 usermgmt   user management menu

Enter a number, a name, the initial part of a name, or
? or <number>? for HELP, q to QUIT: q
Connection closed.
#
```

NFS

NFS — short for Network File System — was developed by Sun Microsystems to network their UNIX-based workstations together. It has become the de facto standard for networked UNIX machines and is widely available on other UNIX machines and even PCs and Macintoshes.

What it does is allow a user on one machine to mount part of another machine's file system so that the file system can be shared. The user accesses the files as if they were local but the access is performed transparently over the Ethernet network and the files never leave the remote system. This allows several people or groups to share files among several machines.

Setting up the link

These files set up the connection links among the various machines and assign the IP addresses to various names. These links are important because the host names that are used within the *mount* command are checked against the lists contained within these files.

```
# cat /etc/hosts
# Sample /etc/hosts file

89.16.32.01 hosts1
89.16.32.02 hosts2
89.16.32.03 hosts3
89.16.32.04 hosts4
89.16.32.05 hosts5
#
# cat /etc/hosts.equiv
host1
host2
host3
host4
host5
#
```

The third file is called */etc/exports*. It defines which parts of the machine's file system can be remotely accessed and by which machine. In the example shown, the machines, *hosts1* and *hosts4*, can mount the root file system while *hosts2* can only mount */usr*. This file is checked every time there is a request to mount a file system using NFS. This file is normally left blank or gives everyone permission to access the whole root file system by simply containing a / and nothing else. If no machine names are on the same line as the file system, then everyone can mount that file system. It is advisable to update this file before re-booting Linux and NFS to ensure that it is correctly read. Once initialized, the file can be updated as and when necessary, although some implementations may require the machine to be restarted.

```
# cat /etc/exports
/   hosts1
/usr hosts2
/   hosts4
#
```

Using NFS

To use a remote file system using NFS, it must be mounted and unmounted in the same way that floppy disks are handled. Not surprisingly, the same commands that handle disks are used with NFS. Due to the implications of unmounting and mounting disks while they are still being used or accessed by other users, these commands are normally designated superuser commands and their use is restricted to the superuser and/or system administrator. The commands can be included in startup scripts that will automatically load remote file systems when the system starts or even when certain users log in.

mount

mount [-r] -f NFS, *options remote-system directory*

This is a version of the normal *mount* command that explicitly uses NFS to access the remote file system and mount it as the given directory. The -r option will make the resulting file system read only.

umount

umount *directory*

This version of the normal *umount* command unmounts NFS remote file systems. Both *mount* and *umount* commands are superuser-only and cannot be executed by a normal user.

```
# dir /mnt
/mnt:
# mount -f NFS hosts1:/usr /mnt
# dir /mnt
/mnt:
3bnet/  bin/   lib/   oasys/  pub/   tmp/
adm/   include/ mail/  options/ spool/  vmsys/
admin/  lbin/  news/  preserve/ src/
# umount /mnt
# dir /mnt
/mnt:
#
```

Once mounted, the remote file system can be used as if it was physically part of the local machine. The file access performance is not as fast as using a hard disk but with Ethernet it is quite acceptable.

If there is an appropriate entry in */etc/fstab* then the directory name can be used with *mount* and *umount* without having to type in all the details.

9   Installing XFree86

XFree86 is a freeware version of the X-windows graphical user interface (GUI) that forms the basis of many common interfaces for UNIX-based workstations such as Sun Microsystem's SPARC workstations. It allows Linux users to have a mouse-based interface that resembles that of Windows or the Apple MAC instead of the normal text-based interface.

It is included in the Slackware distribution and is also available separately, but its installation is a little tricky — there are several links and configuration files to set up — so it is probably best to use the Slackware installer to install and setup the software. The setup utility is called *xfconfig*. This chapter will cover the basic methods of getting XFree86 running and what to do if things go wrong.

Which software packages?

There are four installation packages for Slackware, and apart from the server development package, all of them should be installed. The default choices are sufficient to get XFree86 running and you can go back to install the others at a later date. Before installing, make sure that you select the QUICK mode for prompting. If you don't you will either have to say yes to each package option, which is very tedious, or all the packages will be installed, which will corrupt the installation, because it will load every server option. The chances are that the last one to be loaded will not work with your hardware!

Getting the mouse working

The mouse is assigned a special */dev* file called */dev/mouse* used by the XFree86 software to access the mouse. The file is set up by linking it to another */dev* device that actually represents the physical port that will be used. For the most common mouse interface, the serial port, */dev/mouse* is linked to either */dev/ttyS0* or */dev/ttyS1* which represent COM1 or COM2. This linking can be carried out using the Slackware setup utility as part of the Linux *configure* command. This will ask in turn for the mouse type to be identified followed by additional information about its interface — the COM port number it is attached to. Once completed, the */dev/mouse* link is automatically made so that other software packages, including XFree86, can access it.

gpm and mc

> The problem with the */dev/mouse* link is that there is no easy or obvious way of checking that the link is correct and that the mouse is working. One way of doing this is to run the utility *gpm* and then see if the mouse will move the on-screen cursor. If it does, then the mouse and the */dev/mouse* link are correct. The Slackware configure will ask if *gpm* is to be installed so that it runs automatically when you log in. If you use the utility *mc* (midnight caller) which is a Norton Commander look-alike, then running *gpm* allows the mouse to be used to scroll and select files and directories. However, it may cause problems if XFree86 is used. I prefer to run *gpm* manually by using this command line direct from the console.

Three-button mouse emulation

> XFree86 assumes that it is using a three-button mouse. Unfortunately, most PCs use the two-button Microsoft mouse or equivalent. To get around the problem of the missing button, the third button is emulated by clicking one of the buttons while holding down one of the keyboard keys. This is normally the combination of the right-hand mouse button and the ALT key.

Installing the XFree86 server

> There are many X Free86 servers that are specific to a particular PC graphics card. It is essential that the correct server for the card is used otherwise it will be impossible to get the XFree86 interface to run correctly. The various types fall into several categories:

> **Generic**   These servers assume a standard interface such as 16-color VGA or a monochrome display. They are the best choice to use to get the environment running as they are less likely to cause any problems.

> **Pseudo generic** These are servers that appear to be generic, but I have found problems with them with some graphics cards. The SVGA server is a good example.

> **Specific**   These are servers that are specific to a graphics card, such as Trident 8900c, a manufacturer, such asOrchid or the graphics processor, such as S3 or MACH64. It is important that the right one is used.

> The server is selected by installing the driver software, linking it to a reference file and then ensuring that it has the appropriate entries in a special configuration file. If none of these operations are correctly performed, the XFree86 environment will not run.

Linking the server to X

The next stage is to link the file */usr/X11R6/bin/X* to the required server, for example, */usr/X11R6/bin/XF86_VGA* for a 16-color VGA screen, */usr/X11R6/bin/XF86_SVGA* for a SVGA screen and */usr/X11R6/bin/XF86_MONO* for a monochrome display. The *ln* command with -*sf* options should be used to do this but the links are not straightforward and some documentation wrong or misleading. The following example is taken from my own system that runs XFree86. It shows the full directory entries for */usr/X11R6/bin/x* and */usr/X11/bin/X* and that they are the same. This is shown by the same link and 45235 reference number for the file */var/X11R6/bin/X*.

```
ess2:/usr/X11R6/bin# ls -alsi X
   45235    0 lrwxrwxrwx   1 root     root          16 Nov 16 15:06 X -> /
var/X1
1R6/bin/X*
ess2:/usr/X11R6/bin# ls -alsi /usr/X11/bin/X
   45235    0 lrwxrwxrwx   1 root     root          16 Nov 16 15:06 /usr/
X11/bin
/X -> /var/X11R6/bin/X*
```

This last file, */var/X11R6/bin/X*, is the file that is linked back to the actual server file that was previously mentioned. Again the full directory entry reveals all.

```
ess2:/usr/X11R6/bin# ls -alsi /var/X11R6/bin/X
   14578    0 lrwxrwxrwx   1 root     root          25 Nov 16 15:06 /var/
X11R6/b
in/X -> /usr/X11R6/bin/XF86_VGA16*
ess2:/usr/X11R6/bin#
```

This means that instead of linking */usr/X11R6/bin/X* to the server file, */var/X11R6/bin/X* is used instead .

This linking is automatically done for you when XFree86 is installed using the Slackware distribution. Nearly all my problems with getting it running stemmed from either broken or incorrect links. So it is worth checking that all is well before proceeding.

Adding the path name

Make sure that */usr/X11R6/bin* is in the PATH variable. In some cases, this path name will be */usr/X11/bin* where */usr/X11* is a link to */usr/X11R6*. The end result is the same: the user will automatically be able to access the utilities in the */usr/X11R6/bin* directory.

This can be checked by using the *set* command to display the system variables. If it is not included, edit the file */etc/profile* and add it to the script file. If you are using the *tcsh* shell, the equivalent file is */etc/csh.login*.

Adding the libraries

Make sure that the library files are also locatable by the runtime linker. This is done by appending the entry */usr/X11R6/lib* to the file */etc/ld.so.conf* and then executing the */sbin/ldconfig* command to ensure that the linker is updated. This must be done as root and not as a different user, that is, the system administrator has to do it.

Installing the configuration file

The final point is to install the configuration file. This is not done by the Slackware release and has to be done manually. If the server is a generic one for VGA or SVGA, then all that is needed is to copy the example configuration file to create the actual file. Use the *cp* command to copy */usr/X11R6/lib/X11/XF86Config.eg* to */usr/X11R6/lib/X11/XF86Config*. If changes are needed, then the file will need to be edited to create the new entries. Some have already been provided but others will need new information. This requires detailed data about the video signal timing and can be quite complex. The XFree86 *HOW-TO* document on the CD-ROM gives detailed information about how to do this.

Starting up XFree86

The easiest way of starting XFree86 from the console is to log in as *normal* and then type in the command *startx*. This is a script that will start up the pre-defined server using the definitions stored in the configurations file */usr/X11R6/bin/X11R6/XFConfig*. The screen will change from text-based to a graphical interface with a large cross as a cursor. Clicking on the left mouse button will bring down a menu with the X applications that have been installed.

If *startx* is typed in from another terminal, then the XFree86 environment will not start up at the terminal but will force the console into this mode — even if the console is doing something else!

Closing down XFree86

To close down the XFree86 environment, use the *exit fwm* command from the pull-down menu activated by the left mouse button. This will kill the server and return the system to its normal text-only mode. An alternative is to press the CONTROL, ALT and BACKSPACE keys simultaneously.

10   If it doesn't work...

Despite the best preparation and intention in the world, there are times when a command either does not work or does not function as expected. This can be a frustrating — and sometimes frightening experience. Here are some common problems and suggestions for dealing with them.

The system returns "cannot open file"

- The directory containing the command is not included in the PATH variable. Either change it or specify the full file name.
- The command does not exist. Check the name for any spelling mistakes or letters in the wrong case. Linux commands are case sensitive — *Ls* and *ls* refer to two separate files.
- The file permissions are against you and need changing. This is very common after writing a script and then trying to execute it. The standard write permissions do not allow the file to be executed. Use *chmod* to change them if you are the owner or superuser.
- You may be working using a restricted shell such as *rsh*. Log in as another user that uses the full shell, or ask the system administrator to change your login shell.
- Use *find* to search for the command — it may be in a different directory. If necessary, specify the full path name to access it or change the PATH variable.

The system returns "unrecognized option"

- Check the options for any spelling mistakes. A common mistake is to include dashes when the command does not expect them, as with *tar*. Try the command, if possible, with other or no options.
- Another common mistake is to specify options after file names, when the command expects them before, and vice versa. If the command returns a usage message, check the order.
- Try the command with fewer options. Some older implementations do not support the whole range of options available on more modern systems.
- Check the system and shell. A bash shell command or script will not execute correctly under a tcsh shell, and vice versa.

Checking syntax and existence

If these measures do not work, either the command does not exist on your system or it uses a different syntax. There are still some possibilities left:

- Use the on-line documentation to search for the command and display the documentation. This allows the exact syntax to be checked. The three utilities that are commonly used are *man, usage* and *help. man* takes commands as arguments and searches its database for the documentation, which it formats and displays. The data is basically the same as found in the standard system documentation. It is a good idea to use *pg, less* or *more* to page the data, rather than watch it disappearing off the screen. Be prepared for a delay because the formatting and search may take some time. An alternative to *man* is *help*, which is not quite as all encompassing in terms of its database and information. With Linux commands, using the *--help* option will often display a small help message.

```
ess2:/usr/X11R6/lib/X11# help return
return: return [n]
    Causes a function to exit with the return value specified by N.   If N
    is omitted, the return status is that of the last command.
ess2:/usr/X11R6/lib/X11# ln --help
Usage: ln [OPTION]... SOURCE [DEST]
  or:  ln [OPTION]... SOURCE... DIRECTORY

  -b, --backup               make backups for removed files
  -d, -F, --directory        hard link directories (super-user only)
  -f, --force                remove existing destinations
  -n, --no-dereference       with --force, remove destination that is a
                               symlink to a directory
  -i, --interactive          prompt whether to remove destinations
  -s, --symbolic             make symbolic links, instead of hard links
  -v, --verbose              print name of each file before linking
  -S, --suffix=SUFFIX        override the usual backup suffix
  -V, --version-control=WORD override the usual version control
      --help                 display this help and exit
      --version              output version information and exit

The backup suffix is ~, unless set with SIMPLE_BACKUP_SUFFIX.   The
version control may be set with VERSION_CONTROL, values are:

  t, numbered     make numbered backups
  nil, existing   numbered if numbered backups exist, simple otherwise
  never, simple   always make simple backups
ess2:/usr/X11R6/lib/X11#
```

- If no on-line documentation exists (many administrators remove it to gain disk space and prevent users from using valuable processor time looking up commands) the next resort is the full system documentation.

For most queries, the appropriate HOW-TO document will contain the answers. These have been included along with other documentation on the companion CD-ROM.

- If the command exists in the documentation but not on the system, it may have been removed to save space or for some other reason. At this point, ask the system administrator why the command is not on the system and what alternatives there are to it.
- If the command does not exist in the documentation and is not present on the system, ask other users or the system administrator for help.

Debugging shell scripts

The techniques used to debug shell scripts are very similar to those used to debug BASIC programs a few years ago. These did not have the benefit of symbolic debuggers, which allow the developer to single-step through code, examine variables, and so on. The techniques used in BASIC were based on plenty of *print* statements and control loops, so that variables could be displayed and the program halted at various points. If all else failed, BASIC provides a trace facility, where the statement sequence is displayed as a series of line numbers. By comparing these with the original source, the program flow could be deduced.

Shell scripts do not have a symbolic debugger and therefore rely on the writer's use of *echo* commands to display variables and *read* commands to pause the program.

Other debugging techniques are essentially variations of the command set that is provided. To those accustomed to symbolic debuggers and other more advanced tools, this may appear to be a serious disadvantage — and a good reason for not using shell scripts. In their defense, the lack of a debugger is not that much of a disadvantage and the flexibility and speed of development of shell scripts is more than compensation.

bash scripts

Here are some basic tips for bash scripts:

- Make use of comments in the code. A comment is a line starting with a # and any text that follows it is treated as text and not as a command line sequence.
- Add the *echo* command at the beginning of any line that needs to be disabled from execution. If the line needs to be executed, remove the *echo* command.
- Inserting a # at the beginning of a line effectively disables it as a script command. This is often preferable to deletion for the removal of com-

mand lines. With the line commented out, the contents are still available for restoration.

- Inserting a colon at the beginning of a line prevents its execution but causes the shell to scan the line. Any special shell characters are interpreted and an error causes the script to be aborted.

- Indent subroutines to make their identification clearer. This is extremely helpful in identifying missing *done*, *fi* and other similar command lines.

- When printing variables using *echo*, it is easier to see what is going on if the variable name is printed with a reference to the current point in the script.

- If there are large numbers of *echo* commands, redirect the output to a file and use an editor to inspect it. It is easier to find variables and other data with an editor than to search manually.

- The *set* command can be used to alter the shell response to scripts. For example:

set -n	Read command but do not execute. This prevents a terminal from executing any further commands until Control-Z or Control-D is typed.
set -t	Exit after reading and executing one command.
set -u	Treat unset variables as an error when substituting.
set -v	Starts verbose mode, where each command is printed as it is read. This is useful in identifying syntax errors.
set -x	Prints each command as it is executed and provides a tracing mechanism.

- The # command can be used to find out which commands have been executed and how many times. The table should be cleared before the script is executed using the command # -r. To see the table after the script has completed, simply type #.

tcsh scripts

Here are some basic tips for tcsh scripts:

- Make use of comments in the code. A comment is a line that starts with a # and any text that follows it is treated as text and not as a command line sequence.

- Add the *echo* command at the beginning of any line that needs to be disabled from execution. If the line needs to be executed, remove the *echo* command.

- Inserting a # at the beginning of a line effectively disables it as a script command. This is often preferable to deletion for the removal of command lines. With the line commented out, the contents are still available for restoration.

- Indent subroutines to make their identification clearer. This is also extremely helpful in identifying missing *end*, *endif* and other similar command lines.

- When printing variables using the *echo* command, it is easier to see what is going if the variable name is printed with a reference to the current point in the script.

- If there are large numbers of *echo* commands, redirect the output to a file and use an editor to inspect it. It is easier to find variables and other data with an editor than to search manually.

- The *set* command can be used to alter the shell response to scripts:

  set verbose Starts verbose mode, where each command is printed as it is read. This is useful in identifying syntax errors.

  set echo   Prints each command as it is executed and provides a tracing mechanism.

A   What's on the CD-ROM?

This appendix gives a brief description of what is included on the companion CD-ROM. The basic software is based on Slackware release 3.1 and includes the normal utilities and software needed to create a Linux system. In addition, the kernel sources for all the 1.3 and 2.0 releases have been added. The software is covered by the GNU copyleft license — please read it.

Slackware v3.1

This is complete except for one omission. The *live* directory and its contents have been removed to create enough free disk space to allow the kernel source for all version 1.3.x and 2.0 releases to be included. This means that the option to run Linux from the CD-ROM is not available from this disk.

Extras folder

This contains all the additional documentation that is available from the Sunsite host at the time of writing and covers the more advanced features of Linux. The information is provided in several formats such as PostScript and plain ASCII. This folder includes the HOW-TO and the Linux Documentation Project documents which are the basis of the Linux Bible and cover nearly every aspect of Linux. They can provide a lot more information that is beyond the scope of this book. One word of caution: they can be a little out of date and sometimes the software doesn't quite function in the way it is described. Some of the documents are very preliminary and therefore should be considered as unstable. As one document puts it: "alpha version — trust this and die!"

This folder also contains the source of all the kernels for releases 1.3, 2.0 and 2.1. The files are a mixture of complete releases and patch files. They are generally in a *gzip* compressed *tar* format. Thes files are grouped together in their own directories for easier access.

LINUX_V1.3X

This folder contains the kernel source for versions 1.3.x. Due to space considerations, only every tenth kernel is supplied complete — 1.3.20. 1.3.30 and so on. The interim releases can be created by using the patch files that are also located here.

LINUX_V2.0X

This folder contains the kernel source for versions 2.0.x. These are the latest release and will require version 2.7 or later of the GNU C compiler. Don't worry; this is part of the Slackware release and is installed automatically.

LINUX_V2.1X

This folder contains the kernel source for versions 2.1.x. These are currently at the development stage only and therefore are potentially unstable. For normal use, use a version 2.0.x kernel.

Obtaining more software

The best repository is the Walnut Creek FTP site at *ftp.cdrom.com,* which maintains a mirror of the Sunsite location as well as copies of all the major releases of Linux, including the latest version of Slackware and versions for other processor and computer architectures. Downloading small drivers and programs is not too costly in terms of telephone charges and time and can be used in conjunction with this CD-ROM to expand your library of Linux software. However, this does mean you are on your own in terms of technical support. For some this is part of the enjoyment of using Linux; for others this can be daunting.

Walnut Creek can provide CD-ROMs with this software preinstalled and regular updates to registered users. This service also includes technical support. The site contains gigabytes of software, and purchasing the CD-ROMs is a very cost-effective way of building up a library that can be used to dip into as needed. They are based in California, USA and their telephone number is +1 510 674 0783. Their email address is order@cdrom.com.

Index

Also from Digital Press:

Microsoft Exchange Server: Planning, Design, and Implementation
by Tony Redmond

Microsoft Exchange Server is for people interested in deploying Microsoft's electronic messaging and groupware server in the distributed environments commonly encountered in large corporations.

1996   450 pp   pb   ISBN: 1-55558-162-5   DEC Part No. EY-U042E-DP $34.95

Migrating to the Intranet and Microsoft Exchange
by Randall J. Covill

This book provides critical information for information system managers concerned with providing information and network infrastructure especially for Exchange, enterprise-wide mail systems and the Intranet.

March 1997   250pp   pb   ISBN: 1-55558-172-2   DEC Part No. EY-V420E-DP $29.95

Intranet Development: An IS/IT Manager's Guide
by Judith Hall and James Keenan

Intranet Development: An IS/IT Manager's Guide follows the development of Intranets within a range of companies by using step-by-step case studies. The stages of Intranet development documented in these various businesses can be broadly applied to all organizations setting up Intranets of their own.

March 1997   350pp   pb   ISBN: 1-55558-171-4   DEC Part No. EY-V427E-DP $29.95

Electronic Mail: A Practical Guide
by Simon Collin

A practical guide/source book of tips and ideas for experienced system managers together with all the information to help someone who's just been landed with the project of installing E-Mail. The content covers choosing and installing E-Mail for small peer-to-peer LANs to client server models to WANs.

1995   350 pp   pb   ISBN: 0-7506-2112-5   DEC Part No. EY-T859E-DP $29.95

Available from all good booksellers or in case of difficulty call:
1-800-366-2665 in the U.S. or +44 1865 310366 in Europe.

Essential Linux
Companion CD-ROM

This companion CD-ROM is based on Slackware 3.1 and contains the following Linux software:

- The base system, including boot and root disks for 1.2 Mbyte and 1.44 Mbyte floppy disks.
- Various applications and add ons, such as the manual pages, groff, ispell, joe, jed, jove, ghostscript, sc, bc, and the quota patches.
- Program development. GCC/G++/ObjectiveC/Fortran-77 2.7.2, make (GNU and BSD), byacc and GNU bison, flex, 5.3.12 C libraries, gdb, SVGAlib, ncurses, gcl (LISP), p2c, m4, perl, rcs.
- GNU Emacs 19.31.
- A collection of FAQs and other documentation.
- Networking. TCP/IP, UUCP, mailx, dip, PPP, deliver, elm, pine, BSD sendmail, Apache httpd, arena, lynx, cnews, nn, tin, trn, inn.teTeX Release 0.4 - teTeX is Thomas Esser's TeX distribution for Linux.
- Tcl, Tk, TclX, built with ELF shared libraries and dynamic loading support. Also includes the TkDesk filemanager.
- Games. The BSD games collection, Tetris for terminals, Lizards, and Sasteroids.
- This directory contains extra packages for Slackware, such as an Ada compiler, and the Andrew User Interface System
- The base XFree86 3.1.2 system, with libXpm, fvwm 1.23b, and xlock added. Also includes xf86config, an XF86Config writing program.
- X applications: X11 ghostscript, libgr, seyon, workman, xfilemanager, xv 3.10, GNU chess and xboard, xfm 1.3.2, ghostview, gnuplot, xpaint, xfractint, fvwm95-2, and various X games.
- X11 server linkkit, static libraries, and PEX support.
- xview3.2p1-X11R6. XView libraries, and the Open Look virtual and non-virtual window managers for XFree86.
- The kernel source code and patches for Linux versions 1.3.x
- The kernel source code and patches for Linux versions 2.0.x
- The kernel source code and patches for Linux development versions 2.1.x